Ancient Peoples and Places

SPAIN AND PORTUGAL

General Editor

DR. GLYN DANIEL

ABOUT THE AUTHOR

Born in 1911, Hubert N. Savory was educated at Oxford, where he was awarded a D. Phil. after engaging in studies of the Celtic early Iron Age. From 1936 to 1938, he was MacIver Research Student in Iberian Archaeology at the Queen's College, Oxford. In 1939, he became Assistant Keeper in the Department of Archaeology at the National Museum of Wales, Cardiff; since 1956, he has been Keeper of the Department. He has published many excavation reports and comparative studies connected with the prehistory of Wales. Dr. Savory has returned to Spain and Portugal several times, notably to take part in excavations at the Copper Age fort at Vila Nova de São Pedro, and has published several papers on the later prehistory of the Iberian Peninsula.

Ancient Peoples and Places

SPAIN
AND PORTUGAL

THE PREHISTORY OF THE
IBERIAN PENINSULA

H. N. Savory

66 PHOTOGRAPHS
68 LINE DRAWINGS
23 MAPS

FREDERICK A. PRAEGER
Publishers
New York · Washington

THIS IS VOLUME SIXTY-ONE IN THE SERIES

Ancient Peoples and Places

GENERAL EDITOR: DR. GLYN DANIEL

BOOKS THAT MATTER

Published in the United States of America in 1968
by Frederick A. Praeger, Inc., Publishers,
111 Fourth Avenue, New York, N.Y. 10003
© 1968 in London, England, by H. N. Savory
All rights reserved
Library of Congress Catalog Card Number: 68–16802
Printed in Holland

CONTENTS

ILLUSTRATIONS

Acknowledgments

I HAVE FIRST TO THANK Dr Glyn Daniel and Messrs Thames & Hudson for awaiting so patiently the completion of this book and allowing it to appear as an extra-large volume in their Ancient Peoples and Places series. Next I must thank those Portuguese archaeologists who helped my studies thirty years ago, when I was MacIver Student in Iberian Archaeology at the Queen's College, Oxford and gladly helped me again when writing this book, with photographs or facilities for work in the field: Lieut-Col. Afonso do Paço, Dr Mario Cardozo, of Guimarães, and the staff of the Geological Commission in Lisbon. In Spain I am particularly indebted for help with illustrations to Dr A. Arribas, until recently Curator of the Barcelona Archaeological Museum, Dr J. M. Santa Olalla of Madrid, Dr D. Fletcher Valls, Director of Service of Prehistoric Investigation, Valencia, and the National Archaeological Museum in Madrid.

I should also like to acknowledge the kindness and courtesy shown to me long ago in Portugal by the owners of important private collections and archaeological sites, notably members of the House of Cadaval at Muge, Senhor Ruy d'Andrade at Barbacena, Count H. da Costa Cabaço at Alemquer, Senhor Leonel Trindade at Torres Vedras; and similar kindnesses, more recently, from Dr Concepción Fernández-Chicarro y de Dios and Señor Collantes de Terán at Seville, Señora Viuda Bonsor at Mairena del Alcor and Señor D. José Garcia Berdoy at Antequera. But above all, in the matter of illustrations, I am indebted to Dr Vera Leisner for many photographs, most of which have been previously published in the great series of monographs on megalithic tombs, by herself and her late husband, and for permission to adapt many of the line drawings in

15

these works; Messrs Walter De Gruyter & Co. of Berlin, who published many of these volumes, have kindly consented to their use in this way. I must also thank the British Museum and the Ashmolean Museum for photographs of objects in their care and Mr Michael Walker for allowing me to use his drawings (Figs. 70c, 71) in advance of publication of his monograph on Galician petroglyphs. The sources of the illustrations in this book are acknowledged elsewhere.

Introduction

THE READER OF THIS BOOK on the prehistory of Spain and Portugal may wonder, as the writer himself did at times while engaged on the task, why the effort of compressing so vast a subject into so small a space was ever attempted. The sub-continental character of the Iberian peninsula and its historical tendency to split up, not only into the present two sovereign states but, within modern Spain itself, into a number of centrifugal provinces, separated from each other by massive mountain ranges, different climates, vegetations and economic life, with different cultural orientations and in some cases, until very recently, different languages, are well known.

Fig. 1

Among all this diversity one climatic boundary is particularly marked: that separating 'wet' Spain from 'dry'. The temperate northern coastal strip, with its heavy rainfall and north-west European types of soil and natural forest cover – deciduous oak, elm and ash – has an extension down the western seaboard as far as the Tagus estuary, the eastern limits of which roughly coincide with the western edge of the Meseta or inland plateau of the peninsula, and which is the *raison d'être* of modern Portugal. This western coastal strip has mild, wet winters but a degree of summer drought which has permitted Mediterranean flora to spread westwards and northwards, even, to some degree, as far as Galicia, and mingling, above all between the Tagus and Douro, with the north-west European flora already mentioned, to produce a vegetation of great richness. The whole of this Atlantic coastal strip, turning its back on the Meseta and looking out to sea-ways leading, in early days, equally to the Mediterranean and northern Europe, and more recently to all parts of the world, was the basis in prehistoric times for an 'Atlantic' cultural sphere of great interest for French and British prehistory. It has long been the seat of a numerous and sturdy landowning peasantry prac' tising a mixed agriculture and readily turning to fishing, mining or heavy industry where the opportunity has occurred. The Pyrenees have never been a complete obstacle to these people: the Basques live on either side of them, just as in the Early Iron Age, the locally specialized post'Hallstattian culture of the north'eastern Meseta spread far into south'western France, and settlers from central or north'western Europe, like the Celts in the Early Iron Age and the Swabians in the fifth century AD, have been drawn towards this congenial tract.

By far the greater part of the peninsula, however, belongs to the world of 'dry' Spain with its low, mainly winter rainfall and Mediterranean vegetation, where the natural forest cover has now largely disappeared, to be replaced in favourable areas by wheat, vines and olive trees, and elsewhere by wastelands *(dehesas)* covered with scrub, or lunar landscapes where soil erosion is nearly complete. This dry world falls into two main provinces – that of the Meseta with its harsh extremes of summer heat and winter cold and complicated framework of rugged mountain ranges, and that of the Mediterranean sea' board with its mild winters and local possibilities of intense and varied cultivation. Here, too, the seaboard looks away from the Meseta towards the routes linking it with the rest of the Medi'

Fig. 2

terranean world. It is divided into two rather different regions – one easterly, in Catalonia and Valencia, which is tolerably well endowed by nature, and the other southerly, in Andalusia and the Algarve, which has great natural wealth – by a strange intermediate region around Almeria and Murcia, in which the arid landscapes of Asia and Africa seem to have crossed the narrow seas and nearly engulfed a few intensely cultivated valley bottoms and *huertas*. In prehistoric times, as more recently, the culture and character of the people on the eastern seaboard often seem to have been closely linked with

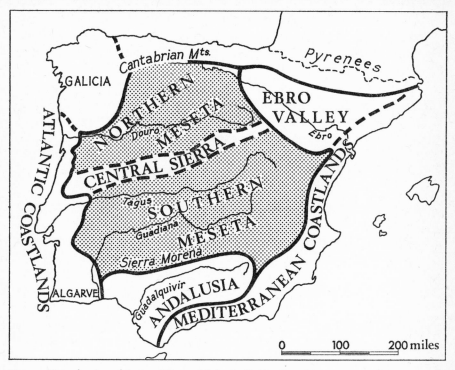

Fig. 1. Natural regions of Spain and Portugal (after L. Dudley Stamp)

those of the inhabitants of Mediterranean France and northern
Italy. Andalusia, on the other hand, not only has an immediate
seaboard with local opportunities for intense cultivation, but
a large river basin – that of the Guadalquivir – which enjoys a
mild winter climate and, in its lower reaches especially, has a
fertile soil capable of a high yield in cereals and livestock. Because of this and its mineral wealth Andalusia in later prehistoric times was more attractive to colonists arriving by
sea-ways from the eastern Mediterranean than any other part of
the peninsula, and was for that reason the region most advanced in civilization; it was, too, the main centre from which

developments in the rest of the peninsula were influenced, its only rival being the much smaller but very attractive region flanking the estuary of the Tagus, which was able for long periods to maintain a distinct and relatively advanced culture of its own.

Then, inland, there is the Meseta – in general much less important in prehistoric times, so far as our present information goes, than it became in the Middle Ages. Here was a vast land given up from the fourth millennium BC until historical times to pastoralism, pursued by people who tended to represent survivals from earlier populations displaced by the more advanced cultivators and metallurgists of the seaboard yet it seems, like the steppe and desert nomads of the Near East in their relations with the urban cultures of the Fertile Crescent, sometimes capable of overthrowing the corrupt rulers and strong places of the interlopers and re-establishing themselves, at least temporarily, near the coast. The rocky western Meseta – León and Estremadura – is nowadays mainly stock-raising country, like the adjacent Portuguese provinces of Beira Baixa and Alto Alemtejo which partially share the climate of the Meseta, and perhaps reached its greatest productivity in this respect under Celtic Early Iron Age cattle men, thereafter reverting to sheep. Some of the clay soil regions, like the *Ribera* on the north bank of the Middle Ebro, parts of Old Castile, and the country around Mérida and Beja on the Guadiana, which are suitable for corn growing, seem also to have been first extensively cultivated by Celtic settlers from the north. In general, however, the Meseta has been given its character, in later prehistoric and early historic times, by influences from the Mediterranean; its peasant culture bears the common stamp of 'dry' Spain – concentration in *pueblos* – villages or small towns which are the basic social and political unit.

In spite of the factors just outlined, which make for extreme provincialism, it remains true that the prehistory of the Iberian

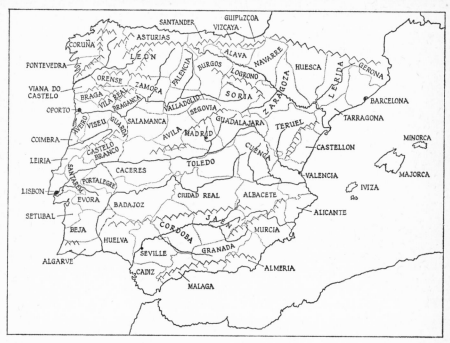

Fig. 2. Provinces and districts of Spain and Portugal

peninsula needs to be surveyed as a whole, for a number of
reasons. The chief of these is an underlying unity which finds
simple expression in the statement that all the inhabitants of
the peninsula are in a broad sense 'Iberians', sharing characteristics that mark them off from other people and are the
results of a long historical process, worked out in relative
isolation among a population the dominant elements in which
have been present since prehistoric times. Isolation is, indeed,
the main key to these distinctive characteristics. It has sometimes
been supposed that Iberia, so like Anatolia its pendant at the
eastern end of the Mediterranean in its physical structure and
relationship to neighbouring land masses, was used in pre-

21

historic times as a bridge for movements of people and culture between Africa and Europe, just as Anatolia was between Asia and Europe. It is now possible to see that by reason of its own natural poverty and isolation, contrasting so markedly with the Near East's dynamism in early times, north-west Africa contributed little in prehistoric times, after the early hand-axe and Aterian cultures, to west European civilization, apart from a limited influence in the Neolithic period. There is thus no true parallel in later peninsular prehistory either to the advance of the Vandals from France through the peninsula to north-west Africa in the fifth century AD or to the reverse move-ment by Islam in the eighth. The way in which the two great peninsulas *do* resemble each other, however, is in their common capacity in prehistoric times to shape their own distinctive cultures and project them far into Europe.

The special Iberian contributions to prehistoric European civilization were made in two dynamic phases, the first in the late Neolithic and Copper Age (*c.* 3500–2000 BC) and the second in the Late Bronze Age and Early Iron Age (700–400 BC), when a power of adapting oriental influences and creating from them a new synthesis was centred in the southern half of the peninsula, but gave the whole of it its unity, transcending the boundary between 'dry' and 'wet' Spain. Most of the latter area remained backward and unimportant from the fourth millennium BC, until the arrival of the Celts; at no time did it play a role comparable to the one it undertook in the Middle Ages, as the springboard from which Christian, European culture recovered its control of the peninsula from Islam and Arab civilization. But one must note, in considering the dynamism of 'dry' Spain, a contrast between prehistoric and historic times. In the later Middle Ages and since, asser-tion of peninsular unity has been the traditional role of the poor but hardy and warlike inhabitants of the Meseta (León, Castile and Aragón) exercised with heavy hand over the much more civilized but centrifugal communities of the seaboard. Nothing quite like this happened in prehistoric times, because Andalusia and the Tagus estuary were the dominant regions; it is only in the origin of 'Beaker' ware possibly, and in the final stages of its tradition ('Boquique' ware) rather more probably, that one may see the beginnings of Meseta overlordships, if only of a temporary nature.

Another, practical reason for treating peninsular prehistory in a single volume is connected with the relatively backward state of the subject, which naturally follows from the economic retardation and isolation of the peninsula in recent times. This retardation, which until very recently greatly restricted the numbers of professional archaeologists fully trained in modern methods of excavation and record in Spain and Portugal, and limited the facilities for training such people in the peninsula, has in turn severely restricted the numbers of archaeological sites from which properly stratified material, or even adequate plans, are available. This difficulty is intensified by the fact that most of the best work by native archaeologists in Spain has been done in northern and eastern areas, within the sphere of Barcelona University, where scientific teaching of prehistory has the longest history, while Andalusia, by far the most important area for the later prehistory, has been, until very recently, the least well endowed with competent local archaeologists, whether professional or amateur. Our knowledge, indeed, still largely depends upon the work of a Belgian mining engineer, Louis Siret, and his brother in one corner of this region, and the wanton destruction of important monuments still frequently occurs. One must add in fairness that certain regions of the peninsula – more particularly Portugal, Galicia, Catalonia and Valencia – have long produced worthy antiquarians, private and official, whose devotion to the recording of local finds and good taste in conservation work compare well with what has recently prevailed, in various countries where technical resources and professional training have gone much further than in the peninsula. The result of all this is that our knowledge of the various peninsular regions and their mutual relations is still most uneven, and liable to be transformed in various respects by future discoveries. Andalusia, in particular, probably has a greater body of important material still awaiting discovery, and more of revolutionary importance still to contribute to European prehistory, than any other part of Europe west of the Baltic and the Adriatic. In such a situation detailed regional treatments must wait, in the expectation that the rapidly improving economic conditions of the peninsula will before long lead to a great increase in competent research in the areas where it is most needed.

In a survey as brief as this, it has been necessary to omit much that would seem important to specialists and to select for special emphasis those cultural phases which represent the peninsula's distinctive contribution to European prehistory; thus the Mesolithic rock shelter art is dealt with more fully than Upper Palaeolithic cave art and the developments of the Copper Age in Andalusia and around the Tagus estuary in more detail than those of this and later periods in other parts of the peninsula. It is hoped that this sort of treatment will be more interesting and useful to the general reader than one of meticulous balance.

CHAPTER I

Primitive Hunters: Palaeolithic Period

THE HABITAT

AT THE BEGINNING of the Quaternary, a million or more years ago, the Iberian peninsula had already taken on a shape differing very little from the present one. It did not rest on a broad coastal shelf such as formerly connected Britain to the Continent, and the straits of Gibraltar already existed, even if the successive Ice Ages periodically had the effect of making them somewhat narrower than they are at present. Long before the end of the Quaternary, Man had learnt how to cross these narrow seas, but distinctive African quadrupeds of the Pleistocene like the giraffe, the camel and the buffalo *(Bubalus antiquus)*, which are known in Algeria and Morocco, do not appear in Spain. On the other hand, the general 'Ville-franchian' fauna which flourished all round the Mediterraean during the early Pleistocene – notably *Elephas meridionalis*, *Rhinoceros etruscus*, *Equus stenosis*, *Trogontherium* (giant beaver) and *Machairodus* (sabre-tooth tiger) – is found in the peninsula and apparently persisted through several glaciations, preceding and including the classic Günz. It seems that the effect of each glaciation was, broadly speaking, to drive the warm-loving fauna southwards in the peninsula, only to return northwards again during interstadial or interglacial phases of warmer climate.

The great mountain masses of south-western Europe – the Pyrenees and Cantabrian Mountains, the Cordillera Central separating the two Castiles and its extension in the Portugese Estrêla, the Sierra Nevada, and even the Atlas Mountains in Morocco – certainly developed ice caps, or extended their existing ones, during the cold phases of the Pleistocene, but it must not be supposed that the intervening country became uniformly inhospitable. The two main climatic regions of the peninsula – the Atlantic coastal strip on the one hand and the Mediterranean seaboard and Meseta on the other – remained distinct: the former was probably only marginally habitable during glaciations, while the latter became moist and fertile; the former growing as congenial as Andalusia between glaciations, while much of the latter became arid. However, we must note that climatic contrasts for fauna would have been broken down to some extent by the valleys of the great westward-flowing rivers and that of the Ebro, which would have permitted movement of large animals in search of a warmer or moister environment, according to the season.

During the Middle Pleistocene period, chiefly in the Great (Mindel-Riss) Interglacial, a new large mammalian temperate fauna spread westwards from Asia, particularly on the north side of the Mediterranean, replacing the earlier species in the Iberian peninsula, as elsewhere. It included *Elephas antiquus*, *Rhinoceros Merckii*, *Hippopotamus amphibius*, *Ursus arctus* or *spelaeus*, *Leo*, *Hyaena*, *Equus*, *Cervus elaphus* and *Bos primigenius* and, like its predecessors, survived a glaciation, lasting until the beginning of the final, Würm glaciation. It was only then that the specialized cold fauna of Pleistocene Europe – the woolly rhinoceros, the mammoth, the reindeer, etc. – appear and find their way into the peninsula. But as far as the evidence goes at present neither the mammoth nor the reindeer spread very far south of the Pyrenees and the Cantabrian mountains, while many of the older, non-specialized species went on

Fig. 3.   Palaeolithic sites and finds

1 Torralba (Soria)	6 Pinedo	10 Carreço (Viana do	15 Vila Nova de
2 Sotillo (Madrid)	(Toledo)	Castelo)	Milfontes (Beja)
3 Manzanares	7 Córdoba	11 Peniche (Leiria)	16 Laguna de la
Valley (Madrid)	8 Gándaras de Bu-	12 Casal do Monte	Janda (Cádiz)
4 S. Isidro (Madrid)	diño (Pontevedra)	(Lisbon)	17 Puente Mocho
5 Villaverde	9 Ancora (Viana do	13 Muge (Santarém)	(Jaén)
(Madrid)	Castelo)	14 Alpiarça (Santarém)	18 Urtiaga (Guipuzcoa)

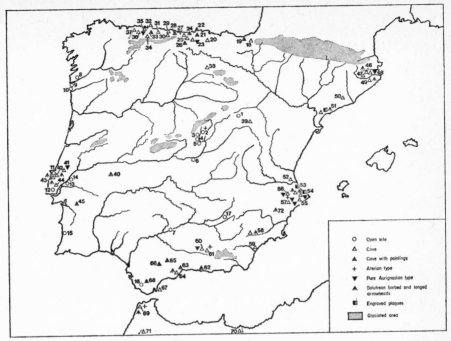

living in the southern parts of the peninsula, which were now a favourable habitat for them. This in shown by the survival of *Rhinoceros Merckii* there, as in southern Italy, and the absence of dwarf, refugee species of *Elephas antiquus*, *Rhinoceros Merckii* and *Hippopotamus* like those of Sicily, Malta and the Aegean. Favourable, that is, but for the presence of Man, who found them caught, as it were, in a trap between the ice barrier of the Pyrenees and the Straits of Gibraltar and was no doubt responsible for the extinction of some of the species before the end of the Pleistocene.

LOWER PALAEOLITHIC MAN

As a result of researches in Africa in recent years, and particularly those of Dr L.S.B.Leakey at the Olduvai Gorge in Tanzania, and elsewhere in East Africa, the important role played by that continent in the evolution not only of the human species but of the earliest human cultures, as represented by tool industries, has become clear. These cultures began in the Early Pleistocene with chopping tools, followed by hand-axes which achieved an extraordinarily widespread and uniform development in the Old World during the Middle Pleistocene (beginning in western Europe during the Günz-Mindel Interglacial, perhaps as much as about 300,000 years ago if we follow the datings based on solar radiation or palaeotemperature curves from ocean cores, or even as much as 400,000 years ago if we follow datings based on the rate of decay of potassium argon in volcanic rocks). The early stages of this evolution have recently been traced, in association with stages of the Villefranchian fauna, at sites in Morocco, and further strength has been given to the assumption usually made by students of the Palaeolithic period in western Europe, that the primitive pebble tools and hand-axes which appear there before the end of the Early Pleistocene were introduced by hominids who

Fig. 4

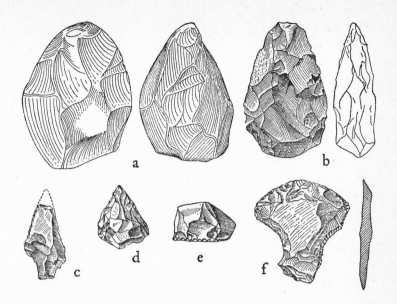

Fig. 4. Earlier Palaeolithic stone tools: a, hand-axe from Casal do Monte (Lisbon); b, hand-axe from Torralba (Soria); c, Aterian point from El Sotillo (Madrid); d, Mousterian point from Cueva Negra de Bellús (Valencia); e, Aurignacian scraper from Cueva Negra; f, tanged scraper from gravel-pit of Valdivia (Madrid) (a after Breuil and Zbyszewski; b after Obermaier; c and f after Pérez de Barradas; d and e after Jordá Cerdá). a-c, 1 : 4; d-f, 1 : 2

spread through the Iberian peninsula after crossing the straits from north-west Africa.

Unfortunately research into the Lower Palaeolithic cultures of the peninsula has lagged behind that being carried on in France and north-west Africa. Primitive-looking quartzite tools, some of them recalling the 'choppers' characteristic of early industries as far afield as Choukoutien in north China, others Abbevillian and 'Clactonian' forms and techniques, have been found in various parts of the Meseta or Andalusia in ancient river terraces (notably in the Manzanares valley near Madrid, at Pinedo near Toledo, Puente Mocho near Jaén and near Córdoba) but research into the chronology of the terraces has not yet got very far and the early Abbevillian and Clactonian tools from the Manzanares are redeposited. The Abbé Breuil and G. Zbyszewski of the Portuguese Geological Services published very extensive studies of the industries associated with various raised beaches on the Portuguese coast,

Fig. 4a

notably at Carreço and Ancora in the Minho province, Furninha and Casal do Monte in Estremadura and Muge, and Alpiarça in the Tagus valley, but their dating of the raised beaches has not been generally accepted. More recently excavations carried out by E. Aguirre at Gándaras de Budiño, near Pontevedra in Galicia, have revealed an industry with quartzite choppers and tools of Acheulian and even Clactonian tradition in an undisturbed layer thought to belong to the early phase of the final (Würm) glaciation. Although conservative coastal industries like this may be derived from ones that flourished in the Guadalquivir valley in Andalusia during the preceding (Riss) glaciation, they seem to lead on to the later 'Asturian' culture of the Portuguese and Biscayan coasts, which are certainly of post-glacial date (p. 48 below).

It is not until the beginning of the Great (Mindel-Riss) Interglacial, 200,000 or even 300,000 years ago, that we can be reasonably sure of the horizon of a Lower Palaeolithic culture in the peninsula. For it is then that quartzite hand-axes of early Acheulian form, like those associated with three lower jawbones and a parietal bone from skulls of Pithecanthropine type at Ternifine in Algeria, and other Middle Pleistocene animals, were deposited near the edge of a former lake at Torral-

Fig. 4b

ba (Soria). This lake was over 3,000 ft up on the watershed between the basins of the Tagus and the Douro and it no doubt provided a cool summer retreat for animals which had passed the winter in the lower parts of the Tagus valley. Implements like those from Torralba and the more evolved one

Plate 1

of flint from San Isidro, near Madrid are characteristic of the later hominid hunters who then frequented the warm forests of

Africa, and those of the Marne, Somme and Thames valleys, hunting the great mammals and using their hand-axes, as it seems, to dig the pits in which they trapped them and to dis-member their carcases after the kill. But we can only infer the appearance of these early Spaniards from the fragmentary bones found elsewhere, in Morocco, near Heidelberg and Steinheim in Germany and at Swanscombe in Kent: for so far no human bones have been reported from Spain or Portugal that could be as early as this. The establshed view that these early hand-axe users spread through northern Africa, across the straits and through the peninsula to north-western Europe remains attractive, but in view of the present concentration of finds of early Acheulian tools in the northern Meseta, and the recent discovery of hand-axes in Greece, it would perhaps be wise to reserve our judgment until similar tools of undoubted Min-del-Riss date have been found in greater numbers near the straits in Andalusia.

MIDDLE PALAEOLITHIC MAN

The oldest human remains so far recorded in the peninsula, like many of the earliest remains from other countries, are fragmentary, but a number of skull fragments have been assign-ed to some phase of development (in most cases a late stage) of the Neanderthal group which represents the final development of the hominids. To the old, unstratified discoveries, of an adult female skull at Forbes Quarry, Gibraltar and lower jaws at Bañolas (Gerona) and Furninha, central Portugal, have been added more recently the stratified ones of a child's skull at the Devil's Tower, Gibraltar, a parietal bone from the Cueva Negra, Bellús (Játiva, Valencia), an adult parietal and an immature frontal from the Cueva de Carigüela, Piñar (Gra-nada) and unpublished bones from the Cueva de la Campana, Piñar. The associations of these more recently discovered bones in stratified caves all appear to be with one stage or other of a local 'Mousterian' culture which was in existence by *c.* 47,000 BC, lasted into the middle phase of the Würm glaciation and survived alongside of elements of Aurignacian culture *c.* 28,000–26,000 BC, to judge by recent radiocarbon datings (GrN-1363, 1455, 1473, 1556, 1678 and 2488). It is therefore not surprising that the bones are thought to represent mainly the highly specialized form of the Neanderthal race associated with the Mousterian culture in south-western France, rather than the earlier less specialized form which flourished in central Europe during the last Interglacial. This increase of material is a by-product of the general tendency for Late Pleistocene man to make much greater use of the entrances of caves, for shelter, doubtless because of a readier command over fire as a protection against dangerous animals at night; but its restriction in the caves to skulls, in place of complete burials, seems to reflect the Neanderthal propensity to separate preservation of heads for ritual purposes.

Clearly, the peninsula cannot have been uninhabited between the Great Interglacial and an advanced phase of the last Interglacial – a gap of at least 100,000 years – and much of the unstratified material from surface sites which has been classified as later Acheulian, Clactonian, Levalloisian and Mousterian must fill the interval and represent the work of earlier hominids. But it is becoming increasingly doubtful whether the old typologically based distinctions between these classes of core and flake tools reflect distinct communities in the Middle Palaeolithic of the peninsula, and in a number of the recently studied caves of the south-east like the Cueva Negra, Bellús, the Cueva del Cochino (Villena, Alicante), and the two caves at Piñar, the levels preceding those with Aurignacian elements apparently show final Acheulian and Levalloisian forms in association with Mousterian. Toolkits were, in fact, becoming increasingly varied and specialized in this

Fig. 4d, e

period, and even in some caves in the Cantabrian area, not-ably that of El Castillo, Puente Viesgo (Santander), the early Würmian levels show the same mingling of industries. Mousterian, in the broad sense, is now fairly well represented in the central and southern parts of the peninsula, but the specialized Levalloisian technique of flake production, which appeared in Western Europe after the beginning of the Late Pleistocene, has a more restricted distribution in the south-east and in the Meseta. Since this technique is now supposed to have been the special contribution of North Africa to Palaeolithic culture, it is possible that the peninsula was here again acting as a bridge between Africa and north-western Europe. It is at any rate certain that the distinctive Aterian forms of tanged points and scrapers which characterize the later stages in this tradition in North Africa do appear on a few sites in south-eastern and central Spain, and nowhere else in Europe. Such forms were apparently already in existence in Cyrenaica by about 34,000 BC to judge by radiocarbon dates obtained by Dr McBurney at Haua Fteah (W-85-6, GrN-2022-3, 2550, 2564), and here at least we can clearly see a specifically North African influence in Spain.

Fig. 4c,f

UPPER PALAEOLITHIC MAN

By definition, the Upper Palaeolithic period is that in which Modern Man and the flint blade industries and other crafts associated with him first make their appearance in Eurasia. Outside of France and Spain, Pleistocene specialists now generally believe that the main centres of this development lay in the Near East and that the spread of men of modern physical type thence westward is related to the diffusion of the Aurigna-cian and Gravettian cultural groups, as now defined, through eastern and central Europe into the old haunts of the western Mousterian culture in south-western France, the former arriving there first, as radiocarbon counts suggest, about 30,000 BC, during an interstadial of the Würm glaciation. The earlier Chatelperronian culture of southern France, in which some French specialists have seen a local transition from Middle to Upper Palaeolithic culture, is very local and does not appear in the Iberian peninsula. Its place must be taken there by a late survival of Mousterian culture. On the other hand the 'typical' Aurignacian has a wide distribution in the peninsula, appearing not only in Cantabrian caves like El Castillo, Hornos de la Peña and Cueva Morín (Santander) and Cueva del Conde, Tuñón (Asturias), but in Catalonia at the Reclau Viver cave, in a cave at Rio Maior, central Por-tugal, on open sites near Madrid, and in the south-east, at the

Fig. 4e

Cueva del Cochino, the Cueva Negra, Bellús and various unpublished caves in the Alcoy district and in the Cueva de Carigüela, Piñar (Granada). But it is noteworthy that whereas in the north the characteristic Aurignacian flint types are accompanied by the distinctive bone points with split base, in the south the latter do not appear and the flints seem to be associated with a Mousterian industry. This has led some Spanish archaeologists to suggest that the Aurignacian may have originated in southern Spain, but it seems more likely that Aurignacian culture reached this area in an attenuated form and at a late date, possibly as a result of renewed cold conditions further north.

Of far more lasting importance for the peninsula is the Gravettian culture, which arrived in southern France *c.* 27,000 BC and spread, after some delay, beyond the Pyrenees, estab-lishing there a persistent tradition of flint-working based on the blade and the battered-back point, which ultimately gained a foothold in northwestern Africa. The Gravettian tradition became particularly strong near the Mediterranean coast of Spain, at such sites as Reclau Viver in Catalonia, the lower

Fig. 5a

levels at the Cueva de Parpalló (Valencia), the Cueva de la

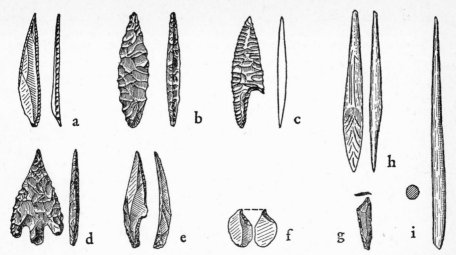

Fig. 5.   Later Palaeolithic artifacts: a, Gravettian point from Parpalló (Valencia); b, Middle Solutrean point from Parpalló; c, Upper Solutrean tanged point from Cueto de la Mina (Asturias); d, Upper Solutrean barbed and tanged arrowhead from Parpalló; e, Epigravettian tanged point from Parpalló; f, Epigravettian microburin from Parpalló; g, Middle Magdalenian microlith from Parpalló; h, Epigravettian bevelled-butt bone lance-point from Parpalló; i, Middle Solutrean bone borer from Parpalló (c after Hernandez Pacheco, all others after Pericot). 2:3

Zájara (Almería) and Hoyo de la Mina (Málaga), forming part of a west Mediterranean province to which the Grimaldi culture of Italy also belonged. This province seems to have shaped the local development of other tool traditions – the Solutrean and Magdalenian – which later spread into it from the 'classic' areas adjoining the Biscayan coast. From now on the cultural distinction between the 'dry' Mediterranean and 'wet' Atlantic zones of the peninsula, which later becomes so familiar, begins to be discernible.

Even more distinctive of the peninsula are the local forms developed there by the Solutrean culture, which flourished in southern France, as we know from radiocarbon counts, between *c.* 19,000 and *c.* 15,000 BC. These are so original, and apparently so indebted to local Mousterian and Aterian types that Spanish prehistorians have been tempted to believe in a local origin for the Solutrean. Unfortunately, a lack of relevant radiocarbon dates from Spanish caves has so far hampered an objective consideration of these views, but it now seems more likely, in the light of P. Smith's careful study of the stratification at Laugerie-Haute in Dordogne and material from caves nearer the Rhône valley, that the typical Solutrean lance- and arrow-heads first evolved in Languedoc and did not spread south of the Pyrenees until the middle phase of their development. It was the distinctive technique of fine pressure-flaking, ultima-tely applied to both surfaces of these weapons, which links the various forms that are considered to be 'Solutrean'; but, whereas

Fig. 5b, c   the leaf-shaped and laterally tanged forms appear in all the areas, the concave based form is distinctive of the Pyrenean and Cantabrian caves, while the remarkable barbed and tanged form which anticipates the finely flaked arrowheads made in eastern Spain in the third millennium BC, is only characteristic

Fig. 5d   along the Mediterranean coast, near Madrid, and in central Portugal. As these fine barbed and tanged arrowheads also occur, with leaf-shaped ones, in caves at Mugharet el 'Aliya, Taforalt and Khenzira in Morocco in levels intercalated with ones in which the locally persistent Mousterian and Aterian forms appear, it seems very likely that our west Mediterranean culture, established by the Gravettians, borrowed a fine flint-working technique from the Solutreans of the north and applied it to a weapon form derived from the final Aterians. Moreover, the marked delay with which elements of the en-suing Magdalenian appear in some parts of the peninsula supports the view that the Spanish Solutrean was a late development. It is necessary, however, to distinguish be-tween the French and north Spanish group of the late Solu-trean, and the Mediterranean group, with bone tools and barbed and tanged arrowheads, which appears at S. Julián de Ramis and Reus in Catalonia, as well as at several sites in the south-east. Whether the bow was invented by one of these groups or by the Aterians of North Africa, is a problem for the future.

The last of the specifically French Upper Palaeolithic cul/tures to cross the Pyrenees is the Magdalenian, with which are associated in France and in the Cantabrian area of Spain the most advanced stages of cave painting, artistic carving of hunt/ing equipment made of bone and antler and a decline in flint/working. Once again there is a local differentiation, go/verned by climatic differences, between the Biscayan area, and the Mediterranean regions, and in the former province and Catalonia Magdalenian forms do not appear until phase III of the French classification of the culture, and their arrival at the caves of Altamira and El Juyo (Santander) has been dated by radiocarbon counts to *c.* 13,500–12,000 BC (M 829–31). On the other hand Dr Pericot's highly productive and well/pub/lished excavations in the cave of Parpalló, Gandía (Valencia), revealed a remarkable sequence of layers in which a true Gra/vettian is followed by Solutrean, and the Solutrean by the early and middle stages of the Magdalenian, beginning, appa/rently, earlier than in the Cantabrian caves and including the characteristic bone and antler javelin heads and harpoons. But the Parpalló Magdalenian has so far proved to be an isolated phenomenon on the east coast; at the neighbouring caves of Les Mallaetes, Barig and Barranc Blanc, Rótova (Valencia), Solutrean is followed by a renewal of Gravettian forms – a tendency already represented in the final Solutrean at Parpalló, as at the Cueva Ambrosio (Almería), by a rendering of the typical laterally tanged Solutrean arrowhead in the unifacial Gravettian technique. Adaption to the warmer climate and smaller game of the Mediterranean lands then seems to lead to the appearance of very small microlithic battered back points made from narrow blades, with microburins as a by/product. These would be needed to hunt the small game which became more important as the large, warm/loving animals like *Elephas*

Fig. 5e

Fig. 5f, g

antiquus, which have usually been thought to be represented by Aurignacian or Gravettian drawings at Castillo and El Pindal and so to have survived in Spain at least until towards 20,000 BC, were hunted to extinction. This began in the Solutrean at Parpalló and continued there in the Middle Magdalenian, spreading about this time to the Cantabrian area (e.g. La Lloseta, Asturias). Spanish conditions would, therefore, have led the way in creating the Mesolithic way of life, later adopted by hunting communities all over western and northern Europe. However, we should bear in mind that the Magdalenian layers at Parpalló must represent a long period of time, during which this outpost of 'northern' culture apparently remained in touch with the parent group, also established, probably, in parts of Andalusia where Magdalenian elements are known (*e.g.* Cueva de la Cala, Málaga [harpoon]) and in other mountainous and still glaciated parts of the peninsula. It may well have been this northern intrusion into the Mediterranean province of the peninsula, during a cold climatic phase, that impelled Gravettians to spread into north-west Africa, founding there the 'Oranian' culture, c. 15,000 BC. On the other hand the 'Epigravettian' reaction which followed in Mediterranean Spain, and the spread of microliths to the Cantabrian area in the Middle Magdalenian, may have helped to create, even in the north, a certain provincialism, which manifests itself in special local forms of late Magdalenian harpoon with a single or double row of barbs and a lateral loop for attachment. Of Portugal we know little in this final Palaeolithic phase, because most of the material from Estremaduran caves has remained unpublished. In Catalonia the later phases of the Magdalenian culture are represented in a number of caves – S. Julián de Ramis (Gerona) Bora Gran d'en Carreras, Seriñá, (Gerona) and Romaní de Capellades (Barcelona).

Plate 2

Plate 8

The men of modern type who introduced Upper Palaeolithic culture to the Iberian peninsula from the north are as yet

very little known to us from local finds of skeletal material. A
number of crania found in Cantabrian caves (Castillo, Camargo, Urtiaga) are incomplete as they have been fashioned into
cups in accordance with a widespread Palaeolithic practice.
A female skull from an early Solutrean level at Parpalló,
however, is held to show Crô-magnon characteristics, as are
bones recently found in the Cueva de Nerja (Málaga), and a
frontal bone from an Epigravettian level in the Barranc Blanc,
Rótova (Valencia) is thought to resemble the specialized
North African variant of the Crô-magnon type known particularly from burials at Mechta-el-Arbi and Afalou-bou-
Rhummel in Algeria, in which Neanderthal traits handed on by
local late Mousterian (Aterian) survivors may appear. But so
far no well-preserved burial, with grave goods, has been recorded in the peninsula, nor have we any well-studied settlements (apart from layers of débris in caves) comparable to
those known, for example, on Gravettian sites in eastern and
central Europe. For the details of the life of Upper Palaeolithic
hunters in the peninsula we must turn to the equipment surviving in cave layers, so much more varied than in any previous phase, and to the animal bones found with them. These
show that horse, deer and many kinds of smaller game were
the main source of food, after the disappearance of the larger
warm-loving fauna which survived from the last Interglacial,
and it is only in Magdalenian times that the specialized cold
fauna, including mammoth and reindeer appeared, at least
in the north. But above all, to realize the increased intellectual
potential of these advanced hunters, we must turn to their
art – something unknown to the Neanderthal folk.

UPPER PALAEOLITHIC ART

The cave of Altamira, Santillana del Mar (Santander) is one
of the most famous of all the painted caves of western Europe,

and its discovery by the Marqués de Sautuola in 1879 began the controversies about Palaeolithic parietal art which continue at the present day. The paintings here and in other Cantabrian caves have often been described and reproduced in colour and there is no space to deal with them in detail here; many of them in any case belong to the final phase of Palaeolithic cave art and represent an extension of the Magdalenian culture of south-west France into the Cantabrian area. In this general survey it is of greater importance to review the spread of Upper Palaeolithic art, especially in its earlier phases, throughout the peninsula.

In the peninsula the existence of distinct Biscayan and Mediterranean provinces throughout this time renders the local application of the various art-cycles worked out in France by Breuil and his successors extremely problematical. One can do no more here than outline what seem to be the main trends, bearing in mind that precision can only come when more discoveries have been made and properly related to stratified deposits. Clearly the material available is much more limited in range than that from north of the Pyrenees. For example, the remarkable female statuettes which spread from eastern Europe with the Gravettian culture during the first main art-cycle have not yet appeared south of the Pyrenees (the 'Venus' of El Pendo (Santander) being part of a Magdalenian arrow-straightener), perhaps because these were household idols kept in semi-permanent dwellings in the open air, the like of which have not yet been found in the Iberian peninsula. Instead there are a few carvings on bone or antler, or on the walls of caves, which seem to belong to the first period of Aurignacian or Gravettian settlement there. Various signs, including the stencilled hands at Castillo and as far afield as the cave of Maltravieso, Cáceres, could belong to the first or the second art-cycle, and be as late as the Solutrean phase of development in the peninsula. Certainly the head of a cervid at Maltravieso is very like some

Fig. 6a

on trial plaques at Parpalló which we shall be considering in a moment, while the recently discovered early group of paintings in a cave at Escoural (Alemtejo) include an ox with horns painted in twisted perspective – usually regarded as characteristic of the Aurignacian Gravettian phase – as are the horns or antlers of various beasts in the Cantabrian area that are now assigned to the Solutrean phase. Moreover, the late Abbé Glory dated the Escoural paintings to the period *c.* 18,000–13,000 BC.

Fig. 6b

The difficulties in applying French systems to the peninsula are clearly shown by Dr Pericot's remarkable discovery of nearly 5,000 small stone plaques, mostly with engravings of animals but some with paintings in similar style, scattered through the successive layers in the cave of Parpalló (Valencia); these, on the basis of flint and bone objects, have been assigned to cultures ranging from the Gravettian, through the Solutrean, to the early Magdalenian. Such plaques have been found in various French cave-deposits of Gravettian or Solutrean date, but never in such numbers. They seem to be trial-pieces connected with the training of artists, who were possibly

Plates 4, 5

Fig. 6.   Early cave paintings: a, stencilled hand, Cueva de Maltravieso (Cáceres); b, bovid with horns in twisted perspective, Escoural (Evora); c, cervids in trap (?) Cueva de la Pileta (Málaga) (a after Almagro, b after The Times, c after Breuil). a, 1:6; b, 1:4; c, 1:6

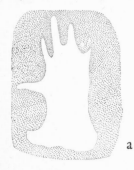
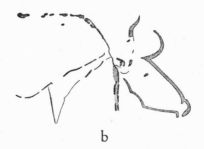

a   b   c

Fig. 6c

also sorcerers, over perhaps as much as 3,000 years – *c.* 17,000–14,000 BC. If this is so, it is strange that this school has appaʹrently left us hardly any cave paintings anywhere near the eastern seaboard of Spain (a possible exception has been published recently from the Sierra de Montsía (Tarragona)), although some of the paintings attributable to this middle phase, at La Pileta (Málaga), show an affinity; these also include what may be the work of a sorcerer practising sympathetic magic – what appears to be a painting of horned animals trapped in a fenced encloʹsure. A few trial plaques of the Parpalló type have been found in Gravettian layers at Les Mallaetes, near by, and at S. Gregorio de Falset in Catalonia. F. Jordá Cerdá is justified in complaining of past underestimation of the Solutrean role in parietal art, but the real point, probably, is that the distinction between Gravettian, Solutrean and Magdalenian, mainly based on tool types, has little significance in the peninsula as far as the art in concerned: outside the Cantabrian area, at any rate, one seems to be dealing with a distinct 'West Mediterʹranean' art province with a tendency to geometric forms as well as simple but naturalistic portrayal of animals, which took shape in southʹeastern France and Italy while Gravettian traʹditions of flintʹworking still prevailed and persisted into the Mesolithic. Most of the paintings at La Pileta (Málaga) could be assigned to this school, but it is noteworthy that at the cave of Nerja in the same area, where more simple paintings of this type have recently been found, the industry represented in the cave deposits is said to be exclusively Solutrean in character.

The highest achievement of the middle phase of Upper Palaeolithic art, about the time when Solutrean flintʹwork was spreading through the peninsula, is represented south of the Pyrenees by the outstanding carving of a horse's head on the walls of the cave of Casares, Saelices (Guadalajara), associated with a group of masked men who recall those of Addaura in Sicily. In the Cantabrian area a distinctive local style of shading, which appears on a number of fine parietal engravings, like those of S. Román de Cándamo (Asturias) and Castillo, also appears on engravings on bone found on Solutrean or early Magdalenian layers at the latter cave and at Altamira as well as on stone plaques of Middle Solutrean date at Parpalló.

In the final art phase (*c.* 14,000–9,000 BC: Jordá Cerdá would confine it to the early Magdalenian) the numerous paintings in the sanctuaries deep in the caves of Altamira, Castillo, Pasiega and Las Monedas are among the greatest achievements of Magdalenian culture in the Biscayan area gener-ally and contrast with the rather poor showing in the same area of the Magdalenian portable art – represented by a comparatively small number of decorated arrow-straighteners of rather deca-dent style like the one from El Pendo (Santander). These con-centrations of paintings, many of them superimposed one upon another in limited areas that seem to have been defined as peculiarly holy or efficacious, extending over a long period, illustrate the importance of magic ceremonies to a primitive hunting community which knew of no other way of ensuring its main food supply. The same tradition of magic shrines, now transferred to the light of day, but still kept in remote mountain retreats, lived on among the Mesolithic hunters of the peninsula and even among their successors, the Neolithic pastoralists of the mountain ranges of the Meseta and the north-west.

Plate 3

CHAPTER II

Primitive Hunters after the Ice Age
(c. 8000-3000 BC)

Fig. 8

THE END OF THE LAST ICE AGE in western Europe as a whole brought considerable economic changes for primitive man, and they are reflected in that part of his equipment which has survived for us to study. The specialized cold fauna, particularly the reindeer, which had formed the staple diet of the Magdalenians, retreated northwards, and those tribes which did not follow their prey in the same direction had to adapt their equipment to the hunting of other animals, including smaller species, to fishing and fowling, and the gathering of shell-fish. This is the explanation usually given of the general reduction in the size of the traditional battered-back points made from flint blades, which characterizes the Mesolithic. In the Iberian peninsula, however, we have already seen that this process of adaptation, and the consequent recourse to 'microliths', had begun long before the end of the final Ice Age, and the spread of microlithic industries north of the Pyrenees in post-glacial times may be partly due to migrations by their users northwards from the peninsula. Moreover, the specialized cold fauna of the Pleistocene seems to have had a relatively restricted distribution south of the Pyrenees: even in the Cantabrian area, reindeer seem never to have become very common. On the other hand the old temperate species like horse, ox and deer evidently remained in the post-glacial period, even though their numbers may have been restricted by the growth of forests, and the climate of the ensuing Boreal climatic phase, dry and somewhat warmer than that of the present day, may in the end have created extremely arid conditions in the Mediterranean areas of the peninsula. If this caused scarcity of game,

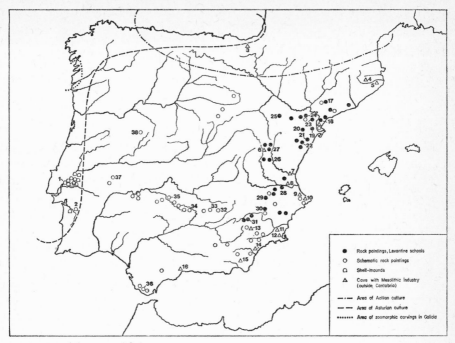

Fig. 7. *Mesolithic sites and finds*

1 Muge (Santarém)
2 Sado Valley (Setubal)
3 Santimamiñe (Vizcaya)
4 Bora Gran d'en Carreres (Gerona)
5 S. Julián de Ramis (Gerona)
6 Cueva de Doña Clotilde, Albarracín (Teruel)
7 Cueva de Llatas, Andilla(Valencia)
8 Cueva de la Cocina, Dos Aguas (Valencia)
9 Cueva de Parpalló (Valencia)

10 Cueva de les Mallaetes (Valencia)
11 Cueva de Palomarico (Murcia)
12 Palomas (Murcia)
13 Cueva Ambrosio, Velez Blanco (Almería)
14 Zajara (Almería)
15 Perneras (Almería)
16 Hoyo de la Mina (Malaga)
17 Cogul (Lérida)
18 Perelló (Tarragona)
19 El Polvorín Puebla de Benifazá (Castellón)

20 Morella la Vieja (Castellón)
21 Barranco de Valltorta (Castellón)
22 Ares del Maestre (Castellón)
23 Calapatá (Teruel)
24 Els Secans, Mazaleón (Teruel)
25 El Mortero, Alacón, (Teruel)
26 Boniches (Cuenca)
27 Tejadas Bajeras and Prado del Navazo, Albarracín (Teruel)
28 Dos Aguas (Valencia)

29 Alpera (Albacete)
30 Minateda (Albacete)
31 Nerpio (Albacete)
32 Cueva de la Graja (Jaén)
33 Aldeaquemada (Jaén)
34 Fuencaliente (Ciudad Real)
35 Almadén (Ciudad Real)
36 Laguna de la Janda (Cádiz)
37 Albuquerque (Badajoz)
38 Las Batuecas (Salamanca)

perhaps this was the reason for the battles between hunters sometimes portrayed by the rock-shelter artists!

Whatever the cause, the flint industries of the peninsula show the same increased microlithic trend as those of the rest of western Europe in the millennia which lie between the end of the last glaciation and the arrival of the first Neolithic farmers. This trend, and the other changes which characterize the Mesolithic, have generally been thought to represent cultural decline and stagnation. This is a natural interpretation in France, for the artistic capacity attested by the cave-paintings and the beautiful reindeer-antler carvings of the Magdalenians disappears there, and the equipment which has survived is obviously very limited and virtually unchanging. In the peninsula comparison between Upper Palaeolithic and Mesolithic achievements was rendered difficult until recently by the long controversy between the Abbé H. Breuil and Dr H. Obermaier on the one hand, and the Spanish school of prehistorians led by J. Cabré, E. Hernández Pacheco and M. Almagro on the other, as to the importance of the North African element in the Upper Palaeolithic and Mesolithic of Mediterranean Spain and the date and authorship of the rock-shelter paintings of this area. For many years the great authority of the first two scholars upheld the conception of a North African 'Capsian' culture based on blades and battered-back points, running parallel with the Chatelperron-Gravette-Solutré sequence in western Europe, ultimately spreading into the peninsula, possibly well before the end of the Ice Age and developing there the rock-shelter art. When the work of French prehistorians, led by R. Vaufrey, in Algeria and Morocco, showed that the Capsian culture proper was confined to southern Tunisia and adjoining parts of Algeria, and that the coastal regions of Algeria and Morocco were occupied by a different blade industry, the Oranian, which might well have been derived from the prolonged Gravettian of west Mediterranean Europe,

46

Breuil shifted his ground and in his later pronouncements attributed the rock-shelter art to Gravettians or Epigravettians, while retaining his view that this art takes the place of the 'Franco-Cantabrian' in the Mediterranean region, and belongs mainly to the Pleistocene. Now, indeed, radiocarbon counts have shown that the 'typical Capsian' cannot have begun very much before the end of the last Ice Age in Europe, and have dated the Upper Capsian at Dra-Mta-el Abiod about 5000 BC. At present, the Spanish view of the rock-shelter art has come to be generally accepted, for reasons that will be examined later (p. 54), and though it is still difficult to say exactly when it began or ended, it must be regarded as a Spanish Mesolithic achievement in the main. To that extent it is surely misleading to present the culture of hunting communities in Mediterranean Spain as in any way inferior in the Mesolithic period to what it was in the Upper Palaeolithic – whatever may be the case with the people on the Biscayan coast.

THE ATLANTIC ZONE

It is, in fact, the Atlantic coastal areas of the peninsula, and particularly the Biscayan coast, which seem to have suffered the greatest decline as a result of climatic change around 8000 BC, and in this respect to have shared, as usual, the fate of south-western France. The decadent heir to the brilliant Magdalenian culture in these regions is called the Azilian after a site in the French Pyrenean department of Ariège; its flint-work shows an increase of microlithic battered-back points and includes small gravers and circular scrapers, while fine, artistic carving of antler tools and weapons has disappear-ed. All that is left is the squat, flat and clumsily carved Azilian harpoon, the chief interest of which is that its perforated base may be derived from the distinctive Cantabrian harpoons of the Magdalenian period, with their lateral loops: perhaps,

47

Fig. 7

therefore, the Azilian culture developed originally in the Cantabrian area and spread northwards along the Atlantic coast, ultimately arriving, with its characteristic harpoons, on the west coast of Scotland. Azilian layers have been found above Magdalenian ones in a number of Cantabrian caves, notably at La Paloma, Soto de las Regueras (Asturias), Valle (Santander) and Santimamiñe (Vizcaya). No good example of the burial of grouped human skulls, associated with this culture at Ofnet in Bavaria, appears to be known from Spain.

Azilian layers on the Biscayan coast sometimes contain large numbers of sea-shells, which indicate the diet of these people. Shell-middens now become a prominent archaeological feature of the area, sometimes overlying Azilian layers and containing few artifacts other than the quartzite pebble 'picks'

Plate 6

to which the name 'Asturian' has been given by Count Vega del Sella. This Asturian industry has a much wider distribution than the Azilian, for its characteristic pebble tools have been collected from caves in the Ampurdán district of Catalonia and a great number of sites on the coast of Galicia and Portugal and on the estuary of the Tagus. It is likely that these tools represent a continuation of the Palaeolithic pebble-tool indus-

Fig. 8. Mesolithic flints: a, trapezoid point from Cabeço da Arruda, Muge (Santarém); b, triangular point from Cabeço da Amoreira, Muge (Santarém); c, pedunculate point from the Covacha de Llatas, Andilla (Valencia); d, 'orange segment' from Cueva de la Cocina, Dos Aguas (Valencia); e, assymetrical trapeze from Moita do Sebastião (Santarém) (a, b, e after Abbé J. Roche, c after Jordá Cerdá, d after Pericot). 1 : 1

a   b   c   d   e

tries of the Atlantic coast (p. 30 above), but their chronology remains to be worked out in detail. It seems probable that these beach-combers moved northwards as the climate got drier, and the Azilians vacated their collecting grounds on the Biscayan coast; they in turn were replaced around the Tagus mouth before 5000 BC by people equipped with geometric microliths, who in turn left great shell-mounds. The Asturians, like the Azilians, had inherited something from the Magdalenians, for what appear to be simplified, undecorated arrow-straighteners made of antler have been found in a number of their middens, at the caves of Balmori, Tres Calabres and Fonfría in the Asturias.

Fig. 7

THE MEDITERRANEAN ZONE

The greater part of the peninsula, as has been said, cannot have suffered as great changes in climate and vegetation as its northern strip when the Ice Age ended, and the immediate post-glacial phase there does not seem to be marked by any transformation of human culture. On the Mediterranean seaboard, where we have most evidence, the latent Gravettian tradition had, as we have already seen, replaced the Solutrean technique in flint-work before the Ice Age came to an end further north, and in some caves where there is an epipalaeolithic layer between the Palaeolithic and Neolithic deposits, e.g. Bora Gran d'en Carreres, Seriñá (Gerona), S. Gregorio de Falset (Tarragona), Parpalló (Valencia) and Hoyo de la Mina (Málaga), we find an essentially epigravettian flint industry, with small battered-back points, microburins and microlithic triangles, crescents and 'rods', recalling the 'Sauveterrian' culture of southern France, which we know from recent radiocarbon counts at the cave of Rouffignac (Dordogne) had evolved by *c.* 7000 BC (GrN-2880). There is, indeed, here a cultural continuum stretching round the western Mediterranean, probably with a northwards trend, as was the case with the Azilian culture about the same time, further west.

Over a large part of western Europe, and, indeed parts of north-west Africa as well, the latter phase of the Mesolithic was characterized by a trend towards more markedly geometric forms in flint-work and the appearance of trapezoid arrow-

Fig. 8

heads, some symmetrical and others lop-sided, some of the more elongated trapezes being mounted transversely. This stage is well represented, with a number of superimposed layers, at the caves of La Cocina, Dos Aguas and Llatas, Andilla (Valen-cia) and in the long celebrated 'kitchen-middens' already mentioned, in the neighbourhood of Muge, close to the Tagus estuary in Portuguese Estremadura – notably those of Cabeço da Arruda, Cabeço da Amoreira, and Moita do Sebastião. Among the simple triangles, crescents and trapezes at these sites occur, alike at Muge and in the Valencian caves, a peculiar-

Fig. 8c

ly Iberian form of pedunculate triangle, and there is a special

Fig. 8d

form of crescent, formed like the segment of an orange, which occurs at Llatas and other sites in eastern Spain. It used to be thought that the kitchen-middens at Muge could be arranged in a sequence, but it is now clear that there is not much diffe-rence in date between Cabeço da Amoreira and Moita do Sebastião. Radiocarbon counts obtained by the Abbé J. Roche after his recent work on these sites have shown that the lowest layers at the former were deposited *c.* 5080 BC, ±350 (Sa-195), while those at the latter were deposited *c.* 5400 BC, ±350 (Sa-16). Most of the characteristic forms of geometric microlith at these Spanish and Portuguese sites would be classed in France as 'Tardenoisian', and assigned to the middle phase of that culture. Particularly characteristic of that phase are the asymmetrical trapezes, common at Muge, which are

Fig. 8e

called 'pointes de Vielle'. As the radiocarbon counts at Rouffignac suggest that the early Tardenoisian forms had replaced Sauveterrian there soon after 6000 BC, it seems very likely that Tardenoisian influences spread from southern France down the Mediterranean coast of Spain and thence across to central Portugal or to north-west Africa, producing the 'late Capsian' before 5000 BC, and the old theories about a North African, 'Capsian', origin of the Tardenoisian must be finally laid aside.

Recent reassessments of the cultural relationships and chronology of the midden folk at Muge are particularly important because this group of sites, as a result of the old excavations by Ribeiro and Paula e Oliveira and the recent ones by the Abbé Roche, have up to now yielded a total of well over 200 burials, constituting the first statistically useful group of human skeletons on which to base the anthropological history of the peninsula. The old view of Professor Mendes Correia, that these were immigrants from Africa (*'Homo Afer Taganus'*) fitted in with the old ideas about cultural origins, but some time ago Professor H. Vallois prepared the way for new archaeological interpretations by maintaining that the Mesolithic folk of Muge were in fact descendants of European Upper Palaeolithic stocks, represented by the skeletons from Combe-Capelle and Crô-magnon, debased by a poor diet of shell-fish. There is no escaping the importance of shell-fish in the life of the Mesolithic inhabitants of Muge, for in the course of centuries a few families built up great mounds formed of broken shells and sand, interleaved with hearths and streaks of scattered charcoal, and in these mounds members of these families were buried in a crouched posture, with occasional flints and poor ornaments of shell and animals' teeth, and sometimes a little red ochre to remind us of Upper Palaeolithic ritual. But bones of ox, horse and deer are also found in the mounds, and if we are to attribute at least some of the rock-shelter paintings to them, the Mesolithic inhabitants of Mediterranean Spain had far better things to do than merely collect shell-fish: they were archers, and so after all were the

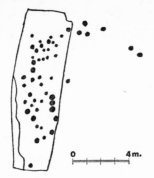

Fig. 9. Mesolithic dwelling, Moita do Sebastião (Portugal). The post-holes (at lower level)
represent a semi-circular wind-break (often rebuilt), the elongated trapezoid outline a hut-floor
sunk in the shell-heap at a higher level (after the
Abbé J. Roche)

Fig. 9   people of Muge, as their flints show. The recent excavations at
Moita do Sebastião have also provided the first tolerably
clear picture of a dwelling. The family group which first began
accumulating this shell mound built a semicircular wind-
break, about 25 ft wide at the mouth, which opened south-
south-east, and would have protected them against westerly
and northerly winds. The post-holes show that this windbreak
was rebuilt several times; the form is found elsewhere on
Mesolithic sites, including one at Badger Slacks, Marsden
(Yorkshire). At a later date, after the midden had grown in
height, what the Abbé Roche considers to have been a
different type of dwelling – an elongated trapeze-shaped hollow
lined with pebbles and breccia – was constructed above the
site of the wind-break, and a layer of charcoal, with Mesolithic
flints, accumulated on its floor.

ROCK-SHELTER ART

It is surely possible now to turn to the paintings which have
been brought to light during the last fifty years or so in remote
rock-shelters in the mountains of eastern Spain, to form a more
vivid picture of the life of Mesolithic man in the peninsula than
we can hope to do from shell-mounds, cave-deposits, or
'surface industries'. Here is an art which undoubtedly has links
with that of the cave-sanctuaries of Magdalenian times, but

which differs from it in a number of important respects. Here are artists who still multiply their pictures, over many centuries, in limited areas deemed to be specially sacred, in remote places in the hills where natural shelters are found at the foot of cliffs, touching-up old pictures or superimposing new ones like their Palaeolithic predecessors, but doing so in the light of day. The pictures are now much smaller, generally from 2 to 12 in. high but sometimes even less; they are simpler technically, usually being monochrome silhouettes, although a number of different colours – various shades of red, black, and white – are used at different times and shading does occur. The greatest difference, however, is in content. The new art of the east coast ('Levantine' to Spanish archaeologists) has lost the old reticence about man and his works. Animals are still the artist's main preoccupation, but they are now often seen in relation to the hunter. Above all, the artist now frequently composes a picture and tells a story, not only about the chase but about the activities of

Fig. 10

Fig. 10.   The Mesolithic hunter: a, encounter with an Ibex (Cueva Remigia, Ares del Maestre, Castellón); b, wolf (or hunting dog?) with a boar (Cueva del Polvorín, Puebla de Benifazá, Castellón); c, hunters following a trail (Morella la Vieja, Castellón) (a after J. Porcar, b after S. Vilaseca, c after H. Pacheco). a, b, 1:6; c, 1:4

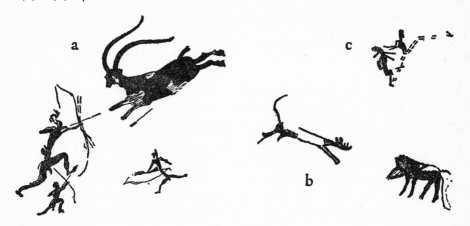

Figs. 12, 14e   the hunter's wife and the strife between tribal groups. Though lacking the detailed observation and technical elaboration of the Magdalenian artist at his best, the Levantine artist some-times achieved extraordinarily dramatic effects with a remark-able economy of means. The geographical range of this art in its dynamic phase, leaving out the decadent and schematized work of a later date, is limited to a strip of mountain country extending from the Catalan province of Lérida through Lower

Fig. 7   Aragon, the kingdom of Valencia and the borders of the Castilian province of Cuenca to Murcia and the borders of Andalusia.

Clearly Levantine art is quite distinct in its nature and distribution from that of the Upper Palaeolithic cave-dwellers. It is natural that a quite different origin should be claimed for it, but the collapse of old theories about 'Capsian' migrations from North Africa into the peninsula now makes an African origin unlikely: if there were any contacts between Levantine art and the late Mesolithic or Neolithic engravings and paint-ings of the Atlas and the Sahara at all, these must have been due to influences from the north like those which produced the late Oranian geometric flint industries. On the other hand it is hard to believe, as Breuil and Obermaier maintained, that rock-shelter art as a whole was contemporary with the offshoots of Franco-Cantabrian art in Castile and Andalusia, especially when one finds that the drawings on thousands of plaques from Parpalló are exclusively of animals, in the Palaeolithic tradition, without any concession to the varied human interests of the Levantine art. Arguments based on the alleged presence, or absence, of representations of distinc-tive Pleistocene fauna in the latter are not very conclusive be-cause it is not known whether any of these species actually still lived in Mediterranean Spain during the last millennia of the Ice Age: indeed, they are not represented in the Solutrean layers at Parpalló.

Fig. 11.   Cogul (Lérida): superimposed paintings (after Almagro). Length 2.3 m.

One of the difficulties here is that Levantine paintings are not only small, but often in a poor state of preservation owing to their comparatively exposed positions, and many are now far more difficult to make out than they were when first recorded. What is certain is that the vast majority of animals portrayed in the rockshelters as the prey of huntsmen are cattle, deer (red and fallow), mountain goats (ibex), wild asses, and boars – species which survived into post-glacial times in the peninsula. However, Breuil was on firmer ground when he pointed to the Palaeolithic tradition in some of the larger pictures of bulls and deer, particularly in the twisted perspective of their horns or antlers and the attempts at polychromy seen in a few, as at Prado del Navazo, Albarracín (Teruel) and in the famous group at Cogul (Lérida). As he pointed out, the sources of this simple but strong style of drawing, with the twisted perspective, lie in the Gravettian and Solutrean, rather than the late Magdalenian art, and it is not unreasonable to suppose that this component, at least, in Levantine art is derived from the

Fig. 11

55

Epigravettian element in the final Palaeolithic culture of the Spanish seaboard, which, as we have seen, took the place of the Magdalenian in most parts of the area.

Like the walls of cave-sanctuaries, the main rockshelters of the Levantine group are really palimpsests in which paintings differing greatly in size, style and subject are superimposed. At Minateda (Albacete) Breuil thought that he could distinguish, and arrange in chronological order, thirteen different styles, and these did not include all the distinct styles to be identified on other Levantine sites. It is obvious that groups of animals, like the bulls of Albarracín, of comparatively large size and without, it seems, originally, any role in a dramatic hunting scene, represent one particular style, which one could readily attribute to a survival of Palaeolithic tradition. As it happens, however, groups of this kind by no means begin the series as worked out by Breuil at Minateda, being later than small and quite stylized human figures, and the bulls at Cogul are not the earliest pictures in their group. The contrast between the

Fig. 12. Mesolithic warfare: Barranco de los Dogues, Ares del Maestre (Castellón) (after J. Porcar). 1 : 5

Fig. 13. Warrior with garters and 'shorts'; Els Secans, Matarraña (Teruel) (after J. Cabré). Reduced

realism of detail with which animals are generally treated in Levantine art, and the stylization – often, it is true, combined with extreme vivacity – with which human subjects are treated, again recalls Palaeolithic art, and no doubt denotes a survival of magic ideas and practices. But, as Breuil and Obermaier noted, there are several distinct traditions of stylization of the human figure ranging from the slender, calligraphic men who aim their bows at each other at Barranco de los Dogues, Ares del Maestre (Castellón), through equally stylized figures with legs of exaggerated thickness, to braves who are depicted with rather more detail, as at Els Secans, Mazaleón (Teruel) with garters and 'shorts' (for protection against scrub vegetation?), and even headgear, as at Cueva Remigia (Castellón), but who still tend to a wasp waist. On the whole it seems wise, on present knowledge, to assume that the earliest pictures in the Levantine group may be as early as *c.* 12,000 BC (this, incidentally, would explain the more credible Pleistocene animals depicted), and that the rest extend through the Mesolithic down to the arrival of the first farmers, *c.* 5000 BC and beyond. The later stage is represented not only by increasingly schematic and symbolical human figures, which have a much wider distribution in the peninsula than the true Levantine art, though

Fig. 12

Fig. 13

Fig. 14. Domestication: a, sheep (El Mortero, Alacón, Teruel); b, roped goat (?) (El Polvorín, Castellón); c, horse and rider (Cueva del Mortero, Alacón, Teruel); d, horse and rider, Boniches (Cuenca); e, woman with basket, Dos Aguas (Valencia) (a and c after Ortego and Almagro, b after S. Vilaseca, d after H. Pacheco, e after Jordá). Much reduced

many occur at the leading shrines, but by figures in a relatively natural style which appear to be engaged in pastoralism or even in agricultural activities.

In the present state of our knowledge it is more profitable to regard the rock-shelter art as a lively reflection of the cultural changes that took place in eastern Spain between the last millennia of the Ice Age and the appearance of the first settled farming communities without trying to date individual scenes at all precisely. The pictures provide some hints of the cultural changes that during this time affected costume, weapons – there are two types of bow, one with a single curve and another with a triple curve, the latter associated at Minateda with men depicted in a different technique, possibly 'foreigners' – and methods of procuring food. Though hunting is the chief preoccupation of Levantine artists and its techniques are shown with fascinating detail – deer, for example being driven by beaters towards a line of archers, as in the often reproduced scene at the Barranco de Valltorta (Castellón), the pair of huntsmen following a long trail left by game at Morella la Vieja (Castellón), and the many indications that hunting magic practised by masked men had been handed down from

Fig. 10c

58

Palaeolithic times – we can also see the first stages of domestication of certain animals. Evidence is growing that dogs had
already been domesticated before the end of the Palaeolithic in
eastern Europe and the Near East, but representations of dogs
in Levantine art are a trifle dubious: the beast which appears
to attack a boar at El Polvorín, Puebla de Benifazá (Castellón)   *Fig. 10b*
may be a wolf. There can be little doubt, however, about the
goat led with the aid of a rope by a man of Mesolithic style at   *Fig. 14b*
El Polvorín: the goat was very probably domesticated by the
end of the Mesolithic in the Near East. Sheep of Asiatic deriva-
tion are likely to have arrived early in Spain, and one is very
probably represented at El Mortero, Alacón (Teruel) although   *Fig. 14a*
its domestication is not clearly indicated. The pictures of
horses being led by a rope or ridden bareback are usually in a   *Fig. 14c, d*
rather poor style and are probably of later date than the pure
Mesolithic. There are several pictures of honey being collected
from cliffs with the aid of rope ladders, and containers, probably baskets, are sometimes shown. Finally we have the lady
at Dos Aguas (Valencia), dressed in a flowing robe and with a   *Fig. 14e*
head less stylized than those of the women who wear short
skirts only, holding in her left hand a basket, very probably to
free her right for sowing.

Fig. 15. Neolithic rock paintings, Bacinete (Cádiz) (after Breuil and Burkitt). 1 : 8

THE SURVIVAL OF ROCK-SHELTER ART

The Spanish school of prehistorians have often sought to strengthen their arguments for the post-glacial date of Levantine art by relating to it surface flint industries which have been observed close to paintings at certain sites – at Cogul (Lérida), for example, and Las Tajadas Bajeras and the cave of Doña Clotilde, Albarracín (Teruel). Such correlations cannot be conclusive but it may be significant, in view of the probable Epigravettian origin of the Levantine art, that these industries are in general of Epigravettian character while the ornamented stone plaques associated with flints of Tardenoisian affinity from the middle layer in the cave of La Cocina (Valencia) are purely geometrical in style. The extraneous influences which began to enter the peninsula in the later Mesolithic and grew stronger in the Neolithic clearly led to the decline of the lively,

Fig. 16.   Schematic rock paintings: a-b, Tejo de las Figuras, La Janda (Cádiz); c, Aldeaquemada (Jaén); d, Almadén (Ciudad Real); e, Laxe dos Cebros, Fentans (Pontevedra); f, La Janda (Cádiz); g, Cueva de la Graja (Jaén); h, Piedra Escrita, Fuencaliente (Ciudad Real); i, S. Blas, Albuquerque (Badajoz); j, Batuecas (Salamanca); k, Aldeaquemada (Jaén); 1, Las Viñas, Zarza de Alange (Badajoz) (a-d, f-l, after H. Breuil, e after Sobrino). Much reduced

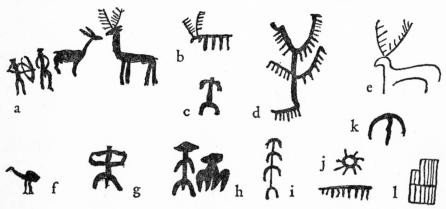

Fig. 17.   Rock Painting, Las Batuecas (Salamanca) (after Breuil). Reduced

impressionistic art of the Epigravettians. This art, however, had a long survival, in a decadent and increasingly conventional and restricted form, after the arrival in the peninsula of the first pottery-using farmers *c.* 5000 BC, not only in its original centres but in wide areas to the west and north where the best style of rock-shelter art is not found but to which the descendants of the Mesolithic hunters were gradually driven by the settled agricultural communities established on the east coast, in parts of Andalusia, and near the Tagus estuary.

The semi-nomadic folk who painted or engraved small symbols, no longer arranged with much dramatic content, on rocks in the Sierra Morena and round the Laguna de la Janda (Cádiz) were pastoralists as well as hunters, and at Bacinete in the latter area we even find stylized men who appear to be wielding Neolithic stone axes and hoes. But the old hunting subjects, mainly deer, are represented in increasingly stylized fashion not only near the Laguna de la Janda but near Almadén in Estremadura; the latest group of incised deer appears in a coastal area of Galicia, sometimes in a secondary relationship to the characteristic local cup-and-ring carvings, and probably belongs to the Bronze Age. To these Mesolithic survivals are added, in the sacred places of the Sierra Morena, painted

Fig. 16
Fig. 15

Fig. 16d
Figs. 16e, 71

Fig. 16   symbols derived from the ancestor-worship of the Neolithic
           agriculturalists (p. 110 below). In various parts of the northern
Fig. 17   Meseta, even as far west as Las Batuecas (Salamanca), paintings
           which retain something of the old naturalism have been found.
           At Cogul (Lérida), one of the principal eastern shrines,
Fig. 11   stylized animals of late date are seen, and even Iberian inscrip-
           tions which suggest that the place still had some superstitious
           value in early historical times.

CHAPTER III

The First Farmers (c. 5000-3000 BC)

THE ESTABLISHMENT of the first farming communities in western Europe was still thought of, not so long ago, as the outcome of a revolutionary phase inaugurated in each district by the arrival of new settlers from the east or the south, bringing with them, at one and the same moment, a whole series of accomplishments deemed to be Neolithic – domestication of plants and animals, bifacial flaking of flint weapons and tools, polishing of stone implements, pottery-making and the construction of permanent villages and communal burial places. That moment was earlier than c. 2000 BC, but how much earlier depended on highly subjective assessments of the speed of folk-movement and culture diffusion in various parts of Europe. During the last ten years, however, the application of radiocarbon methods of dating at a large number of sites in the Near East as well as in various parts of Europe has shown that the invention and diffusion of these 'Neolithic' arts from the original centres in the Near East did not, in fact, take place on the same narrow chronological horizon but were part of a process that began before the last Ice Age ended in Europe and went on for several millennia.

In the Near East certain communities which might be classed, on the basis of their equipment, as Mesolithic, were already evolving in a Neolithic direction by c. 9000 BC and beginning to domesticate the sheep and the goat, and certain wild grasses native to the region, from which emmer and einkorn wheat and barley were evolved. Sickle flints, meant to be set in bone handles, appear in the Natufian culture of Palestine, together with storage pits. This was followed by the growth, in certain areas, of large villages or towns, like Çatal Hüyük in southern Anatolia, or Jericho in Palestine with its

63

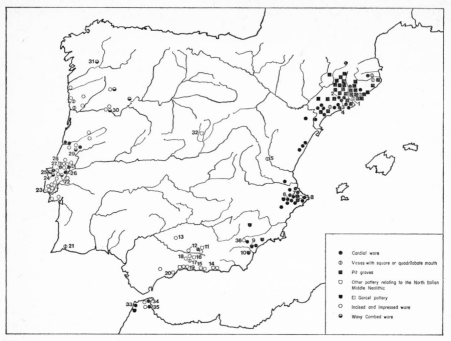

Fig. 18. Neolithic sites and finds

1 S. Quirze de Galliners, Bovila Madurell (Barcelona)
2 Montserrat
3 Cueva Bonica (Barcelona)
4 El Pany, Pontons (Barcelona)
5 Ademuz (Valencia)
6 Cueva de la Sarsa, Bocairente (Valencia)
7 Cova de l'Or, Beniarrés (Alicante)
8 Cueva del Montgó, Denia (Alicante)
9 Tres Cabezos (Almería)

10 El Garcel (Almería)
11 Carigüela de Piñar (Granada)
12 Montefrío (Granada)
13 Cueva de los Murcielagos, Zuheros (Córdoba)
14 Cueva de los Murcielagos, Albuñol (Málaga)
15 Cueva de Nerja (Málaga)
16 Cueva del Agua, Cacín (Granada)
17 Alhama de Granada
18 Cueva de la Mujer,

Alhama de Granada
19 Cueva del Higueron (Málaga)
20 Cueva Tapada, Torremolinos (Málaga)
21 Lagos (Algarve)
22 Rio Maior (Santarém)
23 Olelas (Lisbon)
24 Casa da Moura, Cesareda (Leiria)
25 Gruta da Furninha, Peniche (Leiria)
26 Santarém
27 Cabeço da Ministra, Alcobaça (Leiria)
28 Cabeço dos

Mosqueiros, Alcobaça (Leiria)
29 Eira Pedrinha, Condeixa (Coimbra)
30 Cachão da Rapa, Carrazeda d'Anciais (Bragança)
31 Orense
32 Cantarranas (Madrid)
33 El'Aliya, Achakar(Tangier)
34 Gar Cahal (Tangier)
35 Caf Taht El Gar (Tangier)
36 Cueva Ambrosio, Velez Blanco (Almería)

great walls. In these leading centres the domestication of cattle and the development of pottery came rather later, towards 6000 BC. From the Anatolian centre Neolithic civilization spread up the Danube, and down the Rhine, reaching Holland *c.* 4000 BC. Another wing of the Neolithic advance had spread villages of scattered circular huts, different from the rectangular huts of the Danubians, to southern Italy and Sicily by 5000 BC; these villagers used round-based pots, plain or decorated with nail-impressions, like those made by the Neolithic people on the coast of Cilicia, Lebanon and Palestine. A third wing, passing, at a later date, through Egypt, reached Cyrenaica before the end of the fifth millennium, and led to the development in the northern Sudan, early in the fourth millennium, of a Mesolithic culture which used Tardenoisian types of transverse arrowheads but made pottery quite closely related in its decoration to the Levantine Neolithic ware just mentioned. These hunting folk and others related to them on the fringe of the Sahara in the Fayum, Cyrenaica, Algeria and Morocco soon adapted concave-based and barbed and tanged arrowheads which are of great significance for Iberian prehistory.

Fig. 18

THE NEOLITHIC IN SPAIN AND PORTUGAL

By one way or another, in the course of millennia, the transition from the life of hunters to that of settled agriculturalists was accomplished also in the Iberian peninsula. The process, however, remains obscure because of the almost total lack of adequately recorded modern excavations of stratified open-air settlements of the pure Neolithic phase, and the rarity of radiocarbon datings, which could be the basis of comparisons with the Near East. Our knowledge of such early settlements, indeed, even today hardly goes beyond what was provided by the excavations of Louis Siret many years ago at El Garcel and Tres Cabezos in the province of Almeria. This is all the more tantalizing because the considerable amount of material from excavations in caves, for the most part without recorded stratification, or from burials or partial excavations of open-air settlements or chance finds, includes much that seems to be related directly or indirectly to what is known from the Neo-lithic phase in the central or eastern Mediterranean.

Even the rock-shelter art, as we have seen, contains many hints of domestication of animals, or even of agriculture, some of which may be of Mesolithic date. We must certainly not lose sight of the fact that there was a long 'aceramic' proto-Neo-lithic or Neolithic phase in the Near East, during which micro-liths of Tardenois affinity were used in various regions. Dr Santa Olalla, then, showed prescience when he spoke, some twenty years ago, of an 'Early Neolithic' *c.* 8000–3500 BC, followed by a 'Late Neolithic', *c.* 3500–2000 BC. In view of reports of the identification of bones of domesticated sheep in the pure Tardenoisian levels in the well-stratified cave-deposit of Châteauneuf-les-Martigues, near the mouth of the Rhône, the extraordinary resemblance, in style and content, of many of the Spanish rock pictures to some of those that were painted on the wall-plaster in the Neolithic town of Çatal Hüyük on the Konia plain in Anatolia around 6000 BC, and the evidence that boats were already making quite long journeys in the eastern Mediterranean and that the islands of Cyprus and Crete had been settled by this time, the possibility that some of the microlith-using communities of Mediterranean Spain were already in fact to some degree Neolithic by 6000 BC cannot be ruled out. Early voyagers may well have bypassed Sardinia and the Maltese islands in favour of the more spacious and fertile lands beyond, but we must bear in mind that resemblances in the art of the two cultures may simply be due to a comon inheritance from Upper Palaeolithic, Gravettian ancestors.

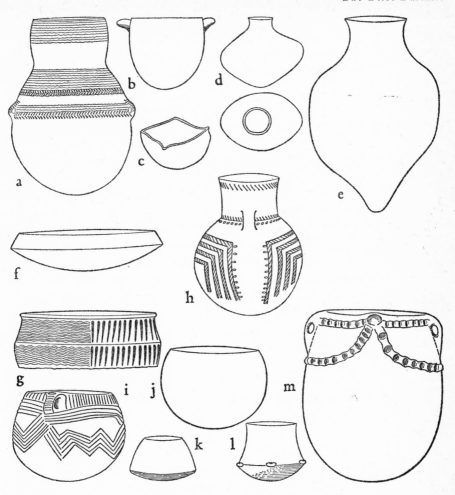

Fig. 19.   Neolithic pottery: a, Santarém; b, Casa de Moura, Cesareda (Leiria); c, Ademuz (Valencia); d-e, El Garcel (Almería); f-g, Gruta da Furninha, Peniche (Leiria); h, m, Cueva de los Murcielagos, Zuberos (Córdoba); j, Dolmen de Poço da Gateira, Reguengos (Evora); k, Las Churuletas 3, Purchena (Almería); l, Loma de la Torre 4, Purchena (Almería) (c after Fletcher Valls, d-e after L. Siret, h, m after Pellicer, i after S Olalla, j-l after G. and V. Leisner). 1 : 6

67

In further classifying his 'Late Neolithic', however, Dr Santa Olalla spoke of a 'Hispano-Mauritanian' culture that was succeeded, about 2500 BC, by an 'Ibero-Saharan', and in so doing he was making implications about the origins of two cultural groups that Professor Bosch-Gimpera had abstracted long previously from the unstratified material available to him – the 'Cave culture' and the 'Almerian culture'. Since that time there has been a reaction amongst Spanish prehistorians of the Barcelona school against what has no doubt been an excessive reliance on Africa as a source of Iberian Mesolithic and Neolithic culture, but an attempt must now be made to assess, from the unsatisfactory evidence, the relative importance of Africa, the northern shores of the Mediterranean, and direct sea-contact, in establishing Neolithic culture in the peninsula. The nature of that evidence is such that the distribution of distinctive ceramic groups and the radiocarbon dates

Fig. 19

obtained at a limited number of stratified sites in Italy, southern France and Spain, where these groups are represented, must be the main guide. In outline, it is clear on the one hand that Cardial Ware, which is so distinctive of Mediterranean Spain, must be derived ultimately from the early Impressed Ware of the Anatolian and Syrian coast, probably mainly by movement round the northern shores of the Mediterranean, and that the later square-mouthed and quadrilobate vessels of the same area must be derived ultimately from the Balkans; on the other hand the plain pottery of the south-east, initially with pointed bases or oval section, and the incised cave-pottery of central Andalusia and Portugal, must have been partly derived from North Africa, all these events taking place roughly between the middle of the fifth and the middle of the fourth millennium BC. But above all it is now clear that a contrast not unlike that which Bosch-Gimpera envisaged, between a 'Cave culture' which maintained a mixed agriculture in the mountains and a south-eastern culture which built villages in the open close to the coast and larger areas of cultivable land, and later exploited mineral deposits, is justifiable, even though the details of his classification may no longer be acceptable.

THE CAVE CULTURE: *c.* 5000–2500 BC

A number of caves in the mountains near the Mediterranean THE CARDIAL coast of Spain, and even a few in central Portugal, have yielded GROUP pottery decorated principally with the edge (sometimes even the side) of a sea-shell – usually *cardium edule* – but very often with nail impressions, incised or notched lines or even finger-printed cordons associated, to form patterns which sometimes cover a large part of the surface of the pot. The patterns are commonly formed of horizontal or vertical bands filled in with transverse or diagonal lines, herring-bones or trellises. The forms are globular or hemispherical bowls or bottles with   Plates 7, 9 lugs, perforated (usually horizontally) or unperforated, or   *Fig. 19a* straphandles which are sometimes peaked or ledged. The ware is often very fine and well-fired, with a pink slip. The main

Fig. 20. Neolithic pottery: decoration. a, painted sherd from Cueva del Montgó (Ali-cante); b-c, incised rayed circles, Cueva de Carigüela de Piñar (Granada); d, incised concentric lozenges, Cueva de la Pastora, Alcoy (Alicante); e, Olelas (Lisbon); f, Carvalhal de Aljubarrota (Leiria); g, Cueva de Nerja (Málaga); h, clay spoon from Cantarranas (Madrid); i, Gruta da Furninha, Peniche (Leiria) (a after S. Valero, b-c, g after Pellicer, d after Ballester). 1:3

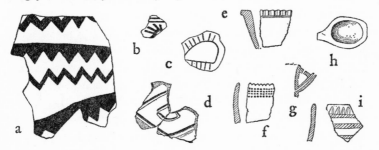

concentration of sites is in the provinces of Valencia and Alicante, but there are a number in Catalonia (notably in the hills of Montserrat) and a few in central and eastern Andalusia. The most famous site, however, is the Cueva de la Sarsa, Bocairente (Valencia) which appears to have yielded pottery belonging almost exclusively to this group, although no detailed record of stratification has been published. Apparently associated with this pottery were a number of the short round-sectioned ground and polished stone axe-heads which generally characterize the pure Neolithic in the Iberian peninsula; a flint industry of triangular or trapeze-sectioned blades, scrapers, awls and trapezes of Tardenois affinity; several bone *spatulae* of the kind commonly associated with querns on Balkan Neolithic sites of the Starčevo group and supposed to have been used for collecting the flour; pottery spoons of the simple type found in most of the Neolithic cultures round the Mediterranean; limestone discs with twin perforations like those from the Middle Neolithic layers at the cave of Arene Candide in Liguria; arc pendants made of schist; and, as a demonstration of the agricultural status of the cave-dwellers, charred grains of barley, saddle querns, serrated flint blades of the kind used in many Mediterranean Neolithic groups as sickle components, and bones of ox, sheep or goat and pig. An equally important, unpublished site in the same region is the Coveta de l'Or, Beniarrés (Valencia), which yielded much cardial pottery of fine quality, some of it with diagonally notched bands and red slip ('almagre') surfaces. The successive layers in this cave apparently produced flint trapezes and crescents in association with a number of barbed and tanged flint arrow-heads, plump ground and polished stone axe-heads, sea-shell necklaces, bone *spatulae* and arc pendants like those from La Sarsa; very recently radiocarbon dates of 4560 ± 160 BC (KN51) and 4315 ± 75 BC (H-1754/1208) have been obtained for samples consisting of charred grains of emmer and

Plate 7

Plate 9a-c

Fig. 21c

Fig. 21b

Fig. 21e

Fig. 22g

Plate 9d, e

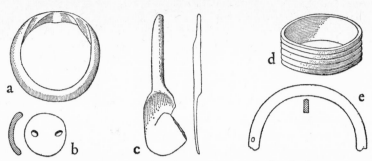

Fig. 21. Neolithic objects of bone and stone: a, pectunculus bracelet from grave; 2, Palaces, Zurgeña (Almería); b, perforated disc (shell) from Palmela (Setubal); c, bone spatula from Cueva de la Sarsa, Bocairente (Valencia); d, stone bracelet from Cueva de Nerja (Málaga); e, stone bangle from Cueva de la Sarsa (a-b after G. and V. Leisner, c, e after S. Valero, d after Illustrated London News). 1:3

einkorn wheat and barley from the lower Neolithic level in this cave, which compares well for the date of c. 4400–4200 BC recently obtained for the lowest levels at Arene Candide. Since, however, a date of 5570 ± 240 BC has just (1967) been obtained for the lower Cardial layer at Châteauneuf-les-Martigues (Bouches-du-Rhône), the Cardial Neolithic may well have begun as early as c. 5000 BC in some Mediterranean areas of Spain.

Discoveries in recent years have undermined the view put forward by Professor San Valero Aparisi in his study of La Sarsa that cardial ware was introduced into eastern Spain from north-west Africa. In the latter area recent work, synthesized by L. Balout, has tended to show how limited is the distribution there of pottery in any way comparable with that from the Valencian caves; its principal occurrence is, indeed, in coastal caves on either side of the Straits of Gibraltar such as Mugharet el 'Aliya (Achakar) and Gar Gahal and Caf Taht el Gar near Tangier, the last two having recently yielded to M. Taradell a stratification in which cardial wares underlie sherds of Beaker and other classes of Chalcolithic pottery, as it does in the Catalan cave of El Pany, Pontons (Barcelona). On the other hand cardial ware closely akin to the Valencian

71

and the Catalan has been found in many caves in southern France, notably in the deeply stratified cave of Châteauneuf-les-Martigues near the mouth of the Rhône, where Escalon de Fonton has found it lying above a pure Tardenoisian layer and underneath successive stages of the 'Chassey' Neolithic culture of France. Cardial ware of a sort also occurs in the lowest Neolithic layers in the finely stratified cave of Arene Candide on the Italian Riviera, underlying Middle Neolithic layers with Chiozza and Lagozza pottery, and with nail impressions largely replacing shell edge decoration. In this respect it stands appreciably closer to the Impressed Ware of southern Italy and the Levant. It is, indeed, remarkable that the best parallels in the Iberian peninsula to the finger-nail decoration, arranged in bands and panels, at Mersin and Arene Candide occur in megalithic Passage Graves at Olival da Pega (Alemtejo) and Guadalperal (Cáceres), both in the Tagus valley, near the route which seems to have been followed by makers of cardial and Chiozza-Lagozza ware on their way from the Mediterranean to the Atlantic. Possibly the earliest stages in the spead of cardial and impressed pottery in the peninsula are hidden from us by a failure to discover the appropriate open-air settlements.

Plate 18

At present, at any rate, cardial pottery is known to us in Spain almost wholly from caves and seems to belong to a cultural context which contrasts with that in which it occurs in the central and eastern Mediterranean. For there it is found in open-air villages which are sometimes fortified and with a very poor flint and obsidian industry, proper to people who used the sling and the mace rather than the bow. In Spain it is associated with projectile tips of the local Tardenois tradition and bone borers which probably represent clothing still largely made of skins. This and its occurrence in caves, in hill country away from the coast, usually above small valleys and limited areas of agricultural land, suggests that the users were mainly pastoralists of local Mesolithic origin, who had picked up some Neolithic arts from the occupants of open-air stettlements on the better land, which are not yet adequately explored. Once established among the upland pastoralists, it seems that in Spain, as in southern France, the tradition of cardial decoration lived on in some districts at least, until late in the Neolithic phase, or even into the Chalcolithic, as the tanged arrowheads and the cardially decorated bottles or costrels of 'El Garcel' affinity at the Coveta de l'Or, and, above all, the premonitions of Bell Beaker ware in the rosy slip and diagonally hatched bands of some vessels, suggest. This south-eastern cardial group, like the parallel central Andalusian incised-ware group, is a counterpart of the Sicilian Stentinello group of late impressed ware, with which it has many patterns in common.

Whatever may still be the uncertainties about the routes by which the cardial tradition was established in the peninsula, there can be no doubt about the source of certain ceramic forms which spread widely there during the early part of the fourth millennium BC. They are characteristic of the Middle Neolithic layers at Arene Candide in Liguria and are well represented in northern Italy generally. The most striking trait, of Danubian or Balkan origin, is the provision of square or quadrilobate mouths on jars or bowls. Vessels of this type have been reported not only from the pit graves and caves of Catalonia but from the neighbourhood of Teruel, caves near Alhama de Granada and in central Portugal (including a quadrilobate vessel from the Cabeço dos Mosqueiros near Alcobaça) and from open sites near Oporto in the north and near Lagos in the south of Portugal. Other characteristic forms of this group occur in the only well-known open settlement of this period on the Meseta—Cantarranas (Madrid), a large group of round hut-floors, recessed into the subsoil, which yielded plain hemispherical and globular bowls, jars with strap-handles and finger-printed cordons, spoons, cheese-strainers and sherds decorated

THE NORTH ITALIAN ELEMENT

Fig. 19c

Fig. 20b

with lines scratched after baking, in the manner of the early Lagozza, Chiozza and Chassey pottery. The patterns in this group are trellised bands, triangles, and chequers, like those which afterwards appear on the schist plaques of the southern Portuguese megalithic culture (p. 100 below), It does, indeed, seem probable that immigrants spreading down the Tagus valley from northeastern Spain in the early fourth millennium BC played a large part in founding the ceramic traditions alike of the central Portuguese cave culture and the southern Portuguese megalithic culture, as we shall see.

In Catalonia the pit graves sometimes contain carinated bowls, with vertically perforated lugs on the carination, which also link with Lagozza and Chassey forms, and bottle-shaped jars like those from the Middle Neolithic levels at Arene Candide appear and are copied by the later cardial ware of the south-east. A more specialized form which seems to derive from Italy, with the handle incorporating a pourer, is known from several caves in central Andalusia. This whole ceramic range is associated in the Catalan graves with trapezoidal arrowheads, bone borers which were apparently worn in the hair, and necklaces composed mainly of large beads of 'callais', a green substance of uncertain origin which here makes its first appearance in Iberian archaeology. Unfortunately no open settlements like Cantarranas have been discovered in Catalonia, but it seems that these new settlers led a mainly pastoral life, like the other cave dwellers, although saddle querns and plump axe-heads associated in Catalonia suggest a mixed agriculture. It is in this phase that the Neolithic occupation of some caves in Old Castile and the Cantabrian area of Spain seems to have begun. In the interior of Catalonia the late phase of the pit and cist grave culture, with its 'Chassey' pottery, seems to have lasted until the middle of the third millennium BC, to judge by a radiocarbon date recently obtained for a burial at Sabassona near Vich (I-1518).

Fig. 20g

Plate 10

A group of caves in the provinces of Málaga and Granada,
which includes the well-known sites of Cueva de la Mujer,
Alhama de Granada, the Cueva Tapada, Torremolinos and
the Cuevas de Hoyo de la Mina, Cala, Higuerón and Nerja
near Málaga, has yielded much pottery which maintains the
traditional shapes of the two previous groups, with a particular
fondness for globular jars with cylindrical necks inspired by   *Fig. 19b, m*
the north Italian Middle Neolithic, fingerprinted cordons of
similar origin, strap-handles linked to the body by a pair of
horizontal cordons, and rich decoration which has much in
common with the East Spanish cardial and Stentinello (Sicily)
impressed ware but prefers heavy incision, punching and comb-
ing to the old cardial technique. The recently published deep
stratification from the cave of Carigüela de Piñar (Granada)
makes it clear that this style succeeds the pure cardial decoration and must be dated in central Andalusia to the middle and
late fourth millennium BC, with some probable survival,
inland, into the third millennium. At the recently explored
cave of Nerja on the south Andalusian coast there is practically no cardial ware and the incised ware seems to follow a
Mesolithic culture without pottery. Broad bangles carved out   *Fig. 21d*
of limestone and decorated with longitudinal furrows are
characteristic of this group.

The distinctive central Andalusian incised cave pottery
does not seem to spread westwards in Andalusia, probably
because other cultural groups, which will be considered later,
had already established themselves in the lower basins of the
Guadalquivir and Guadiana, but a closely related ceramic is
abundantly represented in cave deposits in the limestone country of Portuguese Estremadura. The richest sites are the Casa da
Moura, Cezareda, the Gruta da Furninha, Peniche, the Gruta
de Senhora da Luz, Rio Maior, and further north, the cave of
Eira Pedrinha near Coimbra. In addition to the typical
Andalusian forms and bag-shaped jars with vertical lugs for

Fig. 20i

Fig. 20e, f

suspension there are numerous deep bowls with unperforated lugs, some of them plain and perhaps representing the earlier contribution of the northeastern group last described, but mostly decorated with coarse stabbed herring-bone bands below the rim or diagonally hatched bands anticipating Bell Beaker patterns. Also distinctive of this area are vertically or laterally indented rims. Sherds of these types have been found in the superficial layers of shell-mounds at Muge and else-where south of the Tagus estuary, but they are not characteristic of the pottery from the early cists and megalithic tombs of southern Portugal generally. On the other hand the ware appears in the Passage Graves of Beira and on open sites as well as megaliths north of the Douro. Clear stratigraphical indica-tions are rare on the Atlantic coast, but a layer containing pottery of this type, with microliths, has recently been found under a Chalcolithic settlement at Olelas, north of Lisbon, while on the other hand the abundant bifacial arrowheads of biconcave, rhomboid and leaf form apparently associated with this pottery in many central Portuguese caves, and the presence of collective burials of upwards of 100 individuals at Casa da Moura, Furninha and Eira Pedrinha, suggest that the pottery remained in use at least until the end of the fourth millennium in northern Estremadura, and possibly for very much later further north. Finds of saddle-querns, plump stone axe-heads and hoes as well as bones of ox, sheep, goat and pig in the central Andalusian and central Portuguese deposits, and actual grains of wheat at Carigüela de Piñar, indicate a mixed economy similar to that further east. In the province of Alicante there is at least one cave, that of Montgó, Jávea, which has produced much material that is related to that further west, as well as cardial ware, and seems to continue into the Chalcoli-thic phase. Significantly, a limestone bangle like those from Nerja is preserved from this cave. To this final Neolithic phase at Montgó seem also to belong bowls with sharply furrowed decoration, forming horizontal bands and concentric hanging semicircles, and even some sherds from very large jars of coarse ware, with geometric patterns painted reddish brown on pale buff which must reflect contact with the central Mediterranean, and begin a series of painted sherds of various kinds that crop up locally and occasionally in the southern parts of the peninsula throughout the early Copper Age.

Fig. 20a

Although the central Andalusian and Portuguese groups of cave pottery clearly owe a great deal to their predecessors in Mediterranean Spain, some of their forms and decoration seem inspired from a different direction. This applies particularly to the use of a comb to produce a broad band of undulating furrows near the rim, in a way that recalls the Neolithic pottery of Khirokitia in Cyprus in the sixth millennium BC, and the Mesolithic pottery of Khartoum in the early fourth, on pottery from various caves in central and northern Portugal. Indeed, in various parts of northern Africa, from Neolithic Khartoum to the Sahara and the Mediterranean and Atlantic coasts, bag-shaped pots decorated with a repertoire of incised and notched patterns very similar to that of the Portuguese cave culture have been found. The ultimate source seems to be the impressed ware of the Levant and perhaps to some extent that of Stenti-nello, and the spread of these forms into the peninsula appears to have brought with it, at least in the later stages, the barbed and tanged, biconcave, leaf-shaped and rhomboid flint arrowheads which characterize the later Neolithic cultures of North Africa. The notched or furrowed hanging concentric circles which appear here and there in the late Neolithic of Iberia seem also to be shared with the North African cultures, appearing as they do in the Khartoum Neolithic in the late fourth millennium BC and the Neolithic layer at Caf Taht el Gar near Tangier. On the other hand the growing resort to a lustrous red slip which characterizes some of the later car-dial ware, pottery from the Cueva de Murcielagos, Zuheros

Fig. 19g

Plate 9
Fig. 42

77

Fig. 19i
(Cordoba) with its white-filled incised decoration reminiscent of the Cypriot red-lustre ware, and the plain bowls from early Passage Graves in the Reguengos area of the Alemtejo, reflects maritime contacts with the east and central Mediterranean towards the middle of the fourth millennium, like those which brought painted pottery to the Cueva de Montgó. The influence in this case came from the 'Diana' ware of Sicily, Lipari and Malta and ultimately from the Levant. The incised rayed
Fig. 20b, c
Plate 17
circles from Carigüela are an interesting link with those painted on rocks, with other schematic pictures, at the Laguna de la Janda and in various parts of western Spain and central Portugal.

THE NEOLITHIC PERIOD IN THE NORTH-WEST

The final stage of the Neolithic in the peninsula, it is clear, saw an increasing variety of external influences and a multiplication of regional groups. It is probably now that a pastoral Neolithic economy, adapted to the Atlantic climate of the north-west, became general in Galicia, Asturias and northern Portugal, but it is likely that the Tardenois types of arrowhead were only slowly replaced by the bifacial forms of central Portugal. The pottery recorded here and there from open sites and megalithic tombs shows that the western cave culture was the main influence. One may note in particular the Portuguese cave pottery, with combed wave patterns, from various sites in the provinces of Traz-os-Montes and Orense, including a ledge at Cachão da Rapa, overlooking the Douro gorge in the former province, immediately below some rock-paintings of a purely abstract and geometric kind which are related to many rock carvings, no doubt of later date, in Galicia. Here we can perhaps see the final stage of the long Mesolithic tradition of open-air shrines incorporated in a Neolithic culture which hereabouts may well have belonged to people descended in the main from the Mesolithic hunters of the peninsula.

NEOLITHIC VILLAGERS OF THE SOUTH-EAST: *c.* 4500–3500 BC

The extreme rarity of settlement sites that can be assigned to the Neolithic groups so far described is by now apparent, and this is the justification for grouping them together as a 'Cave culture'. But a few open-air settlements are known in south-east Spain which seem to be purely Neolithic, or at least to have begun in this early phase. The most famous of these is El Garcel near Almería, where a large number of round or oval hut-floors, partly excavated in the ground but with a wattle-and-daub superstructure, were explored by L.Siret on a low hilltop many years ago. The agricultural preoccupations of the inhabitants were indicated by the numerous underground storage pits, like those used for burials at Carmona, saddle and saucer querns, serrated flint components of sickles, plump axe-heads and gouges. Burnt grains, said to be of wheat and rye, were found. Stones of the olive and seeds of the vine suggest that the traditional Mediterranean life had already taken shape locally. The flint arrowheads at El Garcel are exclusively of the Tardenois tradition as in the other Neolithic groups of the peninsula, but the pottery is different from that which must still have been in use further north-east in the modern provinces of Alicante and Valencia, and indeed is known from one or two caves in the province of Almería itself. It is plain, and the characteristic forms are an ovoid jar with a cylindrical neck and a pointed base and a costrel-like vessel with an oval section. These are common types in the 'Neolithic of Capsian tradition' of the north-west African coast and the costrels have analogues in the late predynastic Egyptian and the south Palestinian 'Chalcolithic' cultures of the fourth millennium. The pointed base does appear rarely further north on the west Mediterranean coast, even in the cardial layers at Châteauneuf-les-Martigues, and the costrel form was, as we have already seen, borrowed by the cardial potters at the Coveta de l'Or. But

Fig. 19d, e

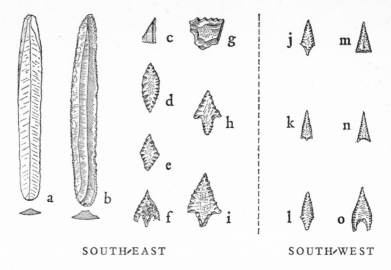

SOUTH-EAST   SOUTH-WEST

Fig. 22. Neolithic and Copper Age flints: a-b, long blades, with and without secondary working, Los Millares (Almería); c, assymetrical arrowhead; d-f h-i, typical arrowheads, Almería-Valencia; g, serrated flint from sickle, Campico de Lebor, Totana (Murcia); j-o, typical arrowheads, west Andalusia and southern Portugal (a-b after Almagro and Arribas). 1:3

the centre of distribution here does seem to lie near the south-western corner of the Mediterranean and it is likely that we are dealing with traits which had spread westwards along the south Mediterranean coast.

A similar culture to El Garcel was found by Siret at Tres Cabezos, near Almería, but here some of the pottery, with its inverted truncated cone-shaped and carinated forms relates to the second phase of the 'Almerian' culture, in which bifacial and leaf-shaped arrowheads appear, large flint blades with or without secondary working are common, and the hints of local metal-working become more definite (even at El Garcel copper slag is said to have been found. The area is, of course, rich in non-ferrous ores, but Siret may be right in thinking that these were worked for export purposes only at first). This second phase, after the middle of the fourth millennium, is

Fig. 19k

Fig. 22

represented at several other villages explored by Siret near Almería – Campos, Parazuelos, La Gerundia; at Cerro de la Cantera, Vélez Blanco (Almeria), explored by F.de Motos; and at the Campico de Lébor, Totana (Murcia), studied by Santa Olalla. At Tabernas (Almería) is another settlement in which stratification has been observed by Santa Olalla but unfortunately not yet published. Like El Garcel and the other sites just mentioned it is built on a hill and may have been defended; the huts in the first phase of occupation are said to have been round, with rectangular hearths.

The fully developed 'Almerian' culture represented by all these settlements constitutes one of the two main poles of development in the earlier Copper Age in the peninsula – one of them south-eastern and favouring the tanged arrowhead, the other south-western and favouring the concave based arrow-head – and the next thousand years or more influences radiating from these two poles control the evolution of the whole of south-western Europe. The development of this early Copper Age culture in the peninsula will be dealt with in Chapters V and VI.

NEOLITHIC VILLAGERS OF THE SOUTH-WEST: *c.* 4000–3500 BC

The Neolithic settlers of El Garcel must have arrived at a time when deforestation and soil erosion had not produced the lunar landscape for which the country around Almería is noted today, for they were, after all, primarily agriculturalists. There must have been many more settlers at this early stage in the lands in the lower valley of the Guadalquivir, which are still fertile. But we know comparatively little of them because no sites as early as this have so far been explored in the area, apart from the sketchy record of his excavations near Carmona left by George Bonsor sixty years ago. From this it is at least clear that large numbers of underground storage pits like those of

Fig. 38c

El Garcel were found at Campo Real in particular and that some of these were also used for burial. They yielded much pottery, including jars with pointed bases, as well as carinated bowls and dishes of the same type as those of the second Almerian phase, saddle querns and flint sickle elements. The ill-explored settlement at Mesas de Asta (Jerez) may begin in this early phase, but reports that some of the painted pottery from here resembles the Italian Middle Neolithic Ripoli ware must be treated with reserve. That the whole of the south-western area was settled by the early fourth millennium BC either by 'Almerians' or by the more pastoral folk who introduced to the area the north Italian Middle Neolithic forms already mentioned, before the spread of incised ware to the central western areas of the peninsula, can perhaps be inferred from the absence from this region not only of the incised ware, but of bifacially worked arrowheads of the biconcave, rhomboid and leaf-shaped types. Their place as the immediate successor locally of

Fig. 22

the Tardenoisian forms is taken by the concave-based arrow-head which, in turn, is extremely rare on the eastern side of the peninsula. Such an arrowhead is said to have been found at the base of the layers with incised pottery at the Cueva de Nerja (Málaga), and in view of the priority of concave-based over barbed and tanged arrowheads in the Fayum, Egypt, in the late fifth and early fourth millennium BC, there is nothing impossible in this. The large flint blade, with or without secondary working, now becomes a frequent element in tomb inventories as well as on settlement sites. The abundant material from burials in the south-western area of the peninsula, to be studied in the next chapter, makes up to some extent for the lack of Neolithic settlement material and confirms the impression that in the late Neolithic a cultural tide began to flow from north-east Africa along the south Mediterranean coast into the peninsula, and that this was reinforced during the early Copper Age. That, at any rate, is suggested by the arrowheads, and the fairly uniform adoption, in south Portugal, Andalusia, Murcia and Valencia, of plain pottery with an 'Almerian' range of forms – carinated, hemispherical and inverted pear-shaped bowls – linking with the Badarian forms in Egypt and ultimately the plain Neolithic ware of the Levant. There is, at any rate, no sign of a similar spread from east to west about this time along the northern shore of the Mediterranean, and the development of a similar range of plain pottery forms about this time in the Chassey, Lagozza and Cortaillod cultures north of the Pyrenees is most probably the result of influences from south-western Europe connected with the spread of megalithic architecture.

THE BURIAL CUSTOMS OF THE FIRST FARMERS

With the Neolithic the human skeletal material found in the caves of the peninsula becomes much more abundant; the communities which occupied the mouths of caves began to bury their dead much more frequently with ceremonial in their deep interiors. It is necessary, however, to make a distinction between the Mesolithic and the early Copper Age phases here, which is perhaps best understood by considering the Catalan pit graves of the early and middle fourth millennium. These were separate burials of crouched bodies in pits which, however, are sometimes grouped together in small cemeteries or even in very large ones, like that of Bovila Madurell, Sant Quirze de Galliners, which contained over 100 graves. Similar separate burials were made by the Middle Neolithic people at Arene Candide, in cists inserted in the cave earth. Some of the Catalan pit graves are, in fact, cists with a Neolithic inventory and relate to the cists with single corpses or only a small number, which precede the communal tombs in Andalusia and southern Portugal (see Chapter IV). Similarly, in cave deposits of the cardial and incised-ware group burials are certainly known but these seem in fact generally to have been separate burials in the earth. It is with the early Copper Age that the practice of burying the dead in communal ossuaries in a single chamber, which might be a natural cave devoted to the purpose or an artificial structure, became general in most parts of the peninsula, and this must be the theme of the next chapter.

It seems desirable, however, to refer here to the light that the skeletal material from these burials throws on the folk-movements in the Neolithic and Copper periods, which have just been discussed. Two main human types seem to have been observed by students of the material: a 'robust' Mediterranean ('Eurafrican') type which seems to owe much to the local Mesolithic population (represented for example at the Cueva de la Sarsa), and a shorter, more refined Mediterranean type which no doubt reflects the Neolithic immigrants from the eastern Mediterranean. Some skulls, moreover, which are broad and have flattened occiputs, have been described as 'Armenoid' and may relate to Asiatic or Armenoid settlers in the Copper Age.

CHAPTER IV

The Megalith Builders

GENERAL

COLLECTIVE TOMBS, of megalithic and related types, are among the most striking prehistoric monuments of western and northern Europe. The Iberian peninsula is one of the richest areas for their study – the remains of several thousand tombs of various types are known to exist there – and it has long been supposed that it was one of the main creative centres from which the practice of building collective tombs spread over Europe during the Neolithic and the Copper Age. Up to twenty-five years ago, however, lack of objective data for the relative chronology of architectural groups which could in theory be distinguished left the field open to largely theoretical studies in which tomb types were classified and arranged in a supposed sequence of development. This was because Louis Siret's very extensive excavations of sites of various types in eastern Andalusia remained unpublished until after his death, and other excavations by G. Bonsor in western Andalusia and by M. Heleno and other Portuguese archaeologists in the Alemtejo were also not fully published. The theories tended, as can now be seen, to oversimplification. The earlier ones, such as those of Cartailhac, Leeds, Åberg and Bosch-Gimpera, assumed an evolution from the simple to the complex, and the last mentioned scholar thought the development began c. 3000 BC in the north-west of the peninsula with simple dolmens which lacked passages, and culminated, towards 2000 BC, with the corbelled 'tholoi' of Los Millares (Almeria) and Alcalá (Algarve). This view was, indeed, an application to the peninsula of the method used by O. Montelius in classifying the megalithic tombs of northern Europe. But already at this early stage Siret himself began a trend, developed further by Wilke and Obermaier, to acceptance of Oriental, or specifically Mycenaean inspiration, of the 'tholos' tombs, and in between the two World Wars Daryll Forde, Fleure and Childe sought to derive the whole series of megalithic Passage Graves and Gallery Graves from exotic prototypes – 'tholos' tombs and rock-cut tombs – built by sea-borne colonists on the souther coasts of the peninsula. Though he substantiates this interpretation with some modifications, Dr Glyn Daniel deprecates the use of the term 'tholos' outside the area of the eastern Mediterranean.

During the last twenty-five years Dr Georg and Vera Leisner have made possible a more objective study of the problem by publishing, systematically and fully, first Siret's and Bonsor's material from Andalusia, then new material from their own and other excavations in the province of Huelva and the Upper Alemtejo, and finally that from many Portuguese excavations, old and new, in the Algarve, the Alemtejo and Estremadura. As a result, although many important excavations conducted by Dr Manuel Heleno, Director of the Portuguese Ethnological Museum at Belém, over the past thirty-five years remain unpublished, one can begin to see the tomb-types as they should be seen, in all their variety and in their proper cultural contexts, defined at least as much by the rich grave inventories as by abstract morphology. It is clear that there is some truth, after all, in the old idea of evolution from the simple to the more complex: the series does, indeed, begin with small, simple chambers that evolve from the single burial cists in Catalonia and southern Portugal, which we have already considered. But these early tombs were built in the southern and eastern, not the north-western areas of the peninsula, and it is clear that many simple polygonal and rectangular chambers in the north-west belong to the end of the series in the second millennium BC. In between lie many different regional or chronological groups which reflect the period of greatest activity and creativeness in the later prehistory of the

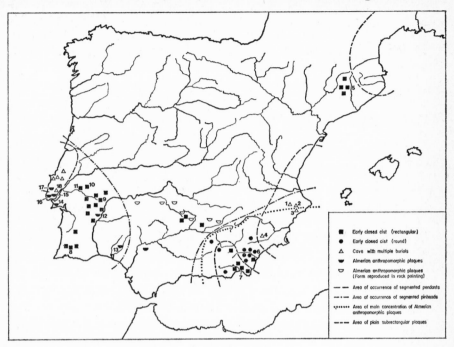

Fig. 23. The earliest communal tombs (fourth millennium BC)

1 Les Llometes
  (Alicante)
2 Cueva de la
  Pastora, Alcoy
  (Alicante)
3 Monte Barsella,
  Torremanzanas
  (Alicante)
4 Los Blanquizares
  de Lébor,

Totana
  (Murcia)
5 Solsona (Lérida)
6 Purchena
  (Almería)
7 Almería
8 Monchique
  (Algarve)
9 Barbacena, Elvas
  (Evora)

10 Madre de Deus,
   Mora (Evora)
11 Azinhal,
   Coruche
   (Santarém)
12 Olival da Pega,
   Reguengos
   (Evora)
13 El Pozuelo
   (Huelva)

14 Lapa do Bugio,
   Sesimbra (Setubal)
15 Dolmen de
   Casainhos
   (Lisbon)
16 Monte Abraão
   (Lisbon)
17 Samarra (Lisbon)
18 Gruta de Salemas,
   Loures (Lisbon)

Fig. 23

peninsula, coinciding with a climatic *optimum* in the moist Atlantic phase in the late fourth and the third millennium BC. It is also clear that this development was shaped to a large extent by external influences which constitute a unifying factor – a growing resort to communal burial, the arrival of new ceramic forms, new types of flint implement and ornament and the beginning of metallurgy – but much of the diversity was due either to the incorporation of indigenous local cultures or to local geological conditions: for example, in the limestone areas of southern Catalonia, Valencia and central Portugal the numerous caves often provided all the chambers that were required locally for communal burial and few artificial ones were built, while the geological contrast between the schists of the Algarve and the Lower Alemtejo and the igneous rocks of the Upper Alemtejo led to structural contrasts, drystone walling coming in early in the former area.

As Dr Arribas has lately emphasized, it is the use of a communal burial chamber in itself which is the principal common denominator in the period which we are now considering. This is a distinctive rite, involving the successive burial of members of a community in a common chamber, crouched very often, it seems, in a sitting position to save space – no doubt with the aid of binding cloths, basketry or cords – against the walls, and possibly in some cases the reburial of skeletalized corpses after exposure elsewhere. Purificatory fires, lit on the occasion of burials, seem to be the explanation of reports of cremated burials left by some excavators, and congestion in some chambers would naturally lead to the disturbance of earlier burials and the piling of bones out of anatomical relationship, as so often reported. Most commonly the number of burials in a chamber would run into tens, but some large artificial chambers have been found to contain more than 100 corpses. Undoubtedly this trend to communal burial reflects influences borne along Mediterranean seaways. It is charac-

teristic of most of the Mediterranean islands, but not of the
Chalcolithic civilizations of the interior of Anatolia, Mesopo-
tamia or Egypt. It is beginning to seem, however, that its main
starting point was in the southern part of the Levant, where a
tradition of houseburial, combined with a form of megalithic
construction, can be traced back to the Mesolithic period at
Einan in Galilee, and many thousands of megalithic chambers,
usually square or oblong, in Israel and Jordan are known to
have covered burials of local Neolithic or Chalcolithic date.
In this area it seems to have been the marginal, semi-pastoral
communities that practised communal burial in megaliths. On
the coast, at Azor near Tel Aviv, a rock-cut chamber of the
fourth millennium BC has recently been found in which more
than 100 persons had been buried. Further inland, settlements
of the Ghassul culture have yielded costrels like those of El
Garcel and stone amulets of anthropomorphic form curiously
like those found in the early stages of the Iberian megalithic
culture on the one hand, and in the Early Bronze Age of
western Anatolia and the Aegean islands on the other. It is
still, indeed, difficult to establish the precise sources and routes
of the colonists who established the megalithic culture in
Iberia. In its earlier phases, however, the exotic elements of the
Iberian megalithic culture stand out fairly clearly; for instance,
the practice of placing with each corpse a small 'idol' or amulet
which may be anthropomorphic or entirely abstract and which
appears to be intended to serve as a seat for the soul of the
departed. But the new-comers were certainly searching for more
than converts to their religion, and the appearance of traces of
metallurgy in certain settlements of the second 'Almerian'
phase is significant: copper had, of course, long been known in
the settlers' old homes. Yet extraordinarily little of the peninsula's mineral wealth found its way into its megalithic tombs,
even in copper-rich areas like Almería, Huelva and the Lower
Alemtejo, until their latest phase of development.

Fig. 24a-f

THE FIRST PHASE IN THE SOUTH-EAST: *c.* 4000–2750 BC

It is in south-eastern Spain that the appearance of new settlers from the east Mediterranean well before the middle of the fourth millennium is most clearly related to that of communal burial. In various parts of this area the same group of exotic types of amulet and ornament has been found with multiple burials in natural caves and chambers cut in the rock or constructed in the open. It is in Valencia and Murcia that the cave deposits of this phase are best defined, at the Cueva de la Pastora and the Gruta and Grieta of Les Llometes, Alcoy; also the caves of Monte de la Barsella, Torremanzanas (Alicante) and Los Blanquizares de Lébor, Totana (Murcia). At all these sites some of the burials were accompanied by bone pins with

Plate 11

segmented cylindrical heads and straight or curving bone pendants similarly segmented. The latter have antecedents at Tell Halaf in Syria and parallels in the Chassey and Cortaillod cultures of Languedoc. At Barsella and Blanquizares were flat, undecorated plaques of bone shaped like the stone amulets of the Ghassul culture of southern Palestine and anthropo-

Fig. 24b

morphic 'double-anchor' pendants which seem to be derived ultimately from the conventional representation of a pregnant goddess, with raised arms and sprawling legs, familiar from painted frescoes of *c.* 6000 BC at Çatal Hüyük in Anatolia. The

Plate 12
Plate 11

Cueva de la Pastora yielded rarer types: a twin-lobed stone pendant of predynastic Egyptian affinity, a crutch-headed pin, no doubt derived ultimately, like the parallels cited from the Danubian lands, from Anatolia, and a sherd which recalls the

Fig. 20d

incised symbolic eyes on the Neolithic pottery of Sicily (Sten-tinello) and the painted eyes on the Chalcolithic pottery of Hassuna (Iraq) and Mersin (Cilicia). All the sites produced

Plate 10

implements of Neolithic types – plump axe-heads and hoes, asymmetrical trapezoid arrowheads, as well as leaf-shaped,

Fig. 22

rhomboid, biconcave based and barbed and tanged, but

hardly any concave-based examples. The pottery at La Barsella is characteristically 'Almerian', plain, with bag-shaped, carinated and cylindrical or truncated cone-shaped forms.

Fig. 19

Some of the exotic types of amulet and ornament which we have just seen associated with Neolithic or early Copper Age flints and pottery in a few south-eastern caves have a far wider distribution in the southern parts of the peninsula, and as they seem to reflect a westward movement of culture, their associations are of great value for the relative chronology of

Fig. 24. Idol-plaques and amulets from Andalusia, southern Portugal and the Near East: a, El Ghassul (Jordan); b, La Pernera (Almería); c-e, Loma de la Lampara 1, Purchena (Almería); f, Beycessultan (Turkey); g, i, Cabeço da Arruda, Torres Vedras (Lisbon); h, Cueva de Blanquizares de Lébor, Totana (Murcia); j, Los Millares (Almería); k, Anta I de Brissos (Evora); 1, Anta de S. Dionisio. (Evora) (a after E. Anati, f after Seton Lloyd, rest G. and V. Leisner) (g-i of bone, rest of stone). 1 : 4

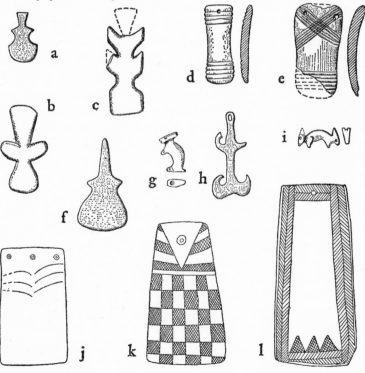

early megalithic groups. They are particularly well represented in a group of simple communal burial-chambers in the province of Almería which Siret assigned to his phases I and II, preceding the development of the 'tholos' cemetery at Los Millares. These are usually circular, from 6 to 10 ft in diameter and built of dry-stone walling, sometimes partially replaced by upright slabs and recessed into the ground, and have no entrance from the side, or entrance passage; some, however, are of similar construction but rectangular in plan. These simple lightly roofed chambers sometimes contained single, but usually multiple, burials. They tend to be poor in pottery, but this when it occurs resembles that from the caves further north. The grave goods consist chiefly of plump stone axes and hoes, asymmetrical trapeze-shaped and tanged or leaf-shaped arrowheads, pectunculus bracelets and plain, flat anthropoid plaques, usually of stone and occasionally with two pairs of arms. A rare element in this early complex is the flint halberd-head with biconcave base, like the associated arrowheads, which seems to be derived from the same source near the south-east corner of the Mediterranean. The oblong, longitudinally curving plaques with St Andrew's Cross and other carvings from Purchena, seem to have a background in Anatolia. On the same horizon flat slate plaques, like those of the Alemtejan megalithic culture but without decoration, appear and seem to be a link, like the former, with predynastic cultures of Egypt.

In the same area, mainly around Purchena, away from the coast, there are a few monuments in which a chamber, about the same size as before, and similarly formed of dry-stone walling or delicate upright slabs, is approached by a short entrance passage, which is sometimes walled up at each end. It seems that these chambers had corbelled roofs of dry stone; because of their primitive grave goods – asymmetrical trapezes and anthropoid plaques – they must stand at the head of the development represented in their area chiefly by the great

Fig. 25a

Fig. 21a
Fig. 24b, c

Fig. 27a

Fig. 24e

Fig. 25b

Fig. 22c

'tholos' tomb cemetery and settlement at Los Millares (see Chapter VI). It would be natural to suppose that these struc-tures represent a local evolution, prompted by the needs of successive burials in a communal chamber, but the idea may in fact have been brought with them by the original colonists or by later reinforcements from the same direction, for a cir-cular structure with entrance passage or rectangular vestibule, used as dwelling or temple, if not primarily as a burial chamber, is characteristic of the Middle Chalcolithic Halafian culture of North Syria in the fifth millennium BC. The Halafian buildings had domed roofs of clay and probably carry on the tradition of the circular huts built 1000 years earlier in the Neolithic village of Khirokitia, Cyprus, which had domed roofs of dry stone, brick or lighter materials. A circular struc-ture with an oblong vestibule has also been found in Cyrenai-ca, and circular communal tombs of dry walling, with various types of roof were being built in the Cyclades and Crete during the third millennium. Passage Graves of this construction, as we shall see, also appear early on in some south-western districts of the peninsula and here again the pos-sibility of a fresh maritime colonization has to be considered.

Still in this early phase, while plain flat anthropoid plaques and trapezoid arrowheads were still in use, another type of Passage Grave begins its development in the provinces of Almería and Granada. This is the truly megalithic chamber built of a comparatively large number of coarse slabs placed vertically to form a rectangular trapezoid or coffin-shaped chamber, usually recessed into the ground, with a short entrance passage similarly constructed, and covered by a circular cairn. Siret excavated some tombs of this type, with primitive elements of the kind described in their inventory, at Los Millares itself and near by at Huéchar Alhama, but the main *Fig. 25c, d* centres of this tradition lie further inland, in the upper basin of the Guadalquivir, around Guadix, Gor and Gorafe in the eastern part of the province of Granada. Their distribution is, indeed, almost wholly exclusive to that of the earlier 'round graves' and 'tholoi' of Almería and must represent a different cultural group composed to a much greater extent of indigenous Neolithic elements. These tombs continued to be built and used throughout the Copper Age in this secluded inland area, and some contain grave goods of Argaric (Mediterranean Bronze Age) character (see Chapter VIII).

There are signs that some of the colonists who introduced the south-eastern forms of arrowhead and amulet managed to extend their influence by land round the northern fringe of the south-western cultural sphere and possibly also by sea, as far as the Middle Guadiana and lower Tagus valleys, and central Portugal. This is strongly suggested by the numbers of rock-paintings of the Almerian anthropomorphic idol-plaques

Fig. 23

which have been observed in various parts of the Sierra Morena, as well as by finds in rock-cut tombs in Murcia and eastern Andalusia, to be discussed later, and by recent reports of settlement sites near the eastern end of the Sierra Morena, in the province of Jaén, with characteristic Almerian material. Actual specimens of the characteristic plaques made of bone or slate are known from a few sites in Portuguese Estremadura – a cave (Lapa de Bugio, Sesimbra), a disturbed communal burial of uncertain character (Samarra, Sintra) and megalithic Passage Graves of the local, partly rock-cut type (Casainhos, Monte Abrão). On these and other sites on both sides of the

Plate 11

Fig. 39f

Tagus estuary the segmented pin-heads are much more plenti-ful, and they are particularly common in cave deposits in northern Estremadura and as far north as Eira Pedrinha, some of which contained a large number of burials. Even the seg-mented pendant appears occasionally, and several were dis-covered recently, with pottery of the local incised Neolithic type, in the cave of Salemas, Rio Maior. Throughout this

Fig. 22

area the associated range of leaf-shaped and biconcave arrow-

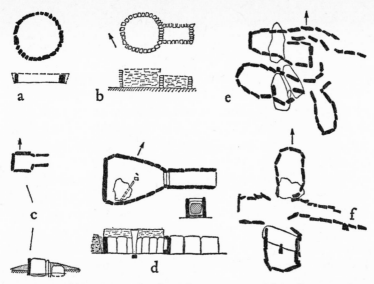

Fig. 25. Andalusian communal tombs: early types: a, Loma de la Atalaya 4, Purchena (Almería); b, Barranco de la Jocalla 4 (Almería); c, Rio de Gor (Granada); d, Los Millares 63 (Almería); e, El Pozuelo 6 (Huelva); f, El Pozuelo 7 (after G. and V. Leisner) Approx. 1 : 250

heads and halberds of the latter form is well represented in cave deposits, megaliths and rock-cut tombs.

Further south, within the area in which the concave-based arrowhead reigns alone, the anthropomorphic plaque and the segmented pin-head appear among the rich grave goods of the megalithic Passage Grave of Olival da Pega, Reguengos (Alemtejo) and in several of the multiple Passage Graves at El Pozuelo (Huelva). The pinhead, indeed, appears in the inventories of several other megalithic Passage Graves, 'tholoi' and rock-cut tombs in the Alemtejo and the Algarve. This distribution is, of course, related to the spread, perhaps partly by sea, of south-eastern flint types, and fine examples of the bicon-cave-based halberd are known from the northern Alemtejo and the province of Huelva. In much of the maritime lime-stone area of central Portugal the new-comers were evidently

Fig. 27a

Plate 17

satisfied with the abundant natural caves for burial purposes, but in the region immediately north of Lisbon megalithic tombs were sometimes built. As many of these are recessed into the rock and their inventories overlap to a large extent with those of the rock-cut tombs which succeeded them, they will be considered in the next chapters.

THE FIRST PHASES IN THE SOUTH-WEST: *c.* 3750–2500 BC

The Neolithic single burials of southern Portugal include, south of the Tagus, oblong or oval cists large enough to contain an extended corpse, built of small granite blocks laid upon the surface and apparently roofed with rough corbelling and covered with circular mounds. These appear to have been most numerous in the western parts of the Upper Alemtejo (Heleno excavations, unpublished), Portuguese Estremadura south of the Sado and around Monchique in the Algarve, but others have been explored near Elvas in the Guadiana valley. The grave goods commonly include one small, plump axe-head and a hoe, which seem to have been placed on opposite sides of the corpse, and a few asymmetrical trapeze arrowheads. As in Almería, the spread of the practice of communal burial provided the stimulus which caused these simple chambers to grow larger, without at first apparently bringing with it any great change in the nature, as opposed to the quantity, of the offerings. In a first stage of development, prob-ably around the middle of the fourth millennium, the rec-tangular form of the single-burial cist was retained, both in the western part of the Upper Alemtejo and in the Monchique district of the Algarve, in closed chambers which might be up to 20 ft long and 4 ft wide. Tombs appear later with an elongated horseshoe plan, open at one end, or with a short entrance passage. Some of these contain concave-based arrow-heads and slate plaques with geometric engravings of the

Fig. 26a, b

Plate 13

Fig. 28

Fig. 26c

Fig. 26d, e

Fig. 24k

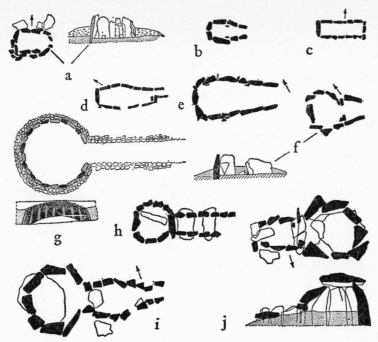

Fig. 26. *Alemtejan communal tombs: a, Azinhal 3, Coruche (Santarém); b, Madre de Deus 2, Mora (Evora); c, d Buço Preto 6, 7 (Algarve); e, Brejo, Ourique (Beja); f, Vidigueiras 2, Reguengos (Evora); g, Folha da Amendoeira, Odivelas (Beja); h, Anta de Brissos 6, Mora (Evora); i, Anta Grande da Ordem, Avis (Portalegre); j, Anta I do Silval (Evora) (after G. and V. Leisner) Approx. 1: 250*

Alemtejan type – two elements foreign to the early Almerian culture, as we have seen. The latter may, indeed, have a com-mon origin with the similarly-shaped plain plaques of the early Almerian graves, and a few examples with engraved decora-tion round the edges are quite close to predynastic Egyptian plaques, but the trellised triangles, chequers and chevrons of the typical plaques of the first phase of the Alemtejan Passage Grave culture probably owe something to the decorative patterns scratched on North Italian Middle Neolithic and early Chassey pottery which, as we have seen already, had some influence on the Neolithic wares of the Alemtejo.

Fig. 24l

Plate 19a, b

97

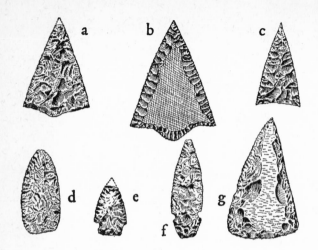

Fig. 27. The evolution of the flint halberd: a, Cabeço da Arruda I (rock-cut tomb); Torres Vedras (Lisbon); b, Casa de Moura (cave), Cesareda (Leiria); c, 'tholos' of La Zarcita (Huelva); d, Alapraia II (rock-cut tomb) (Lisbon); e, Anta Grande da Ordem (megalithic passage grave), Avis (Portalegre); f, S. Martinho ('tholos'), Sintra (Lisbon); g, Anta 6 de Brissos, Mora (Evora) (a, c-g after G. and V. Leisner, b after Aberg). 1 : 4

Further inland, in the Upper Alemtejo, another class of tomb about this time reflects the same trend to successive burial and inaugurates a development which later spread northwards across the Tagus into the uplands of Beira. In this a roughly polygonal chamber, built with a few fairly large granite slabs, is approached by a short passage attached to the chamber without regard for symmetry; there is a circular covering mound with a kerb of stone blocks. The passage is often formed of a single pair of large slabs of the same height as the chamber, and in one case traces of a small forecourt remain. In the region of Reguengos de Monsaraz, at least, where the Leisners carefully excavated many tombs, this type often has a purely Neolithic inventory, without concave-based arrowheads, rectangular-sectioned axe-heads or engraved slate plaques. The associated pottery, too, with its bag-shaped and gently carinated forms and fine wares, which are often in the Neolithic red lustre ('almagre') tradition, contrasts with the later Passage Grave and 'tholos' pottery of the south-west. The latter would seem to have been first introduced by the builders of another form of communal burial chamber which is now known from a number of recent discoveries in the Sado basin. In this a

Fig. 26f

Fig. 19j
Fig. 30a-c

large, circular chamber, from 10 to 15 ft in diameter, is approached symmetrically by a long, straight passage, as in the early 'tholoi' of Almería. Like them, dry-stone walling, favoured by the schist subsoil of the district, is often used to build the passage as well as the superstructure of the chamber; the lower part of this is carefully built of a large number of narrow orthostatic slabs, which in the monument of Folha da Amendoeira, Odivelas are alternately short and tall so as to key in the dry-stone walling of the vault. The grave goods at this site include stone axe-heads and hoes and large flint blades of Copper Age forms, several engraved slate plaques of the early, purely geometric type, and a segmented pin-head. Although this 'tholos' tradition had a long life in southern Portugal and western Andalusia and culminated in monuments like the Cueva de Romeral, Antequera in the second millennium, the early grave goods at Folha da Amendoeira and related sites like Marcella (Algarve) and Barranco de Nora Velha and Monte Velho, Ourique (Beja) show that the form must have begun almost as early in southern Portugal as in Almería. Indeed the plain pottery which appears in some of these tombs, with its fondness for rounded biconical forms with vertical or horizontal tubular lugs for suspension, is very close to the forms associated with the early closed, circular tombs of Almería, and radiocarbon readings which have been obtained for the earliest tholos-inspired Passage Graves in Brittany suggest that we must envisage a date not long after the middle of the fourth millennium for the earliest of these south-western 'tholos' tombs.

In spite of the apparent absence of copper implements from the early 'tholos' tombs of Almería and the Lower Alemtejo, it can hardly be a coincidence that both groups of tombs occur in areas rich in copper ore. The new settlers in the south-west were surely interested in these ores as well as the crops that could be raised in what later became one of the granaries of the

Fig. 26g

Fig. 46g
Plate 21
Fig. 46d

Fig. 30f, g

99

Roman Empire; under their influence the indigenous pastoralists to the north began to adapt their old-established megalithic style of construction, well suited to the granite subsoil of the Upper Alemtejo, to imitate the coastal 'tholoi' with their high vaults, by selecting very large granite slabs to make truncated cone-shaped chambers with massive horizontal capstones which tower above long straight approaching passages. The new, more symmetrically built and sometimes very large Passage Graves used to be called 'Pavian' after a group studied some fifty years ago by Vergilio Correia; the Anta do Silval, Evora and the Anta Grande da Comenda da Igreja, Montemor-o-Novo are well preserved examples.

Fig. 26b
Fig. 26j
Plates 14, 15

It is on the 'Pavian' horizon, about the end of the fourth millennium, that the influence of the earliest Copper Age cultures of the lower Tagus valley on the one hand and the Lower Alemtejo and the Algarve on the other makes itself evident in the grave goods, as well as the tomb architecture of the Upper Alemtejo. It is now that the concave-based arrowhead spreads from the south and the biconcave-based arrowhead and associated forms spread from the north. It is now, too, that the engraved slate plaque spreads from the south and the Almerian, anthropomorphic plaque spreads from the north, together with segmented cylindrical bone pin-heads and amulets in the form of animals. The rich inventory of the Anta Grande do Olival da Pega, Reguengos, from the careful excavations of the Leisners, illustrates this phase. The associated pottery reveals Almerian influence in its forms, but is generally coarser than that of the earlier Passage Graves of the Reguengos district. In the absence of well-preserved skeletal remains – even from careful excavations – upon which to base estimates of the number of burials in tombs of this period, the engraved slate plaques, which were apparently placed with each corpse as a personal amulet, are a guide: at Olival da Pega over 60 plaques are represented, at least by fragments. The standard form, the

Fig. 24g, i

Plates 17, 18

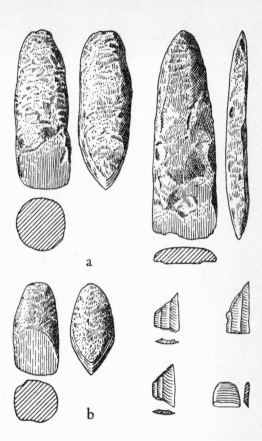

Fig. 28. Grave goods from Early Megalithic cists, S. Portugal: a, Madre de Deus 2, Mora (Evora); b, Azinhal 3, Coruche (Santarém) (after G. and V. Leisner). Axe-heads 1 : 3; flints 1 : 2

prototype, has a purely geometric decoration, probably derived from the North Italian or southern French Middle Neolithic culture, but many, especially in those Alemtejan districts that are nearest to the Tagus valley, have an indented or projecting trapezoid top (in some cases the result of reshaping of a stan- dard plaque) which reflects the influence of the Almerian anthropomorphic plaque. The slate croziers are much rarer and seem to be emblems of spiritual or temporal authority, related to those which are sometimes depicted in the hands of Egyp- tian or Hittite notables (the 'hyg'), and to the classical *lituus*, but perhaps ultimately inspired by the halberd which was one

Fig. 24k
Plate 19a, b

Plate 19c, d
Fig. 53g, b

Fig. 29

of the predynastic Egyptian contributions to the Iberian megalithic culture, rather than the axe, as Dr Heleno has suggested.

Fig. 27a
The actual flint halberds are mainly of the biconcave-based type and were probably imported from the lower Tagus valley;

Fig. 27b
some have polished surfaces with marginal retouching – a predynastic Egyptian technique. The stone axe-heads are now mostly of rectangular section and possibly reflect the influence of rarely found copper axe-heads; the round-sectioned axe-heads of the earlier megaliths become rare. Undoubtedly the rich Copper Age culture associated with the rock-cut tombs of the Tagus Estuary exerted an influence on the 'Pavian' group which is reflected even in the tomb architecture: some monuments, like the Anta Grande da Ordem, Aviz have

Fig. 26i
passages with oval plans, like those of some rock-cut tombs: a similar influence appears in the 'tholos' tomb of Monte Velho, Ourique (Beja). A very large proportion of the megaliths in the Upper Alemtejo, which total well over 1000, belong to this phase, which must have lasted at least until the appearance of Millaran influences, towards the middle of the third millennium BC.

The Alemtejo, of course, is not the only region on the Atlantic side of the Iberian peninsula in which megalithic Passage Graves are plentiful, and a study of some adjoining areas reveals a number of specialized local groups. Some of these clearly represent a development in the Copper Age of the elongated rectangular chambers which we have already considered. One is the elongated trapeze form, which occurs here and there in the Lower Alemtejo, Algarve and western Andalusia, and another is the extraordinary form with multiple elongated chambers, sometimes with a transeptal arrangement,

Fig. 25e, f
set in a circular mound, chiefly known from El Pozuelo near Huelva. Another still is the elongated coffin form which we

Fig. 26d
have already met in the Monchique area, enlarged to massive proportions; it appears here and there in western Andalusia, at

*Fig. 29. Schist crozier, Anta da Her-
dade das Antas, Montemor-o-Novo
(Evora) (after G. and V. Leisner) 1 : 4*

El Pozuelo and Soto near Huelva and Gandul near Seville,
culminating at the Cueva de Menga, Antequera. Here the
enormous megalithic chamber is nearly 100 ft long, up to 20
ft wide and 12 ft high internally. A central line of pillars had
to be provided to carry the weight of the great capstones, and
this feature appears also at El Pozuelo (Tomb No. 4). This
type is also known in Beira. It is only at El Pozuelo that the
primary grave goods have been recovered in sufficient quantity
to establish the date firmly, and here it is clear that use of both
the types of monument began in the Neolithic phase, with
abundant asymmetrical trapezoid arrowheads and round-
sectioned axe-heads, but continued into the early Copper Age
with concave-based arrowheads of the early straight-sided
form, Almerian anthropoid plaques and a few engraved Alemtejan ones; the pottery shows the same Almerian influence as
in the 'Pavian' group. A special feature of the great tombs of
western Andalusia is the mode of construction in a trench cut

Fig. 33

Fig. 30e

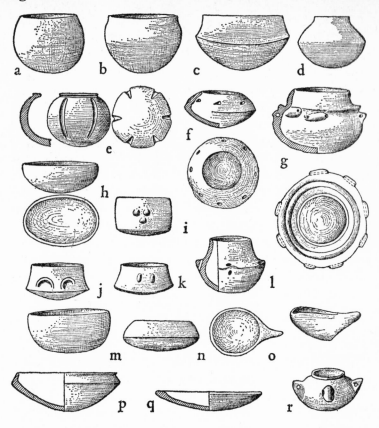

Fig. 30. Pottery from south-western communal tombs: a, Anta 2 dos Gorguinos (early passage grave), Reguengos (Evora); b-c, Anta do Poço da Gateira I (early passage grave, Reguengos (Evora); d, Palmeira 7 (long cist), Monchique (Algarve); e, El Pozuelo 3 (paired, elongated passage graves) (Huelva); f-g, Monte Velho ('tholos'), Ourique(Beja); h-i,k, Anta Grande da Ordem, Avis(Portalegre); j, Anta da Casa Branca 3(Pavian passage grave), Mora (Evora); 1, Anta de Brissos I (Pavian passage grave), Mora (Evora); m-n, Olival da Pega I (passage grave), Reguengos (Evora); o, Antas da Herdade dos Galvões, Alandroal (Evora); p, Praia das Maçãs (rock cut tomb) (Lisbon); q, Dolmen de Casainhos (megalithic passage grave), Loures (Lisbon); r, Penaclara I (Pavian passage grave) (Portalegre) (after G. and V. Leisner). 1 : 6

into the subsoil so that the capstones rest partly on the original surface, over which an artificial circular mound is raised.

The early 'tholos' tombs of the southern Alemtejo and Algarve were by no means an exclusively coastal phenomenon. Two of the 'Pavian' Passage Graves explored by the Leisners in the Reguengos area had had 'tholoi' inserted into their mounds, the lower stages of which, with their numerous delicate uprights, contrast strikingly with the massive orthostats of the adjoining megalith. The same influence appears further east in the Spanish province of the Estremadura, and further north, as well as in the copper-bearing regions of Huelva and to the east on the lower Guadalquivir and near Antequera. Here we find a tendency to elongate the passages of 'tholos' tombs and construct in a trench, a development probably inherited from the local elongated megaliths which we have already considered. These developments are late, however, and will be considered more fully in Chapter VI.

Plates 29, 30

Fig. 31b

Fig. 46g

THE NORTH-WEST: *c.* 3000–2000 BC

The main route of expansion of the Upper Alemtejan Passage Grave tradition northwards lay across the Tagus upstream from Abrantes into Beira. Nevertheless, megalithic Passage Graves are known on the coast, around Figueira da Foz and Viana do Castelo, and there are clusters of them near the coast in Galicia. But as one goes north, specialized forms, like those in which the orthostats are placed diagonally and overlapping, and rise gently in height towards the chamber, appear (as in the Anta da Barrosa, Caminha), and an increasingly large proportion of the polygonal chambers have only a short passage, or none at all. The latter class of monument is common around Vilareal in Tras-os-Montes, while in Galicia many circular mounds (*mamôas*) have proved to contain closed chambers of this or of rectangular form. In northern Portugal there

Fig. 31a

Fig. 31d

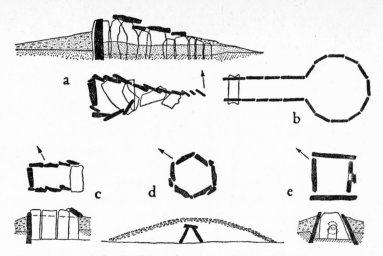

Fig. 31.   Communal tombs of the north-west: a, Val de Cadela I, Vila Nova de Paiva (Viseu); b, Prado de las Navas (Salamanca); c, Antela de Portelagem, Esposende (Braga); d, La Mourela (Coruña); e, Castillejo, Vila Nova de Paiva (Viseu) (after G. and V. Leisner) Approx. 1 : 250

Fig. 31c

Fig. 31e
Plate 16

are a number of more or less elongated rectangular chambers which, however, do not seem to link directly with the early monuments of this type in the south, for their grave goods, so far as they go, seem to be later. One in Beira has a port-hole entrance like those found at Los Millares in the later Copper Age. Comparatively few of the sites north of the Tagus have been excavated and very few indeed with adequate method, but the grave goods are clearly much poorer than those of Alem-tejo: except in the area immediately north of the Tagus, engrav-ed plaques of the Alemtejan type have not been found; the arrowheads are mainly either of the Neolithic asymmetrical trapezoid type, biconcave-based or leaf-shaped; the pottery includes survivals from the local incised-ware tradition, and forms derived from the phase of Almerian influence further south; flat based, truncated cone-shaped cups, steep-sided, round-based bowls with flattened, everted rims, sometimes with grooved decoration, which in Galicia seem to lead on to

the 'hat-shaped bowls' of the Bronze Age, and carinated
bowls, sometimes with handles, seem to belong to the advanced
Copper Age, and rather more of the northern monuments have   *Fig. 67d*
Beaker pottery, probably connected with intrusive burials.
Further east, in Spanish Estremadura and León, the 'tholos'
tradition is well represented as, for example, at Prado de las   *Fig. 31b*
Navas (Salamanca). At some of these monuments the great
size of the chamber enclosed by the thin, regular orthostats – one
is as much as 30 ft in diameter – has given rise to doubts as to
whether they were really covered by corbelled vaults rather
than by wooden roofs like that of the 'tholos' at Praia das
Maçãs (see Chapter VI). In this area, too, the local trapezoid   Plate 23
arrowheads and Neolithic incised ware survive among the
grave goods, but the relative frequency of Beaker pottery,
some of it of late types, suggests a continued use in the Early
Bronze Age.

THE NORTH-EAST: *c.* 2750–1500 BC

The greater part of the Spanish meseta has few recorded
megalithic tombs and this cannot be due entirely to geological
factors. It is possible that a local pastoral culture, which retained separate burial and later made Beakers, was here resist-
ing the spread of communal burial. However, a few of the
builders of communal tombs who had established themselves
on the western fringe of the meseta seem to have reached its
north-eastern fringe, on the watershed between the Duero and
Tagus basins and that of the Ebro, for here are found a few
monuments in the 'tholos' tradition, while a few megalithic
Passage Graves with polygonal chambers are known on both
sides of the Ebro valley in the provinces of Logroño and Alava
(e.g. the Chabola de la Hechicera, El Villar, Haro). But
beyond this, in the Basque provinces, Upper Aragon and
northern Catalonia, is a different megalithic province in which

the dominant form is a large rectangular cist usually made of three to six orthostats as in Galicia or Asturias, probably developed locally from the small single burial cists of the Neolithic period. Only at the eastern end of this Pyrenean belt, in the north-east Catalan district of the Alto Ampurdán, are there a number of megalithic Passage Graves, set in circular mounds. These, however, have rectangular or trapezoid chambers like those of eastern Andalusia, and like similar tombs in parts of Languedoc, reflect actual colonization from south eastern Spain – a connection which is emphasized by the port-holes which separate chamber from passage in two megalithic tombs of Gallery rather than Passage Grave form at Artajona in Navarre. In the same part of Catalonia and further south, in the Gabarras, are other megalithic tombs in which the distinction between chamber and passage is blurred in the same way as it is in a tomb at El Pozuelo and at the

Plate 22

Cueva de Menga – the Cova d'en Diana is an example – and other monuments are quite parallel-sided, qualifying as Gallery Graves, though the cultural significance of this development in Catalonia and other parts of the peninsula should not be exaggerated. The grave goods from a Passage Grave of the Cova d'en Daina type at Puig Roig, Torrent, include plain

Plate 25

bowls of Almerian forms and plain slate plaques like those of the second Almerian phase, as well as Beaker sherds, handled jugs and V-perforated, prismatic bone plaques which represent use extending into the second millennium. This type of assemblage is repeated at many other Catalan Passage and Gallery Graves, and one slate plaque found outside a cave at Burriac (Barcelona) actually has engraved geometric ornament of the Alemtejan type. Further west, in the Pyrenean foot-hills, the standard oblong megalithic cist undoubtedly remained in use among the upland shepherds far into the second millennium, as did the similar tombs on the *causses* of Languedoc (see below, p. 205).

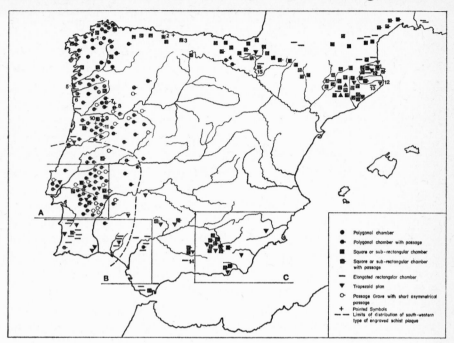

Fig. 32. Megalithic communal tombs

1 La Mourela
  (Coruña)
2 Capilla de Santa
  Cruz, Cangas de
  Onis (Asturias)
3 Peña Tú
  (Asturias)
4 Chabola de la
  Hechicera, El
  Villar (Álava)

5 Anta de Barrosa
  (Viana do
  Castelo)
6 Antela de
  Portelagem
  (Braga)
7 Vila Real
8 Carrazedo de
  Anciães
  (Bragança)

9 Antelas, Oliveira
  de Frades
  (Viseu)
10 Castillejo, Vila
  Nova de Paiva
  (Viseu)
11 Vale de Cadela,
  Vila Nova
  de Paiva
  (Viseu)

12 Puig Roíg,
  Torrent (Gerona)
13 Cova d'en Daina,
  Romañá de la
  Selva (Gerona)
14 Cueva de la Menga,
  Antequera
  (Málaga)
15 Artajona
  (Navarre)

The names of other sites mentioned in the text are given in the lists for the Inset Maps Figs. 41, 45 and 48 of Lower Tagus, the south-east and south-west (=A—C)

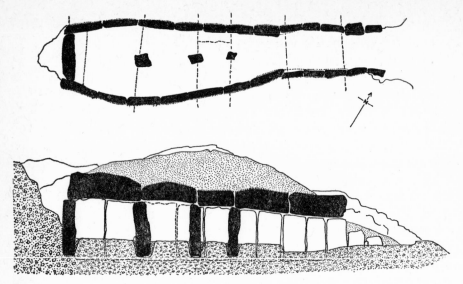

Fig. 33.   The Cueva de Menga, Antequera (Málaga) (after G. and V. Leisner). Length of chamber 25 m.

THE SYMBOLISM OF THE MEGALITH BUILDERS

Wherever megalithic collective tombs built in the southern Portuguese and Andalusian tradition occur in western Europe, a small proportion of the surviving monuments still have, engraved or painted on the inner surface of the orthostats or capstones, abstract symbols of a particular kind, connected very probably, with ancestor worship. Apart from cup-marks, which belong to a distinct, much more widely distributed tradition, these symbols do not seem to be characteristic of the earlier tombs in original centres of megalithic architecture in the Alemtejo and eastern Andalusia; moreover the flat anthro-pomorphic idol form which, as previously mentioned, was copied by the rock-paintings of the Sierra Morena from the

Plate 17 · second Almerian culture about the time the first megaliths were being built in southern Iberia, does not appear among the

symbols found on the orthostats of megalithic chambers. These
seem, in fact, to represent the final stage of schematization of
the abstract human figures which we have already seen (p. 61
above) being taken over by the earliest farming communities
from the Mesolithic artists. Since they are characteristic of a
late stage of the western megalithic culture rather than of the
'tholos' tombs of Almería or southern Portugal, they may represent cultural fusion in the pastoral communities of the interior.
The carvings inside the Cueva de Menga, on the related monument at Soto, Trigueros (Huelva) and at the Pedra dos Mouros,
Belas (Lisbon) are typical: similar carved figures and purely
geometric symbols are often carved on rock surfaces in the
open in Tras-os-Montes and Galicia. Similar figures are
sometimes painted in red or black and this tradition of polychromy is chiefly characteristic of the Passage Graves of Beira,
although a number appear on monuments near Carrazeda de
Anciães in Tras-os-Montes and alongside the painting of a
statue-menhir on the rock of Peña Tú near Llanes (Asturias).
The most remarkable of these paintings are those recently
found in the Dolmen de Antelas, Oliveira de Frades, where a

Fig. 34a, b, d

Fig. 34e

*Fig. 34. Megalithic carvings
and paintings: a, Cueva de
Menga, Antequera (Málaga)
(carving); b, Dolmen 2 de
Soto, Trigueros (Huelva)
(carving); c,Granja de Toniñu-
elo, Jerez de los Caballeros
(Badajoz) (carving); d, Pedra
dos Mouros, Belas (Lisbon)
(carving); e, Peña Tú (A-
sturias) (carved and painted rock
surface) (a-c after G. and V.
Leisner, d after V. Correia, e
after J. Cabré). 1:20*

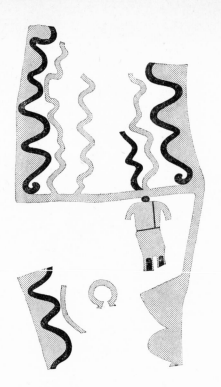

Fig. 35
Fig. 39b-d

Fig. 36

somewhat more realistic human figure is associated with a comb, like actual specimens found in tombs further south (see p. 122 below), a crozier, an anthropoid plaque of the kind common near the Tagus valley, and multiple wavy lines. The latter occur on several other monuments in Galicia and Asturias (Capilla de Santa Cruz, Cangas de Onís) as well as northern Portugal and in some cases at least seem to represent snakes. The schematized human faces at Soto and Peña Tú must be the starting point for the statue-menhirs of southern France, with their croziers, and the Mother Goddesses of the Marne grottoes; the wavy lines of Antelas are repeated quite closely on the central slab of the Bryn-celli-ddu Passage Grave in Anglesey.

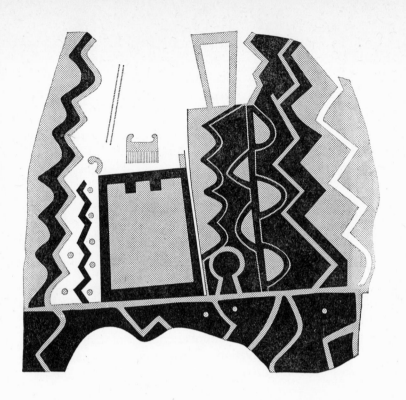

THE SETTLEMENTS AND CEREMONIAL ENCLOSURES

We should be able to follow up the apparent distinction between coastal copper-workers and inland pastoralists and
farmers with greater precision if a few settlements of the megalith-builders had been excavated with modern method, but
unfortunately not a single one has been explored in this way,
or even accurately planned and described. Many years ago
Vergilio Correia partially excavated a settlement near Pavia
in the Upper Alemtejo, which had been built on a promontory
overlooking the river Tera and fortified on the level side with
a dry-stone wall at some stage of its history. The typical plain
pottery, arrowheads and axe-heads (mainly of rectangular
section) and fragments of engraved slate plaques suggest that

Fig. 50e

this settlement belonged to the megalith-builders. Rectangular clay plaques with perforations at the corners and clay crescents perforated at the ends (loom-weights?) occur also at Copper Age settlements in Almería and Ribatejo. Sites yielding similar material are known elsewhere in the Alemtejo, notably at the Castelo do Giraldo, Evora, but here recent trial excavations by Afonso do Paço have shown that the dry-stone wall, 123 yds in circumference, which surrounds the settlement, was built on top of the occupation layer yielding 'Passage Grave' material. The querns and rubbers from these sites at least prove that their occupants were farmers as well as herdsmen. Ritual enclosures are even vaguer: one of the early single-burial chambers near Pavia is set in a dry-walled enclosure some 50 yds long, and in the same area is a horseshoe-shaped enclosure of widely spaced blocks, some 10 yds long. In Galicia are some ancient circular dry-walled enclosures with single entrances, and there are old accounts of alignments of standing stones. Without proper excavations, however, it is impossible to say whether these structures are contemporary with megaliths.

CHRONOLOGY

At the time of writing there are still no radiocarbon dates from the peninsula itself which can be confidently related to a particular phase in the history of a megalithic tomb. The dates from Los Millares (see p. 155 below) do, however, serve as a rough *terminus ante quem* for the main development of megalithic Passage Graves, and general confirmation of the view that the megalithic communal tomb began its evolution in Iberia well before the middle of the fourth millennium is provided by a series of radiocarbon dates which suggest that megalithic Passage Graves, including ones with corbelled roofs in the Iberian 'tholos' tradition, were already being built in Brittany well before 3000 BC: there is really no sound alternative to the old-established view that such tombs must have been inspired from Iberia. That inspiration must have come before the Alemtejan engraved slate plaques and croziers came into general use, for the latter did not establish themselves in north-west Europe.

CHAPTER V

Rock-cut Tombs and the Tagus Culture

GENERAL

IN THE PREVIOUS CHAPTER, when dealing with the spread of collective burial and associated cultural forms westward through the southern areas of the peninsula, we deferred consideration of another type of collective tomb which in its earliest stages, at least, is closely associated with the diffusion of early Almerian types into the interior of southern Spain and the lands around the Tagus estuary: the rock-cut tomb or artificial cave. The earlier form of rock-cut tomb, found chiefly in parts of Andalusia and Murcia where natural caves are not plentiful but the rock is easily cut, is carved deeply into a slope approached only by a horizontal passage or a vertical shaft; it represents the westernmost occurrence of a widespread Mediterranean type in use from the fourth to the second millennium BC and closely connected with maritime colonization, trade, and early metallurgy. Around the Tagus estuary, however, a special form developed which is hardly found elsewhere: the roof of the chamber comes close to the surface of the rock and is pierced by a circular opening which could be sealed by a cover slab. This slab could be lifted to admit successive burials without disturbing deposits and no doubt had a special ritual use. This locally specialized form of collective tomb is one of the distinctive types of a highly original culture which developed around the Tagus mouth during the first half of the third millennium. With the Alemtejan Passage-Grave culture, which it influenced, it was no less important creatively, than in the peninsula the 'tholos' tomb culture of Almería, a culture that finally became focussed, about the middle of the millennium, on the fortified settlement and cemetery at Los Millares.

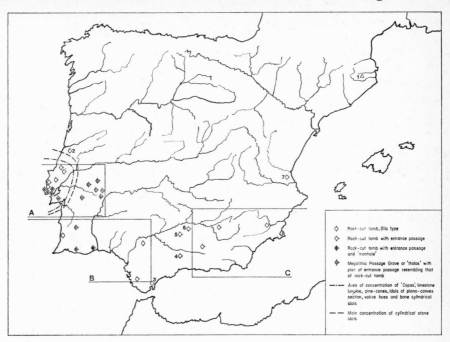

Fig. 37. Rock-cut tombs

1 Cova dels Encantats, Seriñá (Gerona)	3 Jimena de la Frontera (Cádiz)	5 Cabra (Córdoba) 6 Marroquies Altos (Jaén)	7 Castellet de Porquet (Valencia)
2 Pombal (Leiria)	4 Alcaide (Málaga)		

THE MEDITERRANEAN BACKGROUND

In almost every Mediterranean region where collective burial
came into use, during the early part of the fourth millennium,
rock-cut tombs were adopted locally according to the exigencies
and possibilities of the geology: in southern Palestine, Cyprus,
the Aegean islands (notably Euboea), Sicily and Malta. In
Sicily the tradition first appears in the early Copper Age, at
San Cono and in the 'Conca d'Oro' culture of the Palermo

area, but continues, with increasing complication of the lay-out of entrances and subsidiary chambers, until the Early Iron Age. On the Maltese islands, rock-cut tombs appear at an early stage and the kidney-shaped chambers of early examples, like those at Tax-Xemxija, seem to have inspired the first temples built above ground in megalithic style. Here, as in Sicily and further east, the rock-cut tomb became so firmly established that megalithic tomb architecture was not able to displace it. In Sardinia, too, the rock-cut tomb had a long history, for about 1000 'domus de Janas' are known there and an early simple form, with a single chamber approached by a shaft, occurs, as well as the more elaborate tombs which remained in use, at Anghelu Ruju and elsewhere, far into the second millennium and delayed the development of megalithic Gallery Graves until a very late date. Good examples of the classic form are known near Bari in Apulia and Gaudo in Campania, but these, like examples near the mouth of the Rhône and in Champagne, are of somewhat later date; the tombs near Arles, in particular, show the same combination with megalithic architecture which we shall note in Andalusia and around the Tagus mouth.

THE EARLY PHASE *c.* 3 5 00–3 000 BC

Fig. 37
Fig. 38b

The simplest form of rock-cut tomb is represented in the peninsula by ill-recorded examples at Vejer de la Frontera, Jimena de la Frontera (Cádiz), Cabra (Córdoba), Cabra de Santo Cristo (Jaén) and Haza del Trillo (Jaén). These may represent a diffusion from the mouth of the Guadalquivir inland by the main river valley of Andalusia and our lack of information about these sites – some of which were accidentally destroyed during agricultural developments, like various megalithic and 'tholos' tombs of which we have only vague records – emphasizes the unevenness of our general knowledge of prehistoric Andalusia, and the distortion of our ideas which probably results from this. Further east, however, two other tombs are rather better known as a result of recent discoveries. At the Cerro del Greal, Iznalloz (Granada), a symmetrical, domed circular chamber 9 ft in diameter had numerous skeletons placed radially with the skulls against the walls, and one was placed in a shallow recess; the chamber was entered, from a rectangular shaft, by a trapeze-shaped opening with a sealing slab shaped to fit it. With some of the corpses were flat idols made of bone, of the early Almerian type, and the pottery is of plain 'Almerian' forms. The arrowheads are all of the south-western concave-based type. This site, indeed, lies in the Genil basin and outside the early sphere of development of the south-east Andalusian megalithic group. Further east still, at the Loma de los Peregrinos, Alguazas (Murcia) Dr Gratiniano Nieto has studied a more elaborate tomb with an irregular domed chamber roughly 13 ft by 10 which was approached by a short passage opening on to a rectangular antechamber and contained nearly 20 skeletons. The grave goods included several copper awls of rectangular section and stone axe-heads, most of which were oval but some of rectangular section. The numerous flint arrowheads were southeastern types – lozenge-shaped, leaf-shaped and biconcave-based; the pottery of plain 'Almerian' forms, included an 'almagre' (red lustre) sherd. A segmented bone pendant like those already described relates this grave group to the early horizon of Almerian influence, but a flint halberd of the type with recesses on the rounded base and the copper awls suggest that the tomb's use may have continued into the early third millennium.

Fig. 24b

Fig. 38a

Fig. 22

Plate 11

Fig. 27f

Further west, at Aljezur, near the west coast of the Algarve, Estacio da Veiga recorded long ago what must have been a much more complicated monument of the rock-cut group, the upper parts of which had already been destroyed, so that it is impossible to say what form the entrance took. The multiple

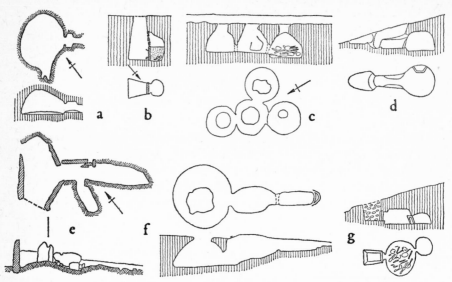

Fig. 38. Rock-cut tombs: a, Loma de los Peregrinos, Alguazas (Murcia); b, Vejer de la Frontera (Cádiz); c, Acébuchal, Carmona (Seville); d, Alcaide I, Antequera (Málaga); e, Dolmen de Casainhos, Loures (Lisbon); f, Alapraia I (Lisbon); g, Alcaide 7, Antequera (Málaga) (a-b after Nieto, c after Bonsor, d and g after Giménez. e after V. Leisner and f after Do Paço). Approx. 1: 250

Fig. 30f

burials, however, were accompanied by grave goods belonging exclusively to the early phase with which we are dealing here – plain 'Almerian' pottery, including a biconical bowl with horizontal subcutaneous lugs, and flint arrowheads which are, apart from a few trapezoid survivals, exclusively of the concave-based type as at Cerro del Greal, stone axe-heads mostly rectangular in section, bone pins with plain or segmented heads, all-over flaked flint halberds with biconcave or concave bases and several Alemtejan slate plaques which are all of the early type with purely geometric engraved patterns. One may have here one of the ports of call of early Almerian navigators on the way to the Tagus and beyond. Around the Tagus estuary itself, as we have said, apart from two unpublished rock-cut tombs of the eastern type at Quinta das Lapas, Torres Vedras, the rock-cut tombs are of the later type with orifice in the roof, but there is at least one remarkable monument, at the Praia das Maçãs, on the coast north-west of Sintra, which provides a link with the earliest sites of the south-east. For here the earliest of a sequence of constructions was a domed chamber, roughly 7 ft in diameter, entirely excavated in the rock, without an opening in the roof; it was approached by a passage from a small antechamber, formed of two lateral compartments partly rock-cut, in a manner that recalls the antechamber at the Loma de los Peregrinos. But in keeping with the subsequent practice of this district these chambers were lined with

Plate 23

Fig. 39. Finds from rock-cut tombs, caves and 'tholoi' (Lisbon area): a, flint sickle blade from S. Martinho, Sintra; b, ivory comb from Samarra; c, votive stone model of a comb from the Dolmen de Casainhos (Lisbon); d, votive stone model of a comb from the south antechamber at Praia das Maçãs (Lisbon); e, bone crozier from the Cova da Moura (cave), Torres Vedras (Lisbon); f-h, bone pins from the Gruta de Cascais (Lisbon); i and k, bone pins from the Dolmen de Casainhos; j, bone amulet from the Gruta de Cascais (a-d, i, k, after V. Leisner). Approx. 2 : 5

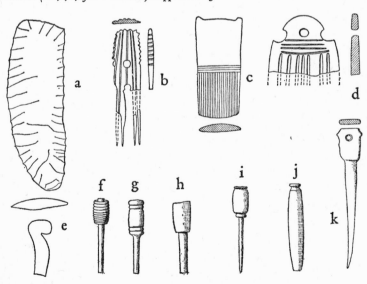

orthostatic slabs or dry-stone walling which no doubt served as a support for corbelled vaulting where this was required. Long afterwards a 'tholos' tomb, partly rock-cut but with dry-stone walling supporting a corbelled vault, with a long approaching passage, was built against the primary antechamber destroying its entrance; its grave goods (p. 152 below) make a complete contrast with those that accompanied the corpses placed against the sides of the primary chamber, which are exactly like those of Aljezur – primary engraved slate plaques,

Fig. 30p

segmented pin-heads, a biconical bowl and large flint blades, but with arrowheads entirely of the local Early Copper Age biconcave-based type instead of concave-based. A new feature

Fig. 39d

is part of a votive comb made of alabaster. The radiocarbon date of 2300 ± 60 BC given for the contents of this chamber (*Madrider Forschungen* I/3, 279) is so much at variance with the other evidence for the date of the early Copper Age in this district that it must be received with caution until more details of the stratification of the sample on which it is based have been published: the chamber may well have been disturbed when the 'tholos' was built and the date given would be quite an acceptable one for this later development.

In the rich territory lying immediately north of Lisbon there are a number of anomalous megalithic tombs the earliest deposits in which belong to the same cultural horizon as those of the primary chamber at Praia das Maçãs, even though most of them have grave goods that suggest renewed use in later periods, including that of the Bell Beaker. One of these, the

Fig. 38e

recently explored Dolmen de Casainhos, Loures, has, however, an almost pure inventory of this early period, with arrowheads mainly of the trapezoid or biconcave-based types, halberds of the biconcave or convex-based types, axe-heads and adzes of rectangular section, a primary Alemtejan slate plaque, part of an 'Almerian idol' of bone, a votive comb of

Fig. 39c, i, k

ivory, a segmented pin-head and other pins of local types. New

types, distinctively Portuguese, are a large limestone 'idol' of
plano-convex section (like Fig. 40l but with a schematic
human face) and a bone amulet in the form of a quadruped
(dog?). The pottery includes broad carinated bowls, platters
with thick rims and hemispherical bowls with several horizontal
furrows below the rim. Bowls like these, of a micaceous ware
with a red slip, occur at many other sites of this phase in the
Lisbon area. The monument itself is an exceptionally large
example of a common local form in which megalithic orthostats are bedded against the sides of a recess excavated in the
limestone subsoil. In this case the form is that of a Passage
Grave, but the unilateral antechamber, wholly excavated in
the subsoil, is evidently inspired by rock-cut tombs like Loma
de los Peregrinos and Praia das Maçãs. Another, partly rock-
cut megalithic chamber which yielded material of this phase,
including an 'Almerian idol' and a segmented pin-head, to
Carlos Ribeiro long ago is that of Monte Abraão, Belas, and
recently a destroyed tomb of uncertain type at Samarra, on the
coast north-west of Sintra yielded an 'Almerian idol' and a
segmented pinhead along with various 'idols' of local types,
and an ivory comb.

Fig. 24g, i
Fig. 30q

Fig. 38a

Fig. 39b

THE MATURE PHASE *c.* 3000–2500 BC

The typical rock-cut tomb of the Tagus estuary, though
peculiar in its use of 'man-holes', has features indicating
renewed contacts with the Mediterranean and, as we shall see,
there are elements in the equipment of the builders of these later
Tagus tombs and the contemporary inhabitants of settlement
sites, like the first village at Vila Nova de São Pedro, suggesting
a fresh movement from some part of the eastern Mediterranean
into the Tagus estuary early in the third millennium which
enhanced the distinctive character of its culture. We know this
culture, in the first place, from the long famous group of four

Plate 24

Fig. 38f

excavated tombs (with several more not yet explored) at Quinta do Anjo, Palmela, south of the estuary, and the single tomb at Folha das Barradas, Sintra, as well as from more recent explorations of a group of four tombs at Alapraia near Estoril by Afonso do Paço, a group of three at Carenque by Manuel Heleno, a group of two at S. Pedro de Estoril by Leonel Ribeiro, and a partly destroyed tomb at Cabeço da Arruda, Torres Vedras, by Leonel Trindade. Apart from the 'man-hole' the most frequently recurring feature of these chambers is the entrace passage, generally opening towards the east like Alemtejan Passage Graves, with outward-curving walls, often giving an elongated egg-shaped plan, and the ten-dency to a kidney-shaped chamber, which is most marked at Palmela. The latter shape appears in some of the earliest Maltese rock-cut chambers, but both features are combined at the newly discovered late Copper Age chambers at Gaudo in Campania and Casal Sabini, Altamura, near Bari in Apulia. The 'man-holes' appear to have no parallels outside the peninsula, but they recall the narrow openings of the beehive-shaped 'silos' explored by Bonsor long ago at the Acébuchal, Carmona, some of which were used for burials. Western Andalusia is, indeed, linked to the Tagus estuary in this period not only by these possible prototypes of the Tagus 'man-holed' chambers but by the practice of burying megalithic or dry-stone burial chambers partly or wholly in trenches cut in the subsoil.

In all the Tagus rock-cut tombs the earlier burials seem to have been placed in an upright, crouching position against the walls, but owing to the disturbances caused by later burials in the Beaker period which took place in most of them, varia-tions in the numbers of bodies recorded – from a dozen or two to nearly 100 – cannot be given much cultural significance, any more than can references to fragmentary human bones found in the entrance passages. In better-preserved examples the

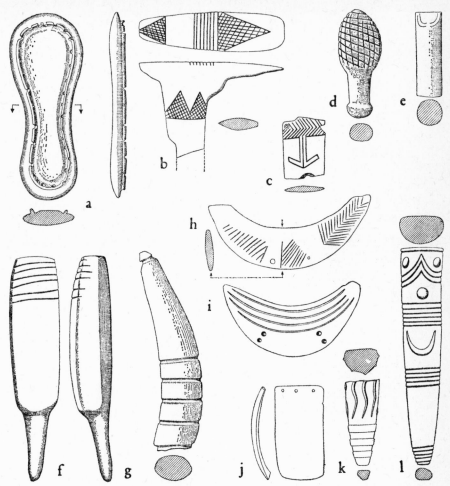

Fig. 40.   Stone amulets and ritual objects of the Tagus Culture: a, Sandal, Alapraia 2 (rock-cut tomb); b, hoe, S. Martinho ('tholos'); c, plaque, Cabeço da Arruda 2 ('tholos'); d, 'pine-cone', Carenque (rock-cut tomb); e, cylinder, Samarra (tomb of uncertain type); f, Cova da Moura, Torres Vedras (cave); g, Cabeço da Arruda 2; h-i, Carenque; j, Estria (megalithic tomb); k, Carenque; l, Folha das Barradas (rock-cut tomb) (a-e, g-l, after V. Leisner). 1:5

entrance passage can be subdivided into a partly arched vestibule, in which it seems that large cylindrical 'idols' were sometimes placed, and a downward-sloping outer passage; the
entrance from the vestibule to the chamber takes the form of
an oval opening which can only be entered in a crouching
position and in some cases at Palmela and Alapraia is known
to have had a door-slab shaped to fit. What may have been the

Fig. 41. The Lower Tagus area

1 Lapa da Bugal-
heira, Torres
Novas (Santarém)
2 Gruta da Galinha,
Torres Novas
(Santarém)
3 Alcobertas, Rio
Maior (Santarém)
4 Senhora da Luz,
Rio Maior
(Santarém)
5 Outeiro da Assenta,
Obidos (Leiria)
6 Casa da Moura,
Cesareda (Leiria)
7 Atougia da Baleia,
Peniche (Leiria)
8 Gruta da
Furninha,
Peniche (Leiria)
9 Outeiro de S.
Mamede, Obidos
(Leiria)
10 Pragança (Lisbon)
11 Gruta de Rocha
Forte, Montejunto
(Lisbon)
12 Vila Nova de São
Pedro (Santarém)

13 Gruta da Erme-
geira, Maxial
(Lisbon)
14 Castro de Ota,
Alemquer
(Lisbon)
15 Castro de Pedra
de Oiro Alemquer
(Lisbon)
16 Gruta da Carrasca,
Torres Vedras
(Lisbon)
17 Gruta da Portu-
cheira, Torres
Vedras (Lisbon)
18 Castro do Penedo,
Runa (Lisbon)
19 Castro da Fornea,
Matacães (Lisbon)
20 Barro, Torres
Vedras (Lisbon)
21 Castro de Zam-
bujal, Torres
Vedras (Lisbon)
22-3 Tombs 1-2,
Cabeço da
Arruda,
Torres Vedras
(Lisbon)

24 Bonabal, Torres
Vedras (Lisbon)
25 Serra das Mutelas,
Torres Vedras
(Lisbon)
26 Cova da Moura,
Torres Vedras
(Lisbon)
27 Quinta das Lapas,
Monte Redondo
(Lisbon)
28 Serra da Vila
Torres Vedras
(Lisbon)
29 Samarra (Lisbon)
30 Praia das Maçãs
(Lisbon)
31 S. Martinho,
Sintra (Lisbon)
32 Folha das Barra-
das, Sintra
(Lisbon)
33 Penha Verde,
Sintra (Lisbon)
34 Monge, Sintra
(Lisbon)
35 Bela Vista Colares
(Lisbon)
36 Olelas (Lisbon)

37 Cova da Raposa,
Sabugal (Lisbon)
38 Estria (Lisbon)
39 Monte Abrãao
(Lisbon)
40 Carenque (Lisbon)
41 Gruta de Salemas,
Loures (Lisbon)
42 Casainhos,
Loures (Lisbon)
43 Conchadas,
Loures (Lisbon)
44 Trigaches, Loures
(Lisbon)
45 Grutas de Cascais
(Lisbon)
46 Alapraia (Lisbon)
47 S. Pedro de
Estoril (Lisbon)
48 Castro de Licêa
(Lisbon)
49 Montes Claros
(Lisbon)
50 Vila Pouca de
Monsanto
(Lisbon)
51 Castro de Chi-
bannes, Palmela,
(Setubal)

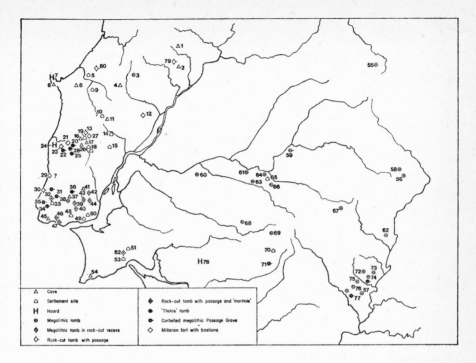

Legend:
△ Cave
◌ Settlement site
H Hoard
◉ Megalithic tomb
◈ Megalithic tomb in rock-cut recess
◇ Rock-cut tomb with passage

◈ Rock-cut tomb with passage and 'manhole'
◐ 'Tholos' tomb
◑ Corbelled megalithic Passage Grave
◇ Millaran fort with bastions

52 Quinta do Anjo, Palmela (Setubal)
53 Castro de Rotura (Setubal)
54 Lapa do Bugio, Sesimbra (Setubal)
55 Anta da Marquesa, Marvão (Portalegre)
56 Penaclara I (Portalegre)
57 Anta do Passo, Reguengos(Evora)
58 Fontalva, Barbacena (Evora)
59 Anta Grande da Ordem, Aviz (Evora)

60 Azinhal, Coruche (Santarém)
61 Madre de Deus, Mora (Evora)
62 Herdade dos Galvões (Evoro)
63 Anta de Brissos, Pavia (Evora)
64 Anta de Casa Branca, Estremo (Evora)
65 Castro de Pavia (Evora)
66 Antas de Pavia (Evora)
67 Anta da Casa de Bragança, Estremoz (Evora)

68 Anta da Comenda da Igreja, Montemor-o-Novo (Evora)
69 Anta do Silval (Evora)
70 Castro do Giraldo (Evora)
71 Vale de Rodrigo (Evora)
72 Poço da Gateira, Reguengos(Evora)
73 Olival da Pega, Reguengos (Evora)
74 Anta and Tholos da Comenda, Reguengos(Evora)

75 Anta dos Gorginos, Reguengos, (Evora)
76 Anta da Vidigueira Reguengos (Evora)
77 Anta and Tholos da Farisoa, Reguengos (Evora)
78 S. Martinho, Alcacer do Sal (Setubal)
79 Ribeira Branca, Torres Novas (Santarém)
80 Caldas da Rainha (Leiria)

'man-hole cover' was recovered at Alapraia in the form of a fragmentary circular slab that had been shaped with metal tools. The burials were richly equipped with offerings, some of them practical, others ritual and in many cases peculiar to the region. These distinctive grave goods do, indeed, occur in some of the local megalithic tombs, already referred to, in some natural caves which have burials of this period, and in certain 'tholos' tombs of a special local type (Barro, S. Martinho, Cabeço da Arruda 2 and Praia das Maçãs), built of coarse dry-stone walling from the ground up, with rather large circular or oval chambers which seem, at least in the case of Praia das Maçãs, to have had a wooden roof, and rather short, straight passages of similar construction (the latter are probably late in the period). But they do not occur outside of a limited area in central Portugal, and as they lack really close parallels in Mediterranean lands, must be regarded as, to a large extent, the creations of this district.

The exclusively central Portuguese ritual and symbolical grave-gifts include various objects made of the local limestone.

Fig. 40k, l

Among these are plano-convex 'idols', mostly tapering towards one of the ends, with a zoned decoration of transverse or longitudinal furrows: in one fragmentary example from Carenque these zones are in relief and the longitudinal lines are wavy, perhaps with the same symbolism as the 'water' lines or snakes of the Beira dolmen paintings. Those from the dolmen of Casainhos and the rock-cut tomb of Folha das Barradas have vague suggestions of a human face and the latter has an upturned crescent in relief which evidently relates to the actual limestone lunulae to be described later. A variant form with sub-rectangular section and a sort of stem occurs at Carenque

Fig. 40f

and the cave of Cova da Moura, Torres Vedras. A few idols of somewhat similar form but without the stem are known from the Algarve. 'Pine-cones', sometimes plain and sometimes with furrowed lattice decoration are known from the

rock-cut tombs, 'tholoi' and the caves of Cova da Moura and
Lapa do Bugio, Sesimbra, but lack close parallels elsewhere.
Lunulae (never of metal in this early phase) may be quite
undecorated and unperforated, as in the case of the large example found lying on the floor at the middle of the second rock-
cut chamber at Alapraia, or decorated with incised longitudinal or transverse lines. Some are perforated at the tips, others
near the middle, as though for suspension with the mouth
upwards or downwards, but there are no records to suggest
that any of them had been fastened to a corpse in any particular
way. It is, of course, possible to surmise a distant connection
with the pectorals worn by Egyptian Old Kingdom nobles
and to point out that lunar cults are characteristic of matriarchical societies, among which the Iberian Copper Age builders
of collective tombs are likely to have numbered. Models of
hoes mounted on their handles, with engraved decoration
suggestive of bindings, recall the symbolism of the ossuaries in
the rock-cut tomb at Azor in Palestine. Other specialities are
phalli (or sickles?) like that from the 'tholos' at Cabeço da
Arruda; the extraordinary hornlike object with projections,
from Carenque, which (if not a sickle) may relate to antler
symbolism connected with that indicated by late rock-paintings already mentioned (p. 61 above); curving plaques with
perforations; and the plaque from Cabeço da Arruda 'tholos'
with anchor (or double axe?) symbolism. Also characteristic
at least of the earlier phase of this culture, are the amulets,
usually of bone, but in one or two cases of callaïs, in the shape
of quadrupeds (dogs or hares?). These must have been suspen-
ded on the person, probably as fertility charms, and have a
distant connection with Egyptian amulets, including Old
Kingdom ones shaped like hares; they have a somewhat wider
distribution and are particularly common in the natural cave-
deposits, including those of the Gruta da Carrasca and the Gruta da Galinha, further up the Tagus valley than the rock-cut

Fig. 40d

Fig. 40h, i

Fig. 40b

Fig. 40g

Fig. 40j

Fig. 40c

Fig. 24g, i

Plate 17

tombs and 'tholoi'; some, moreover, have been found in the northern Alemtejo, notably at the Pavian Passage Graves of Olival da Pega and Comenda da Igreja.

Other 'idols' from the Tagus tombs are variants of types which are well represented in the later collective tombs of Andalusia, especially Almería: above all, this applies to ones like the *baetyls* of Los Millares which seem sometimes to have been used, as in the latter cemetery, in the antechambers or forecourts of tombs. They differ from the Millaran idols, how^ever, in being cylindrical and not expanded towards the base. A

Fig. 40e

small proportion, indeed, make some concession to Millaran iconography in having a pair of engraved double semicircles, allusive to the 'Eye^Goddess' cult which will be described in the next chapter (p. 160). They occur fairly plentifully not only in all types of collective tomb used during the early third millennium but in settlements, from the Tagus estuary as far north as the neighbourhood of Torres Novas and Alcobaça. Related idols, of other stones, are found fairly commonly, along with thin finely polished stone axe^heads and sometimes copper tools whose influence the axe^heads reflect in the late megalithic tombs of Galicia and Asturias. Further south, in Algarve and

Plate 33a

Huelva, there are some cylindrical idols which portray the Millaran 'Eye Goddess' more fully (they will be discussed later), while one cylinder from the Palmela rock^cut tombs has an inverted crescent engraved at half height. Closely related to the limestone cylinders are the smaller cylinders made of bone,

Fig. 39j

which often have a head demarcated by an encircling groove, and these too occur in the settlements. As they are particularly common in 'tholos' tombs, they probably belong to a late phase in the Tagus culture, when Millaran influences were growing: they have, indeed close analogies in the later Almerian culture, where, however, the base tends to expand, as in the stone *baetyls*. A few examples, in Portugal as at Los Millares, which have the head tilted, emphasize the connection with predynastic Egyptian forms. Idols made from the phalange bones of quadrupeds – in most cases probably of horses – occur in the Tagus culture, and a few are decorated with furrows as at S. Martinho and Carenque, or with a pair of rayed circles in the Millaran manner, as at the Gruta da Bugalheira and the Castro of Olelas. The miniature bone crozier from the Cova da Moura, Torres Vedras stands apart from the Millaran elements just described, as evidence for connections with the Alemtejan Passage Grave culture at the beginning of the phase. Finally, the extraordinary life-size models of a pair of sandals, from the second rock-cut tomb at Alapraia should be mentioned. These have a predynastic Egyptian background as well as analogies in Andalusia, as will be seen (p. 145 below), which are all much more schematic and may be late derivatives of the Tagus form. It is hardly surprising that this great variety of new types of 'idol' and amulet drove out of use the Alemtejan engraved slate plaques, which are rare in later Tagus tombs.

Grave goods with a more practical significance include the combs already mentioned, and others representing an indigenous round-topped type and a more elaborate type, with projections at the top, which may relate to Egyptian forms. There are also bone or ivory unguent pots which often have the same engraved lattice pattern as those from Los Millares; pins with various forms of head, some recalling early Egyptian forms while others, with bird-like heads, resemble some from the Early Cycladic culture of the Aegean. Beads of stone, bone, pottery, jet and callaïs occur – this last a speciality of the Tagus culture which is extremely rare in the Millaran culture of eastern Andalusia and, in view of the probability that it was imported originally from the Near East, may represent survival from the local Neolithic culture and ultimately from that of Catalonia. The small bowls or mortars made of limestone, marble or alabaster are a trait in common with the Millaran culture and reflect connections with the eastern Mediterranean.

Plate 33b

Fig. 39e

Fig. 40a

Fig. 39b-d

Fig. 47a
Fig. 47r, s

Fig. 47i, j

Plate 10
Fig. 42e, f

Weapons and tools made of flint are taken over, in the main, from the native culture of the final Neolithic phase, but as the period advances the concave-based arrowhead, originally a

Fig. 22 southwestern form, gains ground against the biconcave-based Almerian form north of the Tagus. Similarly, the primary

Fig. 27f Almerian form of flint halberd is replaced by elongated halberd and dagger-blades with a pair of recesses near the base, inspired by the fastening of copper daggers of the Millaran culture but with fine pressure flaking, sometimes after polishing, which recalls that of late predynastic Egypt. Throughout this phase, polished stone axe-heads, hoes and chisels of rectangular section like those of late predynastic Egypt are normal, and single-piece flint sickles with Egyptian, as well as north-west

Fig. 39a African analogies are common.

Pottery occurs in great abundance in all types of tomb, as well as in many settlement sites which were clearly occupied during the early third millennium around the Tagus estuary, and as is natural in such a highly developed culture, there is a considerable variety of forms, wares and styles of decoration. The

Fig. 30 great bulk of the pottery is undecorated and perpetuates wares and forms derived from the Almerian or south-western cultures of the end of the fourth millennium – hemispherical and carinated bowls, globular bowls with short necks, low platters with thickened rims, often in fine grey- or brown-burnished ware. Flat bases become more common, and biconical hanging bowls with multiple subcutaneous lugs, horizontal or vertical, are popular. But from the earliest stage of the Tagus culture exotic forms appear: first of all the very fine hemispherical bowls of micaceous ware with polished brown- or red-slipped surface and soft horizontal furrowing below the rim, then cylindrical or truncated cone-shaped beakers of very fine thin

Fig. 42a, b micaceous ware with a dark chocolate-coloured wash, having flat or slightly convex bases and slightly concave sides with broad furrowing in horizontal zones near the rim or the base and extremely fine furrowing in between. These are the *copas* of Portuguese archaeologists and, as we shall see, they are characteristic of the earliest phase at Vila Nova de São Pedro, Santarém.

The Tagus 'import' wares are of great importance for determining the source of the extraneous influences that gave the local Early Copper Age culture its distinctive character, for they do not occur in south-eastern Spain and they point clearly to contacts, not with the southeast Mediterranean, as is the case with many elements in the Almerian and south-western groups, but with the Aegean and the Anatolian seaboard. The important feature here is the technique of the ware, with its dark brown wash on a light body, recalling the *Urfirnis* wares which appear in various final Neolithic or early metal age cultures in Greece, the Aegean and the Anatolian and Syrian seaboard. The form and decorative patterns of the *copas* have particularly close parallels in the pottery *pyxides* found in graves of the Pelos (Early Cycladic I) group in the Aegean. These vessels are in *Urfirnis* ware which, however, is thicker and coarser than that of the *copas*, and it is important to note that they accompanied single burials in cists and that other distinctive features of the Early Cycladic culture do not appear on the Tagus. On the other hand another form of Tagus *Urfirnis* vessel, with flat base and concave sides, is rendered in stone in the Early Minoan 'tholos' culture of the Mesará, and another contemporary Cretan form is reproduced closely by a pottery bowl from a north Alemtejan Passage Grave of Pavian type. About the same time in Crete there is a great fondness for decorating pottery with incised concentric semicircles. Fluted decoration of this kind, arranged like a basket-work pattern, is found on large ovoid or hemispherical *Urfirnis* vessels in the bottom layers at Vila Nova da São Pedro, and although this pattern was already being applied with different techniques in the fourth millennium in north-east Africa, fine concentric fluting

Fig. 42b

Fig. 30r

Fig. 42c, d

seems to spread at the time of the Tagus culture, westwards through the Mediterranean not only to Sardinia and southern France but to Morocco (Caf Taht el Gar) and the Canary Islands. The fluted *Urfirnis* wares of the Tagus estuary are not only represented in several of the rock-cut tombs and mega-lithic chambers of the area and natural caves – the Cova da Raposa, Sabugal, and those of Cascais – but on a number of settlement sites.

THE SETTLEMENTS

In contrast to the pure Neolithic, there are now many settlement sites around the Tagus estuary which have yielded material similar to that found in the local rock-cut tombs, megaliths and 'tholoi'. Some of these settlements, moreover, are known to have had defensive walls built round them at some stage of their history. Unfortunately many of these sites – the *castros* of Licêa and Vila Pouca de Monsanto north-west of Lisbon, Rotura and Chibannes near Palmela, and Pragança, Outeiro de São Mamede and Outeiro da Assenta, further north in Estremadura – were explored long ago without proper record, and even those which have been explored more recently, with somewhat greater regard for the record and at least an attempt to prepare a plan, have not been excavated throughout with proper stratigraphical method – as far, at any rate, as one can judge from publications to date. This is all the more unfortun-ate in that it is quite clear from the miscellaneous unstratified finds which can be studied in museums and publications, that most of the sites were occupied in several successive phases, beginning in the late Neolithic or the early Copper Age. At Vila Nova de São Pedro, near Santarém, Lt Col. Afonso do Paço has been exploring, at intervals for the past 25 years or more, what is by now the most important and productive of these sites. Here, at least, a good deal is now known about

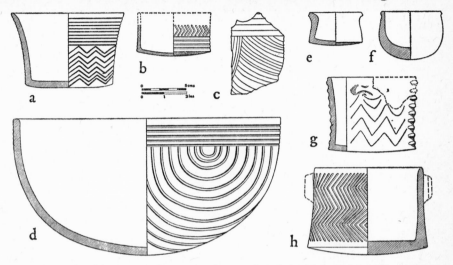

Fig. 42. Pottery of the Tagus Culture: a-d, Vila Nova de S. Pedro (Santarém); e, Folha das Barradas, Sintra (Lisbon); f, Cascais (Lisbon) (stone); g, Rocha Forte de Montejunto (Lisbon); h, Melos (Cyclades) (h after E. M. Bossert and S. Ehrhardt). 1: 4

structures and though the bulk of the published material is unstratified, the writer was generously permitted, in 1959, to cut a section, in collaboration with Miss B. Capstick, down to bedrock. It showed that there were three main phases of occupation, of which the earliest, before the construction of the fort which will be described in the next chapter, belonged to the same phase as the rock-cut tombs of the Tagus estuary – in fact to the time when engraved slate plaques of the Alemte-jan type were still occasionally used in the district, but cylin-drical limestone 'idols' were taking their places. This earliest settlement at Vila Nova contained many pits of varying size and shape like the early settlements near Carmona in Andalu-sia and at Aljezur in the Algarve, and most of these seem to have been silos. Large-scale horizontal digging with modern techniques would alone enable us to arrive at reliable conclusions

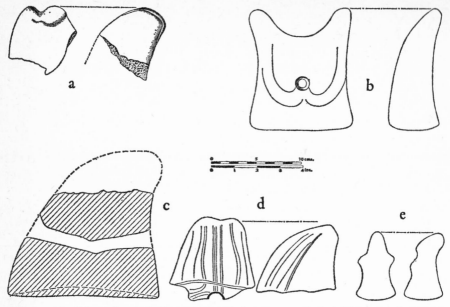

Fig. 43.   Clay idol-spits from Period I at Vila Nova de S. Pedro, a-e with clay 'idol' from Büyük Güllücek, Turkey, f after Kosay. 1 : 4

as to the above-ground structures connected with these storage pits, but the 1959 section revealed various wall-foundations in the occupation layers which accumulated in and above the silos before the Millaran fort was built.

The finds from the bottom pre-fortification layers at Vila *Fig. 52 (Per Ia)* Nova include a great quantity of potsherds, mostly plain, and of wares and forms derived from the Almerian and south-western *Fig. 42a-d* cultures, but many fragments from fine *copas* appear, especially at the very bottom. The numerous stone querns and rubbers as well as the flint sickles, axe-heads and hoes, mainly of rectan-gular section, show that agriculture was an important activity of the inhabitants. At various times burnt grains have been found on the site, and identified as wheat (*Triticum compactum* or *sphaerococcum*), barley and beans; the last-named are particularly common. In addition flax and olives were grown. Animal bones include the main domestic species, with ass and, apparently, horse. In one of the silos was found what appears to have been a ritual burial of an ox with a large hemispherical pottery bowl placed above it. The 1959 section produced few worked flints or metal objects in the bottom layers, in marked contrast to the abundance of concave-based arrowheads and evidences of metal-working in the Millaran phase on the site. This apparent poverty in copper matches that of the rock-cut tombs before the Beaker phase, but cannot be taken to mean a complete ignorance of the metal. The large, well-constructed potter's kiln at Vila Nova, with a domed chamber 12 ft 6 in. in diameter and crushed pots still in position against the walls, seems to have been built in this early phase before the adjoining inner rampart of the fort was built, and its technical sophistication is a hint that metal-working was not completely unknown in the culture which constructed it. Plain subrectangular clay plaques with perforations at the corners, possibly loom-weights, occur in the early levels, as they do in the megalithic settlements of the Alemtejo. A distinctive feature of the earliest settlement at Vila Nova, apparently unknown elsewhere, is the numerous fragments of baked clay supports for spits, usually with horns and a vague allusion to contemporary anthropomorphic idols. Similar supports with horizontal perforations occur about the beginning of the third millennium in the Aegean and western Anatolia; at an earlier date still, clay 'idols' of related form occur at Büyük Güllücek in central Anatolia and, indeed, at various sites in the Balkans. This Anatolian connection reinforces the evidence of the *copas* at Vila Nova for a strong influence on the Tagus culture from the north-east corner of the Mediterranean near the beginning of the third millennium, which differentiated it from the 'tholos'-building groups south of the Tagus and in Andalusia to be discussed in the next chapter.

Fig. 52

Fig. 50e

Fig. 43

CHAPTER VI
The First Metal-Workers

GENERAL

ALREADY DURING THE TWO previous chapters we have been considering cultural developments which were assigned, more or less theoretically, to an early phase of the Copper Age in the western Mediterranean, remarking from time to time on the possibility that exploitation of copper ore deposits near the coast in southern Spain and Portugal may have begun in the time of the earlier collective burials in the area, even though early occurrences of copper objects in these burials, like the awls at the Loma de los Peregrinos (p. 119 above) were extremely rare. We also noted the contrast between two distinct cultural groups among the users of collective tombs in this same area south of the Tagus, one responsible for 'round graves' or 'tholos' tombs and the other for megalithic Passage Graves. Whereas the tombs of the latter group mainly lay well inland in Andalusia and Portugal, the earliest tombs of the former group lay near the coast and may well have inspired the development of megalithic Passage Graves by the inland farmers and pastoralists. Despite their poverty in metal, the concentrations of these early 'tholoi' in close juxtaposition to the copper ore deposits, in southern Alemtejo and Almería, can hardly be accidental, and it is precisely in the later tombs of this cultural group in Almería and the Algarve, that copper objects become relatively plentiful. Moreover it is in this late phase that collective tombs occasionally occur in real clusters – 13 at Alcalá in the Algarve, about 80 at Los Millares in Almería. At the latter site we know the reason for this apparently unique concentration: a fortified settlement which was clearly of exceptional importance. The construction of forts with structural details like Los Millares is associated in central Portugal with the arrival of a number of specifically 'Millaran'

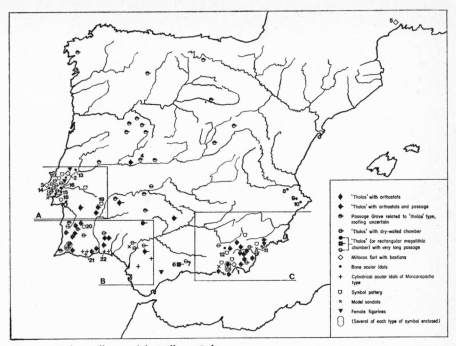

Fig. 44. Early metallurgy and the Millaran Culture

1 Los Millares (Almería)

2 Vila Nova de São Pedro (Santarém)

3 Zambujal, Torres Vedras (Lisbon)

4 Guadalperal (Cáceres)

5 Lébous (Montpellier)

6 Cueva de la Viera, Antequera (Málaga)

7 Cueva de Romeral Antequera (Málaga)

8 Ereta del Pedregal, Navarrés (Valencia)

9 Cueva Bolumini (Valencia)

10 Cueva de la Pastora, Alcoy (Alicante)

11 Almizaraque (Almería)

12 Los Castellones, Gor (Granada)

13 Lapa de Buga-lheira, Torres Novas (Santarém)

14 S. Martinho, Sintra (Lisbon)

15 Carenque (Lisbon)

16 Olelas (Lisbon)

17 Rocha Forte, Montejunto (Lisbon)

18 Palmela (Setubal)

19 Olival da Pega, Reguengos (Evora)

20 Monte do Outeiro, Aljustrel (Beja)

21 Moncarapacho (Algarve)

22 Conquero (Huelva)

types of pottery, ornaments and religious symbolism as well as a marked increase of metallurgical activity. Los Millares may well have been a centre of power the influence of which was felt widely in southern Spain and Portugal, and fortification may well have gone with the presence of a noble or royal household and its rare and valuable dependent craftsmen. It must not be forgotten, however, that the presence of a large minority of concave-based arrowheads among the barbed and tanged arrowheads characteristic of the Almerian culture in the tombs at Los Millares, is an indication of a reverse current of cultural influence from the south-west of the peninsula.

The Millaran culture is distinguished from that of the rock-cut tombs in Portugal not only by its greater metallurgical activity, but by its somewhat different range of connections. Whereas the Tagus culture seems to owe most to contacts with Anatolia and the Aegean, the Millaran culture, like the Almerian culture out of which it grew, seems to be indebted rather to intermittent connections with more remote parts of the Mediterranean sea-board, as a result presumably of southerly contacts along the intervening coast. Probably no large-scale immigration from the Near East took place in this phase and the common ethnic, and to some extent perhaps linguistic basis, would still have served to link the two separate regions. The Millaran culture, however, did not exercise so strong an influence beyond the lower Tagus as did the preceding Alemtejan megalithic and Tagus cultures, or even the builders of the earliest 'tholos' tombs, and the collective graves around the Bay of Biscay and in the British Isles continued to receive offerings of purely Neolithic character.

THE LATER 'THOLOS' TOMBS IN THE EAST: *c.* 2750–2250 BC

Even the earliest corbelled Passage Graves, in the Almerian culture, were, as we have seen, sometimes built entirely of dry-stone walling. But these were soon replaced, in Almería and southern Portugal, by large circular chambers walled with slender orthostats which were either continuous, with access to the chamber from above, or with short passages separated

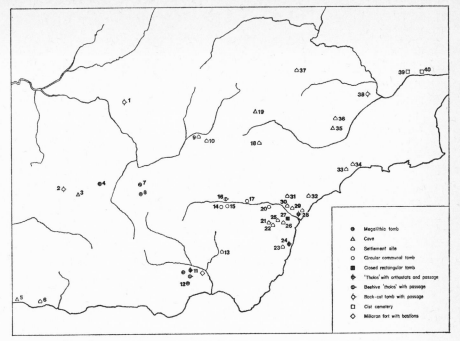

Fig. 45. The south-east

Legend:
- ◉ Megalithic tomb
- △ Cave
- ⌂ Settlement site
- ○ Circular communal tomb
- ■ Closed rectangular tomb
- ◈ 'Tholos' with orthostats and passage
- ⊕ Beehive 'tholos' with passage
- ◇ Rock-cut tomb with passage
- ☐ Cist cemetery
- ◇ Millaran fort with bastions

1 Haza del Trillo (Jaén)
2 Cerro del Greal, Iznalloz (Granada)
3 Carigüela de Piñar (Granada)
4 Los Eriales, Laborcillas (Granada)
5 Nerja (Málaga)
6 Laurita de Almuñecar (Granada)
7 La Sabina, Gor (Granada)
8 Castellones, Gador (Granada)
9 Galera (Granada)
10 Orce (Granada)
11 Los Millares (Almería)

12 Huéchar Alhama (Almería)
13 Tabernas (Almería)
14 Las Churuletas, Purchena (Almería)
15 Llano de la Lampara, Purchena (Almería)
16 Barranca de la Jocalla, Purchena (Almería)
17 Cantoria, Purchena (Almería)
18 Cerro de la Cantera, Velez Blanco (Almería)
19 Cueva Ambrosio, Velez Blanco (Almería)

20 Palaces, Zurgeña (Almería)
21 Fuente Vermeja (Almería)
22 Lugarico Viejo (Almería)
23 Gatas (Almería)
24 Loma de Belmonte, Mojacar (Almería)
25 La Gerundia (Almería)
26 El Argar (Almería)
27 La Pernera, Antas (Almería)
28 Almizaraque (Almería)
29 Tres Cabezos (Almería)
30 Campos (Almería)

31 Fuente Alamo (Almería)
32 El Oficio (Almería)
33 Parazuelos (Murcia)
34 Ifre (Murcia)
35 Los Blanquizares de Lebor, Totana (Murcia)
36 Campico de Lebor, Totana (Murcia)
37 Cehegín (Murcia)
38 Loma de los Peregrinos Alguazas (Murcia)
39 S. Anton de Orihuela (Alicante)
40 Callosa de Segura (Alicante)

Fig. 46a

Fig. 46c, d

Fig. 26g

Plate 20

Fig. 46f

Fig. 47o

Fig. 47k

from the chamber by a slab of nearly the same height as its orthostats, as in tombs 1 and 2 at Los Millares and at the Barranco da Nora Velha, Ourique, in southern Alemtejo. The plump axe-heads and arrowheads of trapezoid as well as concave-based types at the latter site, demonstrate its early date. Sites like Amendoeira Nova in southern Alemtejo and Los Millares 40 illustrate the next stage. Many more of the tombs at Los Millares, however, represent a local type which is hardly found in south-western areas of the peninsula, where the 'tholos' tombs pursue a parallel but distinct line of evolution. These typical Millaran tombs have a lengthened passage, built wholly of orthostats and divided into two or three segments by septal slabs which have port-holes, round or squarish with rounded corners, through which a body could be passed and which have sealing slabs. At several of these tombs Siret's excavations revealed the lower parts of the corbelled roofs still in position and some had central pillars to support the apex of the vault, even though some of the pillars interpreted as such by Siret are now considered by Almagro and Arribas to have ended far short of the roof and to have been ritual steles corre-sponding to the groups of miniature pillars or *baetyls* that stood in enclosures outside the entrances of the monuments. The latter are a distinctive feature of the Millaran culture and are of a different shape from the cylindrical 'idols' of the Tagus culture – swelling towards the base and tending to a larger size – from 6 in. to 2 ft high. They sometimes show traces of red paint and seem to have been connected with periodic observances which also led to broken pots being deposited outside the entrances of the tombs. Their counterparts inside the tombs are similarly shaped 'idols' of stone or bone which sometimes have features relating them to the Mother Goddess cult, and other 'idols', made of phalange bones of quadrupeds (sometimes horses) which are only occasionally painted with 'Eye-Goddess' symbols.

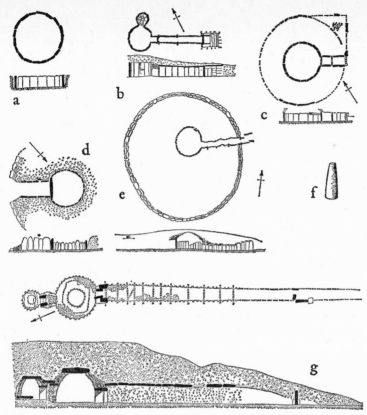

Fig. 46. The evolution of the 'tholos' tomb: a, Loma de la Atalaya 3, Purchena (Almería); b, Alcalá 3 (Algarve); c, Los Millares 7 (Almería); d, Barranco de Nora Velha (Beja); e, Monte do Outeiro (Beja); f, Los Millares 16 (Almería); g, Cueva del Romeral, Antequera (Málaga) (a and f after G. and V. Leisner, b after E. da Veiga, c after Leisner, Almagro and Arribas, d-e after O. da Veiga Ferreira, g after C. de Mergelina and R. Velázquez Bosco). Approx. 1 : 400

Structurally, the typical Millaran tombs show a sophistication which is emphasized by the records of fragmentary
painted wall-plaster found in some of the chambers: gypsum
seems to have been used for plaster and decoration to have
consisted of red geometric patterns, but details are too scant for

comparison with the archetypal frescoes of Neolithic Anatolia. The covering mounds are invariably circular, up to 50 ft in diameter, and sometimes built on specially prepared platforms with a surface of beaten earth. They have orthostatic or dry-stone revetment walls, some of which may be concentric and hidden in the body of the mound, while others may simply be built on the surface of the mound as a decorative feature, the latter especially where the mound is a natural one adapted for the purpose, as in some tombs in western Andalusia. When Almagro and Arribas re-excavated the megalithic Passage Grave No. 8 and the 'tholos' No. 37, with triple-segmented passage, it seemed to them that they must have been built at the same time because they shared the same natural hillock equally. Another of the tombs re-excavated by them (19) has yielded a radiocarbon date of 2430 ± 120 BC (KN 72). Its structure, however, with drystone walling in the chamber and passage, lateral niches and triple-segmented passage with port-hole slabs, suggests a fairly late date in the series at Los Millares. The multiplication of side-chambers, indeed, seems to increase in the later stages at Los Millares, and at the same time orthostatic construction tends to be replaced by dry-stone walling, both in the chambers and the passages, and grave goods become much poorer. Another feature of the final stages of the 'tholos' tradition is the building-up of the courtyard as a theatre for ritual. The early tomb, No. 40, simply has two stone pillars flanking the approach to the entrance, whereas the late tomb, No. 20, with walls mainly of dry stone, had a semicircular forecourt outside the entrance and the mound framed with orthostats. The late tomb of Encantadas I, Almizaraque, some distance from Los Millares, had a trapezoid forecourt flanked by dry-stone walling. Such forecourts may be related to free-standing peristaliths or precinct walls, traces of which were noticed by Siret at one or two monuments. The lateral chambers seem in some cases to have been used for children, while adults were placed in the chambers and passages. The total number of corpses, as in the case of the large and early tomb No. 40, can reach 100.

Some of the characteristic Millaran grave goods have already been referred to, especially those of a ritual nature. The more utilitarian forms must first be considered now as a clue to the chronological horizon of these later tholos tombs. Flint is still well represented in the tombs, but except in the few megalithic Passage Graves at Los Millares trapezoid arrowheads are practically unknown. In their place Copper Age types reign supreme, but as befits a centre lying close to the frontier between the south-western and south-eastern flint-working zones, leaf-shaped and barbed and tanged arrowheads compete with concave-based ones: among the latter are ogival ('mitriform') arrowheads with deeply concave bases. The characteristic *Fig. 220* large blades remain in use, but halberds and daggers are of the late form with lanceolate blades, sometimes with recesses on the base for hafting which relate to metal weapons, though some *Fig. 27c, f* concave-based halberds occur, like those of the Algarve and Huelva. Objects made of ivory are fairly common, including combs of the native round-based type as well as a much more *Fig. 47a* elaborate winged form which recalls Egyptian examples. The ivory dagger-pommel from the early tomb No. 12, resembles one from the trapezoid grave at Nora in the Algarve. Ivory un- *Fig. 47p* guent pots are common, as in the Tagus tombs, but the decora-tion is almost invariably an incised trellis. Similar pots are sometimes made of alabaster, as are plain mortar-like pots like those from the Tagus. The ivory seems sometimes to have been derived from the hippopotamus and like the vases made of ostrich eggs, emphasizes the North African and Egyptian connections of this culture. Among ritual objects, the ogival Almerian flat 'idols' have practically died out, the plain trapezoid slate plaques appearing only in the early tombs, Nos. *Fig. 24j* 12 and 40: the former tomb also yielded an ivory sandal, less realistic than that of Alapraia, and another early tomb, No. 7, yielded a curious little 'idol' recalling one from an early Minoan 'tholos' tomb at Kumasa.

Fig. 47l

The pottery from the 'tholos' tombs at Los Millares and other late Passage Graves in Andalusia for the most part perpetuates the forms of the earlier 'Almerian' phase but the increased wealth of this new semi-urban centre is reflected in the comparative abundance of the decorated wares, and the variety of their techniques. For not only is there painted pottery, but pottery with incised decoration of which some relates to the Mother-Goddess cult and some seems to borrow rayed circles and schematic representations of deer from the indigenous Mesolithic and Neolithic groups of the interior; there is too another class of ware, which also appears in Passage Graves further west and settlements in Almería, which uses ribbon-like bands filled in with pittings. The Mother-Goddess symbolism appears on stone, bone and pottery 'idols' and will be discussed separately; painted pottery also deserves separate discussion elsewhere. Another class of decorated pottery, Bell-Beaker ware, is in a separate class because it is later in date and may be presumed to have accompanied secondary burials in the cemetery (see Chapter VII); the same goes for tanged copper daggers, wristguards and arrowheads which are generally associated with Bell Beakers. But not all the copper objects which occur in some of the Millaran tombs are of Beaker type: there is a specifically Millaran copper repertoire, consisting of awls, rectangular in section, which carry on the tradition established centuries earlier at the Loma de los Peregrinos rock-cut tomb, elongated axes and chisels and daggers or halberds with a pair of niches near the butt for the hafting and mid-ribs on one or both faces. These forms appear also at the smaller contemporary group of 'tholos' tombs at Alcalá in the Algarve: their technical aspect will be discussed later in the chapter, and all that need be stressed immediately is

Fig. 51g-k

Fig. 51l, n, r

Plate 26

Plate 18

Fig. 50d

Fig. 50i, k, q

the resemblance of the nicked daggers to flint forms, and the fact that copper objects are characteristic of the earliest types of 'tholos' tomb at Los Millares, e.g. Nos. 2, 7 and 40.

THE LATER 'THOLOS' TOMBS AND ROCK-CUT TOMBS IN THE WEST: *c.* 2750–2000 BC

We have already seen that corbelled Passage Graves of refined construction begin early enough in certain districts of western Andalusia and southern Portugal to influence the development of the truly megalithic Passage Graves of the interior; but it is certain that this tradition was as enduring in the coastal districts of the west as it was at Los Millares. The later 'tholoi' of the west exhibit structural features which suggest that their builders were in touch, to some degree, with Los Millares, as the grave goods also indicate: thus the splendid Cueva de Romeral, Antequera, a group of tombs near Seville of which the Cuevas del Vaquero and de la Pastora and the Domen de Matarrubilla are the most famous, and several of the tombs at Alcalá in the Algarve show the same tendency to add side chambers and build almost exclusively with dry-stone walling as the later tombs at Los Millares. But these same monuments have other divergent features which show how much they depend upon local antecedents. Those of western Andalusia inherit the local tradition of constructing in a trench and the side chambers are commonly round and connected to the main chamber by a passage, while roofing, as at the earlier Cueva de Menga and Dolmen de Soto, is formed by extremely massive capstones resting partly on the edge of the trench. But what differentiates the western tombs from those of Los Millares more than anything else is the extreme length of their passages and the absence of a system of septal slabs and 'port-holes'. The Cueva de Romeral had a passage over 100 ft long and the covering mound was about 275 ft in diameter and 30 ft high:

Fig. 46g
Plate 21

Fig. 46b

it is the finest Passage Grave surviving in the peninsula, but little of interest remained from its burial deposits. Matarrubilla was shown by a recent re-excavation to have had a passage nearly as long. The outer part of the passage still had several crouched burials with rich offerings: these included parts of an elephant's tusk with remains of an ivory necklace, including spacer plaques which suggest that it was a lunate pectoral; part of an ivory model sandal; and some ornamental gold leaf. In the same area are monuments with long passages and side chambers which retain orthostatic construction, as at Cañada Honda, Tomb G, Gandul. Another distinctive feature of this area is the use of a large stone basin or platform, in the main chamber, as in the Irish 'Boyne' Passage Graves, for some ritual purpose: the best example is at Matarrubilla. Only the Cueva de Viera, Antequera, has port-hole slabs leading to its long, orthostatic passage and into its small, square chamber, but the port-holes are square and resemble those in the group

Fig. 38d, g of seven late rock-cut combs of the eastern type at Alcaide, Antequera: here the approaching passages often still have the convex sides characteristic of the Tagus tombs, but the multiplication of side chambers places them in the same late stage of development as later Millaran tombs: scanty grave goods suggest late use, about the beginning of the Second millennium.

In southern and central Portugal, too, 'tholos' tombs were still being built at a late date in the third millennium, but here again, a pre-existing tradition was followed with only partial adaptation to trends elsewhere. At Alcalá in the Algarve the

Fig. 46b passages lengthen, though not so much as in western Andalusia, but the septal slabs of Los Millares are replaced by pairs of jambs which narrow the passage at two or three points, rather in the manner of northern Irish court cairns. This type of construction occurs in monuments built wholly of orthostats, wholly of dry-stone except for the megalithic roofs, or with dry-stone chambers and orthostatic passages. Side chambers or

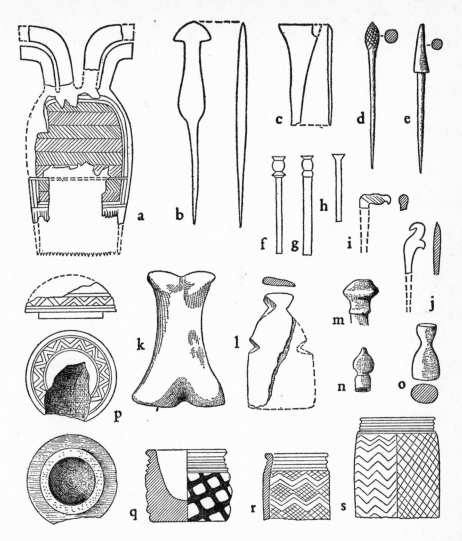

Fig. 47. Copper Age objects of bone and ivory: a, ivory comb, Los Millares 12; b, d-e, i-j, bone pins from Vila Nova de S. Pedro; c, bone pin from Alcalá 2 (Algarve); f-h, bone pins from Pragança (Lisbon); k, phalange from Los Millares IV; l, bone idol from Los Millares 7; m-n, clay phalli from Alcalá 3 (Algarve); o, miniature stone baetyl from Los Millares 40; p, ivory dagger-pommel from Nora (Algarve); q, stone unguent pot from El Carlero (Seville); r, ivory unguent pot from Belas (Lisbon); s, ivory unguent pot from S. Martinho (Lisbon) (a, c, k-q after G. and V. Leisner; b, d-e, i-j after Do Paço). Approx. 1 : 2

niches opening above floor-level occur in monuments of all these types and the whole cemetery (except for tomb 1) must be regarded as late, following on Marcella and the Monte Velho group of orthostatic 'tholoi' with simple short passages. Tomb 3, which yielded a rich inventory of copper flat axes, chisels, knives, saws, daggers and halberds all associated with burials in the niche, must be fairly early in this group. Concave-based arrowheads occurred in this and some other tombs of the group, but it is noteworthy that the finest and most extravagantly barbed arrowheads from this cemetery came from the earliest-looking tomb, No. 1. Tomb 3 also yielded several phallic pendants and bone pins (?) with spatulate heads. The fragments of engraved gold leaf from tombs 4 and 11 suggest secondary burials in the Bell-Beaker phase, although no actual Beaker is recorded from the Algarve. In southern Alemtejo the Anta dos Tassos, Ourique, with its dry-stone chamber and short orthostatic passage, has a radiocarbon date (*c.* 1850 ± 200 BC) (Sa-199) which accords with its late form, and the small dry-stone chamber with short orthostatic passage, forecourt and double sill at Serro do Gatão, Ourique, is also probably late. But the west Andalusian tendency to an extra long passage asserts itself in the exceptionally well-preserved monument of Monte do Outeiro, Aljustrel with its multiple jambs, impassably low passage and 'Mother-Goddess' pot. In central Portugal a different tradition of 'tholos' construction established itself, using the 'cyclopean' construction suggested by the igneous rock of the Serra de Sintra. The medium passage without jambs, at Cabeço da Arruda 2, is followed at Monge and Barro by a very short passage with remains of a forecourt. The rich grave goods from these tombs are predominantly of the Tagus culture with only a few Millaran forms, like the decorated phalange bones at São Martinho: they probably belong to the middle of the third millennium. The secondary 'tholos' at Praia das Maçãs, with its possible radiocarbon date, has

Fig. 50k, m-o

Fig. 47c, m, n

Fig. 46e

Plate 33b

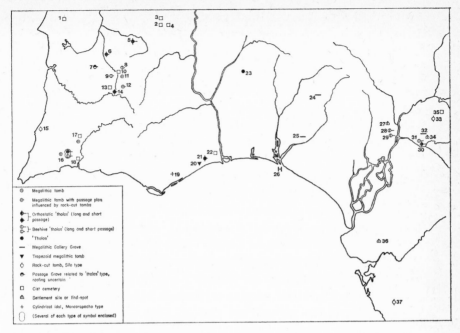

Fig. 48. The south-west

1 Santiago do Cacem (Setubal)	11 Anta de Brejo, Ourique (Beja)	21 Marcella (Algarve)	30 Cañada Honda, Gandul (Seville)
2 Mombeja (Beja)	12 Monte Velho, Ourique (Beja)	22 Castro Marim (Algarve)	31 Cueva del Va-quero, Carmona (Seville)
3 Beja	13 Atalaia, Ourique (Beja)	23 La Zarcita (Algarve)	32 Cañada del Car-rascal, Gandul (Seville)
4 Trigaxe (Beja)	14 Nora Velha, Ourique (Beja)	24 El Pozuelo (Huelva)	33 Acebuchal, Carmona (Seville)
5 Monte do Outeiro, Aljustrel (Beja)	15 Aljezur (Algarve)	25 El Soto, Tri-gueros (Huelva)	34 Mairena del Alcor (Seville)
6 Malha Ferro, Aljustrel (Beja)	16 Alcalá (Algarve)	26 Huelva	35 Carmona (Seville)
7 Folha de Amendoe-ira, Odivelas (Beja)	17 Buço Preto, Monchique (Algarve)	27 El Carambolo (Seville)	36 Mesas de Asta (Cádiz)
8 Serra do Gatão, Ourique (Beja)	18 Figueira (Algarve)	28 Cueva de la Pastora (Seville)	37 Vejer de la Frontera (Cádiz)
9 Anta de Tassos, Ourique (Beja)	19 Moncarapacho (Algarve)	29 Matarrubilla (Seville)	
10 Panoias de Ourique (Beja)	20 Nora (Algarve)		

already been mentioned (p. 122 above). It is exceptionally large and wholly of dry-stone construction, set in an oval pit 19½ ft by 16½ ft and 3 ft deep, with an approaching passage cut in the rock like a Tagus rock-cut tomb and a central socket for a pillar which is thought to have been of wood, like the upper part of the vault itself. The estimated number of burials – 150 – is the highest for a Portuguese collective burial chamber of any kind, and the inventory belongs almost wholly to the Tagus culture, with no Millaran influence on the pottery and very little descernible in the idols. It is hard to believe that the radiocarbon date of 1690 ± 60 BC (MF I/3, 281) obtained for a sample from this 'tholos' can really relate to its building and it is more likely to have been connected with the late Bell-Beaker burials in the chamber and passage. We have already suggested that the date of *c.* 2300 ± 60 BC (MF I/3,278) ob-tained from the primary rock-cut chamber here is likely to be the real date for the building of the 'tholos'. The curious minia-ture Passage Grave at Bela Vista, Colares (Sintra), enclosed with large blocks and with a single massive capstone, closes this series with its late Beaker ware and gold ornament.

THE SETTLEMENTS

Fig. 49

The exceptional size and wealth of the cemetery at Los Millares concentrates attention on the settlement which Siret found and partially explored on the tip of the spur between the valley of the Andarax and the Rambla de Huéchar. Here, according to his brief description, he discovered a bank about 300 yds long cutting off a triangular area of 12½ acres in which there were traces of many houses built in two groups, according to the lie of the land, possibly with an inner line of defence: two of the houses, of which details are recorded, were of rectangular plan and comparatively large, but no detailed plan was made of the settlement or of the 'aqueduct' which was thought to

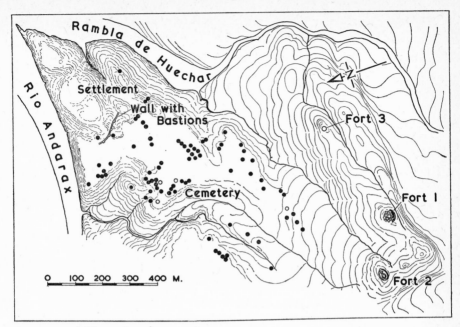

Fig. 49. Los Millares: Area plan

have brought water into it from a spring one kilometre outside
it. At a similar distance from the settlement, spread out along
a ridge to the south-west of it and its cemetery, Siret examined
four 'forts' of which the most elaborate, No. 1, enclosed an area
about 97 ft in diameter, with a double wall from which pro-
jected six bastions of oblong plan, with the outer end convex,
and traces of an inner enclosure or tower linked to the perimeter
by radiating walls. Since Siret's day the whole area covered by
the sites just described has been subjected to denudation and
vandalism and the recent re-excavation by Professor Almagro
and Dr Arribas was less successful in checking Siret's results
at the settlement and forts than in the cemetery. These scholars
were, however, able to show that the settlement was in fact
defended by a wall about 8 ft thick, of rough masonry pointed
with clay, against the outer face of which had been built at

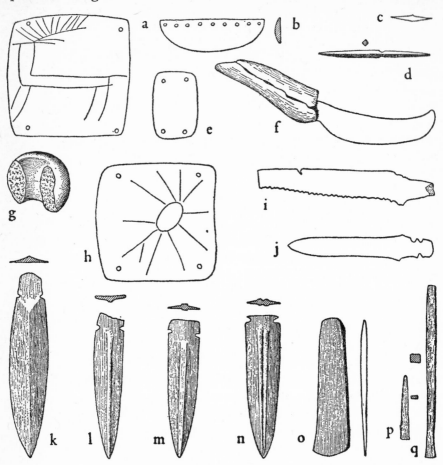

Fig. 50. Copper Age metalwork and other types: a, b, decorated clay plaques from Vila Nova de S. Pedro; b, bone model of an axe-head of Egyptian Early Dynastic type from Los Millares 7; c. copper awl from Vila Nova de S. Pedro; d, copper awl from Los Millares 16; e, clay plaque from Pavia (Evora); f, copper knife with bone handle, from Vila Nova de S. Pedro; g, stone mace from Vila Nova de S. Pedro; i, copper saw from Los Millares 37; j, copper knife from Vila Nova de S. Pedro; k, m-o, copper knives, halberd (m) and axe-head from Alcalá 3 (Algarve); l, copper knife from Los Millares 12; p-q chisels from Vila Nova de S. Pedro (a, c, f-h, j, p, q after Do Paço, e after V. Correia, b, d, i, k-o after G. and V. Leisner). 1 : 4

irregular intervals semicircular bastions, and which was pierced by a gateway 13 ft wide with walls flanking the road leading into the interior. Against the back of this wall, and at various points further into the interior, the foundations of circular huts generally about 15 ft in diameter were found. Owing to the denudation of the site, and the limited nature of the excavations, it is still uncertain at which stage of what must have been a long history (to judge by the tombs and the different types of dwelling present) Los Millares was fortified. Nor does the information so far published enable us to judge how soon after the construction of the wall was deposited close to its outer foot a piece of burnt wood for which the radiocarbon date of 2340 ± 85 BC (H-284/247) has been obtained, though the date of 2200 ± 120 BC (KN-73) recently obtained for charcoal from a layer attributed to the Los Millares culture at Almizaraque may be compared.

It is unfortunate that other Millaran settlements in the province of Almería, though evidently better preserved than Los Millares and better represented by finds available for study, have been the subject of excavations carried out with inadequate method and so far without proper publication. We are indeed still without a single adequate plan of any settlement of the third millennium BC anywhere in southern Spain. Some of these settlements – *e.g.* Tres Cabezos with its circular or polygonal huts, Campos with its double wall and bastions – were excavated by Siret, while another site, Almizaraque, was excavated and summarily published by him and by J. Cuadrado Ruiz, who left a brief account of a mound 100 × 50 yards and 3 or 4 yards high, surrounded by a ditch and containing a considerable depth of deposits, with constructions of various dates. The houses are said to have been oval and built of lath and plaster, with storage pits, and objects preserved include a female 'idol', a schematized 'sandal' and a flat 'Eye-Goddess' idol. There are many barbed and tanged arrowheads, flat

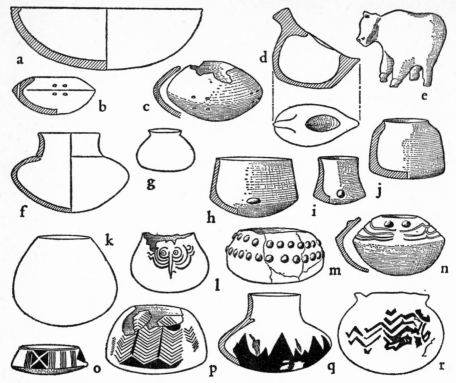

Fig. 51. Millaran pottery: a, S. Pedro de Estoril (Lisbon); b, Nora Velha (Beja); c, Las Churuletas I, Purchena (Almería); d, La Zarcita (Huelva); e, La Sabina, Gor (Granada); g, Los Millares 55; h-i, n, q, Los Millares 40; j-k, Los Millares 7; l, Los Millares 21; m, Los Millares 47; o, Almería; p, Los Millares I; r, Rambla de Huéchar 2, Gador (Almería) (a-n, p-r after G. and V. Leisner, o after L. Zambotti) 1:4

Plate 18

copper axe-heads and awls, and slag from copper and silver working. The pottery includes sherds with white-encrusted dotted bands, Beaker ware and the familiar clay plaques with perforations at the corners. The charred grains include wheat (*Triticum compactum*) emmer, barley and bean (*Vicia faba L.*, var. *celtica nana*). Equally obscure are the results obtained by Santa Olalla at Tabernas (Almería), which remain unpublished. Here a large hill-top, which may have had a defending wall, had layers representing several successive periods and with

Beaker pottery in the upper ones, and large circular houses in the lower ones. Small circular or oval huts, with storage pits, characterize the small hill-top settlement at Campico de Lébor, Totana (Murcia). In central and western Andalusia, and Portugal south of the Tagus, there are virtually no accounts of settlements which give any real idea of their character (Mesas de Asta, Jerez with its dubious 'stroke burnish' ware of supposed Aegean Chalcolithic or Early Bronze Age origin is no exception) and it is not until one returns to Vila Nova de São Pedro that one can form any idea of the spread of Millaran culture in the west from settlement, as opposed to tomb material. Here, after a long life, the unfortified 'Tagus' village was overlain by a fortified settlement in which a small central area about 80 ft wide was surrounded by a massive rampart faced with rough walling pointed with a mixture of clay and pounded limestone, up to 25 ft thick, and resting on a layer of mixed clay and pounded limestone spread over the site of the earlier settlement. Against the outer face rested bastions faced with large blocks of stone and its thickness at the south-west corner was pierced with a narrow entrance passage. About 60 ft out from this main rampart an outer, roughly concentric wall with similar semicircular bastions has been traced and in the interspace were hut foundations, one of them a roughly circular hut which was built against the foot of one of the inner bastions. The potters' kiln described in the last chapter was enclosed by the main rampart, the inner face of which curves inwards to contain it; there are also indications that the settlement had a third, outermost enclosing wall. Not only is the construction of this fort at Vila Nova strongly reminiscent of Los Millares with its semicircular bastions – especially, indeed, of the first outlying fort at the latter site – but the contents of the occupation layer contemporary with it, lying on the prepared surface of clay and pounded limestone already mentioned, are Millaran in character, with abundant evidence of metalworking, various copper

Fig. 52

Plates 31, 32

Fig. 50c, f, j

157

Fig. 50a, b

Fig. 47f, g

axe-heads, awls, chisels, saws, daggers and knives, pottery and clay plaques decorated with symbols and abundant concave-based arrowheads, many of them mitre-shaped. It is to the later stages at Vila Nova that the vase-headed bone pins so common there, as at other sites in central Portugal, belong. It is probable that Vila Nova was not the only fortified site of this kind in the Lower Tagus area: at the Zambujal near Torres Vedras a small walled enclosure with towers and bastions has been explored in recent years, and has yielded a radio-carbon date of 1690 ± 100 BC (KN-115) for a Beaker culture level; it is also possible that the ill-recorded defensive walls at Chibannes and Rotura on the Setubal peninsula and at Licêa, Pragança and Olelas north of Lisbon, may belong to this period. It seems probable that Millaran cultural influence in this area brought with it a great development of metallurgy by imported craftsmen in the service, perhaps, of intrusive rulers whose activities demanded protection by walls and bastions.

The distinctive types of concentric fortifications with bastions, at Los Millares and Vila Nova, have encouraged Dr Blance to speak of Early Bronze Age colonists coming from somewhere in the eastern Mediterranean about the middle of the third millennium, and following Sangmeister, she has drawn attention to the particular resemblance of the Early Cycladic fortifications at Chalandriani on Syros to the Iberian forts, with their semicircular bastions and outer line of defence. But we have already seen that whereas the earlier, Tagus culture which, as far as we yet know, did not build forts with bastions, has special connections with the Aegean, the later, Millaran culture seemed to show a renewed relationship to the south-east Mediterranean. As it happens, towns with semi-circular bastions are known in Palestine, too, in the third millennium (*e.g.* Jericho and Ai) and the Egyptians recognized this difference from their own tradition of square bastions when they showed, on tomb reliefs (*e.g.* in the tomb of Anta,

VILA NOVA DE S. PEDRO, 1959.

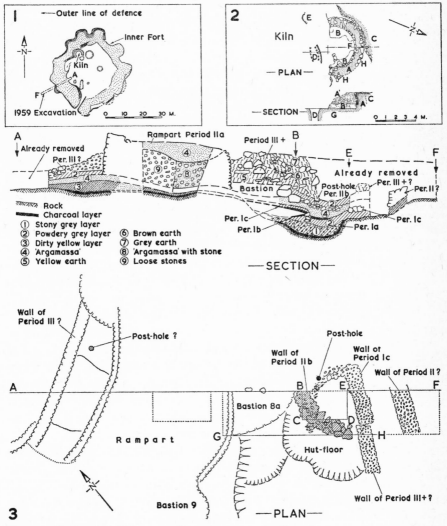

Fig. 52. Vila Nova de S. Pedro, 1959: plans and sections. 3 A to F = 18 m.

Deshashe) Egyptian soldiers assaulting Palestinian towns with semicircular bastions. If there was, indeed, any fresh infusion, at least of a governing class, into south-eastern Spain in this period, it is likely to have come from the Levant rather than the Aegean. But that it can have been no more than a governing class which defended its authority over a much more numerous indigenous 'Almerian' or 'Tagus' population by fortifications like those of its native land is suggested by the many differences of detail between the cultures associated with the 'Millaran' forts and tombs on the areas to which they spread from the original centre. Yet, that there was a new element in the population at Los Millares which exercised religious as well as military power is also suggested by its distinctive magic symbolism.

THE MILLARAN 'EYE GODDESS'

Various references in earlier parts of this book have shown how ancient in the Near East and Iberia are more or less schematic representations of a Mother Goddess. But emphasis on the eyes as opposed to the particular sexual features, and to the exclusion of all else save hints at necklaces or facial tattooing, is a specialization which seems to appear in Syria about the end of the fourth millennium and to be related to a particular cult, identified with Ishtar, at the temple at Brak with its numerous clay idols. Not until much later was the eye symbol adopted in Egypt as the sign of Horus. The characteristic owl face, with its concentric rings, sometimes allied with a long nose, appears on a red lustre vase from Lapithos, Cypus: an almost identical schematization is painted on a

Fig. 51l

vase of Almerian form from the 'tholos' tomb No. 21 at Los Millares. The realistically carved ivory head from a 'tholos'

Fig. 53a

tomb of the Tagus group at São Martinho, Sintra indicates that some of the lines below the eyes are meant to represent tattooing of the cheeks, and similar tattooing occurs on a more

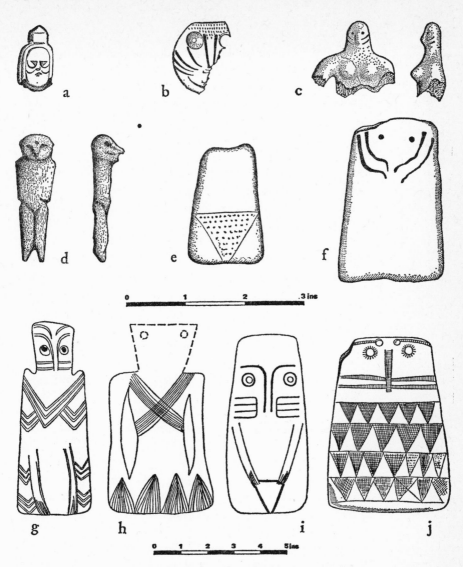

Fig. 53. Anthropomorphic idols from Portugal: a, S. Martinho, Sintra (Lisbon) (ivory); b, Quinta de Macheia, Carrasca, Torres Vedras (Lisbon) (bone); c–f, Vila Nova de S. Pedro (c and e clay, d and f stone); g–h, Idanha-a-Nova (Castelo Branco) (slate); i, Montemor-o-Novo area (stone); j, Mertola (Beja) (slate) (c–f after Do Paço, g–j after G. and V. Leisner)

Fig. 53c

schematized female figurine of clay from Vila Nova. This schematization, usually without indication of the nose, is characteristic of a whole series of 'idols' made of bone, stone or pottery – sometimes painted, sometimes carved – found as far east as the Cueva de la Pastora and the Ereta del Pedregal in Valencia, in the settlement at Almizaraque, in a megalithic tomb near Gor (Granada), on stone cylinders from the provinces of Huelva, Estremadura and the Algarve, but only in one early 'tholos' (No. 7) at Los Millares. At Vila Nova and other Tagus sites the symbol only appears on cylinders in an attenuated form. The phalange bones with 'ocular' decoration occur as far west as the Lapa da Bugalheira near Torres Novas in central Portugal and may be connected with the same ancestor cult as ritual sandals and carvings of feet in megalithic tombs in north-west Europe. Another form of female 'idol' is more plastic and harks back to the Gravettian figurines. The best examples are from the settlement at Almizaraque but more schematic ones occur at Vila Nova. The emphasis on a pubic triangle filled with pittings, and beaked bird-like heads at Vila Nova and Monte do Outeiro is another link with predynastic or early Dynastic Egypt. At Los Millares itself and the 'tholos' at Almizaraque, the owl-faced symbol is chiefly found on pottery, and on pottery elsewhere the emphasis sometimes shifts from the eyes to the tattooed zigzags, as on vases from the Palmela tombs and the cave of Rocha Forte, Montejunto, in Portuguese Estremadura. This specifically Millaran symbolism has only a limited distribution northwards to Languedoc, Brittany, Ireland and, somewhat dubiously, the Galician group of cup-and-ring carvings. The last-mentioned group includes a few 'Mother Goddess' faces and has a distribution which Mr Michael Walker has shown to be different from that of megalithic tombs in the area, and may be related to settlement in the local Copper Age, like similar carvings in Ireland.

Plate 33d-g

Plate 33a

Fig. 53f

Fig. 53d
Plate 33e, f

Fig. 53e
Plate 33c

Fig. 42g

PAINTED POTTERY

We have already encountered a few scraps of painted pottery on southern Spanish sites at an earlier stage (pp. 77, 82) but only in the Millaran culture can we at last assemble a small number of complete pots seemingly representing a distinctive style, which can be related in a general way to the painted wares of the Neolithic and Chalcolithic cultures of the Near East and the eastern Mediterranean. Such ware appears to be almost absent from the Tagus culture but at Tabernas and Los Millares there are several bowls of Almerian form which are decorated either with light colours on a red base, or red on a light base, to produce simple geometric patterns of multiple chevrons, zigzags and filled triangles; these seem to relate to sherds found below the Beaker level in the Gar Cahal cave near Tangiers and in the 'silos' of Campo Real and other sites near Carmona. Some sherds from the latter area are from a hemispherical bowl with multiple chevrons on the inner surface while others are from a similar bowl with a trellis pattern on the outer surface. Multiple chevron patterns also appear on a bowl from a 'tholos' of Millaran affinity at Rambla de Huéchar near Almeria and on a stone vessel from the cave of Los Blanquizares de Lébor, Totana (Murcia). It is easy to find distant parallels to these patterns at such early sites as Hačilar and Mersin in Anatolia, and the typically Almerian carinated bowl from San Andrés has light on dark saltire patterns curiously reminiscent of Tell Halaf; but a distinguished authority, Professor Bernabò Brea, has noted a general affinity of both form and decoration with the contemporary Serraferlicchio culture of Sicily which is probably much more relevant to the problem of Millaran origins. Painted ware seems to belong to the opening phase of the Millaran culture and to be closely connected with the foreign element moving along the North African coast—an element that gave it its distinctive character.

Fig. 51l, p-q

Fig. 51r

Fg. 51o

METALLURGY

Fig. 500

Fig. 50k, l, n

Fig. 50f, i

It has often been asserted that the earliest forms of copper weapons and tools found in southern Iberia can only be related in a general way to those of the Near East. The slender axe-heads, certainly, are a form very widespread in the latter area. The ribbed and notched daggers are not easy to parallel exactly in the East, although there is a distant relationship to early Minoan forms, while saws and curving knives like that from Vila Nova seem to relate most closely to early Egyptian ones, though a similar knife is known from Eutresis in Boeotia. But recent spectrographical analyses, particularly those carried out by Sangmeister and Junghans, have shown that from the technical point of view the Iberian implements represent an extension through the Mediterranean of a great Anatolian province in which effective implements were produced from the fourth millennium onwards by reduction together of cop-per and arsenic ores. The early implements in Iberia to which we have so far referred generally consist of copper with a moderate admixture (up to about 6%) of arsenic. Once established, the technology of arsenical copper endured in Iberia for many centuries, but the localized character of Mil-laran implements show that by this phase Iberian ores were no longer being exploited mainly for export, as they probably were in the days of the earlier 'tholoi' and rock-cut tombs, but for local customers. It is stated that at the Almizaraque settlement more than a hundred implements of various types were found. This accords with the account of several furnaces with bases like large crucibles and the upper parts formed of clay arcs being found there, together with stocks of carbonate ore. Silver also may have been exploited at Almizaraque, since its ore occurs near by, but there is no definite proof of this. At Vila Nova a pile of $13\frac{1}{2}$ kilos of limonite ore was found, but this must have been brought from a considerable distance since there is no local supply. In the occupation layers of the fortified settlement many fragments of copper-stained crucibles, some of them oblong, with feet at the corners, were found, and at other sites similar crucibles are sometimes zoomorphic. Cast-ing, however, seems generally to have been rather primitive, in open moulds (hence the blades with a midrib on one side only, *Fig. 50k, l* though bivalve moulds must sometimes have been used (*e.g.* to produce the Alcalá 'halberd' with midrib on both faces). *Fig. 50m* The various copper mines actually recorded from the penin-sula, in which waisted mauls and sometimes Copper Age or Bronze Age implements were found, cannot as yet, however, be certainly dated as far back as the Millaran epoch.

THE END OF MILLARAN CULTURE

The walled and bastioned forts of Almería and the lower Tagus, whatever their precise origin, are a distant reflection of a phase of highly developed social and military organization in the eastern Mediterranean, represented above all by Old King-dom Egypt. That kingdom finally collapsed, *c.* 2200 BC, under the attacks of nomadic tribes, and the same fate overtook the second city of Troy about the same time. It seems that the Millaran culture met a similar fate: at Vila Nova de São Pedro the occupation layers which formed on top of the ruins of the inner walls contained Bell-Beaker pottery instead of Millaran types, and at Los Millares and near Seville the communal tombs received secondary burials with Beaker pottery, weapons and gold ornaments. All over the peninsula in the last quarter of the third millennium the Beaker nomads become culturally dominant, and soon afterwards spread rapidly to most parts of western and central Europe. This remarkable phenomenon, Iberia's most original contribution to European prehistory, will be considered next.

Chapter VII

The Beaker Culture

THE BELL BEAKER EXPLOSION: *c.* 2250–2000 BC

TWENTY YEARS AGO Dr Santa Olalla drew a picture of a 'Mediterranean Bronze Age I' in Spain (2000–1700 BC) in which Bell Beakers were the ceramic, and communal Passage Graves of all types the architectural, expression of an age of Spanish greatness. Only a few years ago Professor Almagro was still maintaining this concentrated chronology, in the face of numerous radiocarbon dates from adjoining parts of Europe, while recognizing the distinct cultural origins of Bell Beaker pottery. During the last three chapters we have been separating the main elements of this over-concentrated picture – culturally and chronologically distinct as they are – and now, after more than 1000 years, we have reached the day of the Bell Beaker, and seen it appearing as a new and intrusive element at Vila Nova de São Pedro after the decay or destruction of the Millaran fort. At none of the many unstratified Early Copper Age settlement sites and collective tombs in the peninsula which have yielded Bell Beaker pottery can it be proved that it belongs to a primary phase, and at some Passage Graves in the south there are indications that this pottery and its associated copper weapons and gold ornaments in fact accompanied secondary burials. We have already hinted that the makers of this distinctive pottery may have played a role akin to that of the nomads from the desert who disrupted the advanced cultures of the Near East about the beginning of the last quarter of the third millennium and, indeed, that they spread from the interior of southern Spain to overwhelm the Millaran overlords of coastal Andalusia and the lower Tagus about this time. This involves a conception of the 'Beaker Folk' not unlike that which prevailed among British archaeologists in the early decades of this century, as nomadic pastoralists who

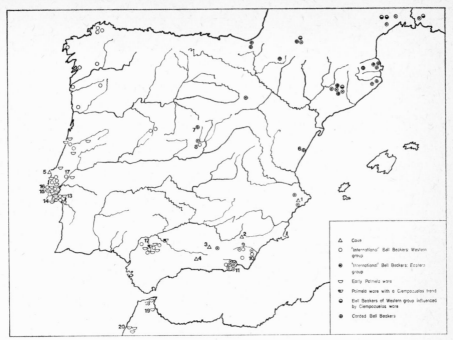

Fig. 54.   Bell Beakers, phases I-II

1 Cova de l'Or, Be-
  niarrés (Alicante)
2 Cueva Ambrosio,
  Velez Blanco
  (Almería)
3 Cueva de Cari-
  güela de Piñar
  Granada)
4 Cueva de Alhama
  de Granada
5 Cova da Furninha,

  Peniche (Leiria)
6 Filómena
  (Castellón)
7 Entretérminos,
  Villalba (Madrid)
8 Arenero de Miguel
  Ruiz (Madrid)
9 Loma de la
  Atalaya, Purchena
  (Almería)
10 Loma de Belmonte,

  Mojacar
  (Almería)
11 Los Millares
  (Almería)
12 Cañada de Car-
  rascal, Gandul
  (Seville)
13 Palmela (Lisbon)
14 Alapraia (Lisbon)
15 S. Pedro de
  Estoril (Lisbon)

16 Penha Verde,
  Sintra (Lisbon)
17 Vila Nova de S.
  Pedro (Santarém)
18 Gar Cahal, Tan-
  giers (Morocco)
19 Caf Taht El Gar,
  Tangiers
  (Morocco)
20 Dar es Soltan
  (Morocco)

spread from beyond the Pyrenees to most parts of western and central Europe, bringing with them the earliest metallurgy of those regions and which was synthesized in 1928 by A. del Castillo in his classic work.

During the past thirty years the conceptions of a Beaker Culture and a Beaker Folk have been passing through a phase of severe criticism, in which many different interpretations have been put forward. The late Professor Gordon Childe played a prominent part in spreading doubts as to whether the makers of Bell Beakers originated in south-west Europe or played any real part in spreading early metallurgy, or indeed whether they were a 'folk' at all. The most extreme view put forward was that Bell Beakers merely represent a tradition of craftsmanship and that their distribution reflects trade and not folk movement. This idea does not stand up to close examination of typological detail because the Beaker 'empire' in Europe in fact comprises many regional groups each of which is linked to the others by many common traits but differs from them enough to forbid the idea of trading except within very narrow limits, and though there is undoubtedly a simple 'International' form of Bell Beaker (the Leisners' 'Maritime' type) with an extraordinarily wide distribution in Europe, the individual examples of this tend to show a decline in the quality of the fabric and finish the further they are found from south-western Europe. However, the comparatively narrow horizon on which Beakers appear in most countries outside the peninsula and the lack, at any rate until recently, of means to a reliable and accurate chronology have permitted doubts as to the way folk movements went. As a result attempts have been made, culminating in that of the Neustupnýs recently in Czechoslovakia, to reverse the movement and to make the rich central European concentration of Bell Beakers the primary group. Professor E. Sangmeister in 1961 put forward a somewhat more plausible theory; this made the 'International' Bell Beaker originate in the peninsula but attributed the varied forms and more elaborate patterns that succeed it in the same area to a 'Reflux' movement (*Rückverkehr*) back from central Europe to the peninsula, which brought with it types of ornament and metalwork thought to be of Danubian origin. I regret the haste with which this unfortunate theory has been accepted by some leading authorities in France and Great Britain, although I agree that certain corded Bell Beakers from eastern and central Spain suggest some degree of 'Reflux'. Evidence for technical continuity and evolution in the peninsula makes it hard to accept Sangmeister's theory entirely.

The doubts about the accomplishment of the Bell-Beaker makers as metallurgists and, indeed, the existence of a general range of associated weapons, tools and ornaments that would justify the phrase 'Beaker culture' arose in the past, of course, partly from the rarity of stratified sites and exclusive grave groups in the peninsula. There are now, however, as will be seen, a number of closed finds from separate burials in Spain and Portugal as well as beyond the Pyrenees which make it clear that certain types of copper dagger and arrowhead, archer's wristguard, dress fastener and gold ornament are regularly associated with Bell Beakers, almost wherever they occur in any numbers, and these types are different from those of the Millaran culture in southern Spain and Portugal. At the same time, the work of Sangmeister and his associates on metal analyses of the Copper Age and Early Bronze Age on the continent, and of Coghlan and Case on similar analyses in the British Isles, has now largely reinstated the Beaker Folk as disseminators of much of the early knowledge of working in copper and gold in western, northern and even central Europe. It must, in fact, be accepted that there was a distinct range of metal forms which was evolved in the peninsula by the makers of Bell Beakers as a result of their contacts with the early metallurgists of Andalusia and that these and other types spread, with Beaker ceramics, to many parts of Europe. Moreover, a number of radiocarbon dates now available, especially from the Low Countries, show that this expansion was so rapid as to justify the phrase 'Beaker explosion': it must have been accomplished within a few generations after the original expansion from the interior to the coast of Spain and Portugal, *c.* 2250 BC. When we come to the familiar phrase 'Beaker Folk', however, there remains the difficulty that the physical type which has come to be regarded as characteristic of Beaker graves in central Europe and the British Isles – strong build, broad skull with rugged face and flattened occiput – has not so far apparently presented itself to any appreciable extent in burials with Beaker pottery in the peninsula. It is likely enough that the Mediterranean types which seem to predominate in burials of the Beaker phase in the coastal regions of Spain and Portugal represent the indigenous Neolithic and Early Copper Age population of these areas, among whom any immigrant minority from the Meseta would quickly have been absorbed. This Mediterranean element has remained predominant in the peninsula ever since, but we have already noted an 'Armenoid' element in the Early Copper Age population of south-eastern Spain (p. 84 above) while a broad-skulled element which is said not to be strictly 'Beaker' in its characteristics has long been known from Beaker burials at Ciempozuelos and other sites near Madrid. Broad-headed 'Alpine' folk are known today on the middle Tagus and along the northern seaboard of Spain: the former, indeed, can be traced back to the time of megalithic tombs in the Basque provinces. It is quite possible that the typical Beaker men of northwestern Europe owe something to the survival of Crô-magnon characteristics among the pastoral-ists of the Meseta in the third millennium BC, who developed a tendency to brachycephaly either through contact with the Armenoids or Alpines already mentioned, or through an internal process of development; but so small a proportion of the Neolithic and Copper Age skeletal material from the peninsula has so far been adequately studied and published that it seems wise to suspend judgement until more work has been done.

I myself, at any rate, am prepared to believe that the Bell Beaker originated in the Iberian peninsula not only because its
tradition lasted longer there than anywhere else but because in
contrast to the situation in central Europe its background can
be traced back there for at least a thousand years before its
classic form, with its characteristic red-slipped ware and notched decoration, spread throughout the coastal regions of the
peninsula and thence far beyond the Pyrenees, partly, at
least, by sea-routes previously opened up by the Iberian Passage
Grave builders. From that moment, as isolation on the Meseta
was exchanged for contact with more advanced agriculturalists
and metallurgists in various parts of Europe, specialized groups
of Beaker pottery begin to appear, first of all among the forms
of the 'Maritime' Beakers, then among the patterns and techniques of decoration applied to an increasing number of different
shapes of vessel. The classification of these groups is vital to
the understanding of Beaker evolution beyond the Pyrenees,
which similarly led to the development, within a century or
two, of numerous local groups, most of which cannot truly be
said to have a precise counterpart in the peninsula.

THE ORIGIN OF THE BELL BEAKER: *c.* 3500–2250 BC

We have already had occasion more than once (p. above)
to refer to pottery decorated in a way that seemed to anticipate
Bell Beakers. Even the early cardial pottery sometimes shows
decoration of diagonally hatched bands and at the Cova de   *Fig. 55 a-d*
l'Or (Valencia), the Cueva Ambrosio (Almería) and the
cave of Carigüela de Piñar (Granada) the true cardial impressions are sometimes replaced by notching with some sort of
tool in the manner of Bell Beakers, sometimes red- or white-
encrusted, sometimes with a red lustre ('almagre') surface. It is
characteristic of these early vessels with diagonally hatched
bands that the hatching is regularly in the same direction

171

throughout – a feature which occasionally appears on some 'Maritime' Beakers in Spain and Portugal but is usually replaced on them by hatching in alternate directions. As far as can be judged from fragments, these early vessels were normally bag-shaped rather than of true Bell-Beaker form. The replacement of shell-edge impression by notching in the Beaker manner is probably due to influence on the later cardial ware of south-eastern Spain by the 'Hispano-Mauritanian' incised wares which, as we have seen, were stratified above cardial ware at Carigüela and spread from the Straits of Gibraltar into central Andalusia and across to northern Portugal. Pottery with an over-all decoration of incised or notched lines, sometimes forming transversely or diagonally hatched bands, is characteristic of the Neolithic in a vast area of northern Africa stretching from the Sudan to Rio de Oro, and the influence of it seems to spread to the Sicilian Neolithic pottery of Stentinello. Another element of the Beaker decorative repertoire – the trellised band – appears on this horizon and similarly spreads to Andalusia and Valencia with 'almagre' ware and red encrustation. It is interesting to note that the practice of surmounting the topmost band with a series of triangular or sub-triangular shapes filled in with hatching begins at the Cueva Ambrosio and continues in the Portuguese incised 'cave' pottery at Furninha. This is clearly handed on to true Bell Beakers. The incised diagonally hatched band now (in the latter part of the fourth millennium) becomes a widespread feature of pottery outside the areas in which the Almerian and megalithic cultures developed – the Cueva de la Mujer, Alhama de Granada is a typical site – and red lustre is well established in this context. At this time, as we have seen (p. 98 above), fine red-slipped vessels, sometimes resembling Bell Beakers in form but without decoration, occasionally appear in the earliest Alentejan megalithic Passage Graves. Thus it seems that the elements of the classical Bell Beaker

Fig. 55a
Fig. 20i

Fig. 19b

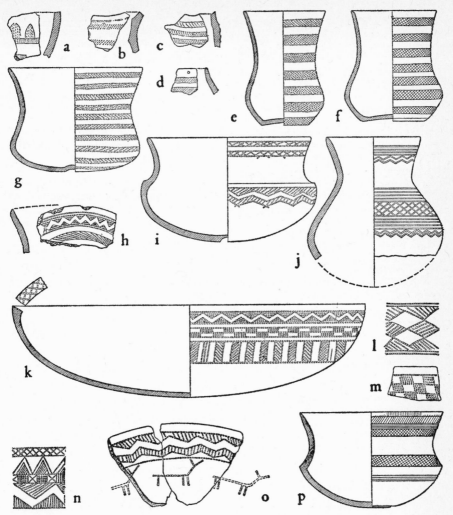

Fig. 55. The development of the Bell Beaker: *a-d,* Pre-Beaker ware from Cueva Ambrosio (Almería) (*a-b*) and Carigüela de Pinar (Granada) (*c-d*); *e,* Filomena (Castellón); *f,* Los Millares XIII (Almería); *g,* Alapraia 2 (Lisbon); *h,* Los Millares (Almería); *i,* Vila Nova de S. Pedro (Santarém); *j,* Cañada del Carrascal, Gandul (Seville); *k,* Alapraia 2 (Lisbon); *l,* S. Martinho, Sintra (Lisbon); *m,* Carmona (Seville); *n,* Acébuchal, Carmona (Seville); *o,* Palmela (Setubal); *p,* Cova da Moura, Torres Vedras (Lisbon) (*a-b* after E. Jimenez, *c-d* after M. Pellicer, *e* after F. Esteve, *f, j, l, o* after G. and V. Leisner, *h* after Almagro and Arribas, *i, k* after Do Paço, *m* after Aberg and *n* after S. Olalla). 1 : 4

were taking shape over a long period among the pastoralists of the interior of southern Spain: it is probable that if the material at our disposal were more evenly spread about the Guadal-quivir and Guadiana basins we should be able to follow the development with greater continuity down to the moment when the pastoralists began to encroach upon the coastal areas; but as these people in all probability still adhered to the Neolithic tradition of separate pit burial, in areas where caves do not occur, finds have been most unevenly distributed.

THE MARITIME BEAKERS: *c.* 2250–2000 BC

Nearly twenty years ago I stressed the contrast in distribution of the simple 'International' or 'Maritime' forms of Beaker and the more elaborately and variously shaped 'Palmela-Carmona' and 'Meseta' wares. The former were prominent in the 'Beaker explosion' beyond the Pyrenees and are mainly coastal in distribution in the peninsula. The latter comprise the great bulk of the pottery of Beaker tradition from secondary burials in the rock-cut tombs of the lower Tagus, the settle-ment sites explored by Bonsor near Carmona on the lower Guadalquivir, the pit graves of the Meseta, and the caves of southern Catalonia, but had a much more limited impact on Beaker evolution beyond the Pyrenees. After some controversy it is now generally accepted that these two groups are culturally distinct and it is probable that the first is the earlier, growing as it clearly does out of local Neolithic traditions and leading on to the second group. Dr Blance has lately suggested that Bell Beakers arose from fusion between indigenous Neolithic groups and the Tagus culture, but she seems to have over-looked the significance of a regional differentiation within the 'Maritime' group which Del Castillo pointed out in 1954. Whereas the classic Bell Beakers of the western seaboard are comparatively broad, with gentle curves and sometimes an

Fig. 56. Bell Beakers, phase III

1 Ermegeira, Torres Vedras (Lisbon)
2 Cova da Moura, Torres Vedras
3 S. Pedro de Estoril (Lisbon)
4 Alapraia (Lisbon)
5 Palmela (Setubal)
6 Montes Claros (Lisbon)
7 Carmona (Seville)
8 Fuente Palmera (Córdoba)
9 Tabernas (Almería)
10 Almizaraque (Almería)
11 Ciempozuelos (Madrid)
12 Las Carolinas (Madrid)
13 Cueva de Somaén (Soria)
14 Cueva de Toralla (Lérida)
15 Pago de la Pena, Villabuena del Puente (Zamora)
16 Montilla (Córdoba)
17 Grajal de Campos (León)
18 Puentes de García Rodríguez (Coruña)
19 Bela Vista, Colares (Lisbon)
20 Montelavar, Sintra (Lisbon)
21 Casas do Cañal, Estremoz (Evora)

omphaloid base, as in a fine example from one of the rock-cut
tombs at Alapraia and others from Galicia (this is the form
which spreads to Biscayan France and from Brittany to the
Paris Basin), those of the eastern seaboard are generally tall and
angular with a narrow and flat or gently hollowed base. This

Fig. 55g
Plate 37

Fig. 55e, f

175

Plate 35

early type of Beaker spreads through southern France, reaching Avignon *c.* 2150 BC (GsY 705), and up the Rhône valley to the Rhineland, where it was influenced by north European corded ware recently introduced into the same area. Now arises an undoubted 'Reflux' movement, whereby tall Beakers with horizontal corded lines and diagonal notching appear in *Fig. 55e* Catalonia, Valencia, and even Biscayan France and the Basque provinces. In this same Mediterranean group of Beakers *Fig. 55b* bar-chevron bands make an early appearance alongside the *Fig. 55f* diagonally hatched ones, as well as trellised bands and marginal chevrons and hatched triangles, and vessels of this family appear not only in southern France but in Sardinia and Sicily: in the latter island a Beaker has lately been found in the cave of Palombara near Syracuse, in association with local 'Malpasso' ware assigned to the end of the third millennium BC. The special importance of this Mediterranean group of Bell Beakers is that its makers adopted the barbed and tanged form of flint arrowheads which had long been used in eastern Spain, and spread it to France and north-western Europe generally. With a growing north European 'corded' element these people later played a leading part in founding the various local Beaker groups of the Low Countries and the British Isles.

We have no means of determining at present which was the earliest of the two groups just described: in view of the evidence already mentioned for a long germination of the Beaker style of ornament on Neolithic pottery in the peninsula and north-west Africa, it seems likely that both the groups sprang from a common stock somewhere in the interior, between the Atlantic and Mediterranean coasts, and differentiated as they established themselves in the coastal areas. In view of the speed and mobility of these pastoralists, it is hardly surprising that sherds of true 'Maritime' Beakers have lately been reported from the fringe of the Sahara in Algeria, in the area where we have already noted ancestral forms of pottery deposited by similar nomads long before. But it is difficult to pin these early Beaker Folk down to their own burial and settlement sites, away from sites where their relics occur mixed with those of other cultures. One such burial appears to be a pit grave, covered with a stone slab, found at the sand-pit of Miguel Ruiz near Madrid, where two early Beakers approximating more to the Mediterranean than to the Atlantic form were associated with a tanged copper dagger of Beaker type. In the same area, at Entretérminos, a tall Beaker with partially corded decoration was found with a similar dagger, a copper arrowhead, a copper axe-head and a diadem of gold strip in a megalithic Passage Grave, and else-where in the coastal areas Beakers of these early types regularly occur with secondary burials in Tagus rock-cut tombs or Mil-laran 'tholoi', or in the upper levels of settlements founded by local, sedentary groups. At Vila Nova de São Pedro, in particular, 'Maritime' Beaker pottery predominates.

THE LATER BEAKER WARES: *c.* 2000–800 BC

We have already suggested that the pastoralists who introduced the primitive Bell Beaker form to the centres of settled popula-tion on the lower Tagus and Guadalquivir were probably absorbed fairly rapidly. This process seems to be reflected in the subsequent history of Beaker pottery. Manufacture of this ware now passed to specialized craftsmen working at a limited number of centres using kilns like that found at Vila Nova de São Pedro (p. 137 above) and perpetuating techniques already long established in the area, like the use of micaceous stiffening of the clay and a dark wash over a red slip: the technical continuity from the early to late forms of Beaker in the cultur-ally dominant centres in the lower Guadalquivir and Tagus valleys refutes any idea of immigrant 'Reflux' barbarians from central Europe. These craftsmen served a market which required a wider range of forms. In addition to the archetypal

Fig. 55k

Bell Beaker we now have hemispherical bowls, often with broadly flattened rims, taken over from the Tagus culture, broad platters with thickened rims, similarly derived, pede-

Plate 34

stalled bowls which anticipate Argaric forms and seem in fact to belong to a late stage of the Beaker tradition, and necked bowls with a rounded or carinated body (the *cazuelas* of

Fig. 55i
Plate 40

Spanish, and the *caçoulas* of Portuguese, archaeologists). The necked bowl had begun to develop at Vila Nova, where most of the Beaker pottery is early, but the full development of the form is best seen around Carmona and in the rock-cut tombs of the Tagus estuary. Corded decoration did not spread to the western regions of the peninsula; at first notched decoration, applied with the aid of a comb or cogwheel-like tool, reigned supreme and only later did continuous furrowing replace it. Patterns became much more varied and elaborate – bar chev-rons, multiple chevrons, cross-hatching (transverse or diago-

Fig. 55k-m

nal), chequers (transverse or diagonal) – and there is a growing tendency for the multiple bands of decoration to contract into

Fig. 55j
Plate 36
Fig. 55n

two or three bands of varied decoration – 'zone contraction' – and even for the patterns to vary horizontally, with 'metopic' arrangements.

In the opening phase, at the beginning of the second millen-nium, when these new developments were still overlapping with the earlier forms, emigration from the coastal regions continued, as we may conclude from the existence of an im-portant central European and north Italian group of Bell Beakers in which the broad form predominates, but which shows the influence of the later range of patterns. Hemispherical bowls with flattened rims occasionally appear in this group, and the associated concave-based arrowheads show that the in-fluence here is coming from the western rather than the eastern side of the peninsula. Traces of the passage of this second wave can be seen among the later Beakers of southern France, and the influence of its patterns spread among the hybrid Beaker groups

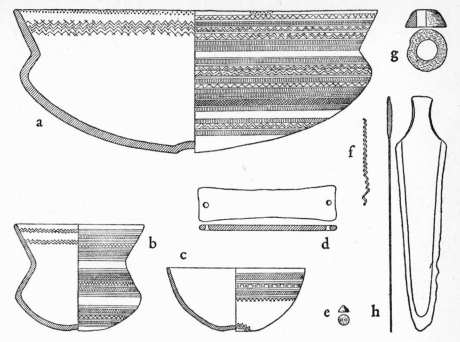

Fig. 57.   A Late Beaker burial: Pago de la Peña, Villabuena del Puente (Zamora) a-c, pottery; d, stone; e, g, bone; f, gold; h, copper (after Maluquer). 1 : 4

of north-western Europe, being particularly noticeable on the Dutch 'Veluwe' and the British 'short-necked' Beakers. It is to this horizon too that most of the Beaker pottery from caves in the Tangier area (Gar Cahal and Gaf Taht el Gar) and far down the Atlantic coast of Morocco (Dar es Soltan and Temara) belongs. Some of this pottery, however, may represent trade rather than emigration. In Portugal the early stage, with decoration still mainly notched, is represented almost exclusively at the settlement of Penha Verde (Sintra), while the later one with the same patterns incised is represented almost exclusively at the settlement of Montes Claros near Lisbon. The pottery from the settlements near Carmona is mainly notched, but on the Meseta the bulk of the pottery of

Plates 39, 40
Ciempozuelos near Madrid is incised and often heavily encrusted with white. At this late stage the necked bowls develop a special squat form which is practically a platter.

Particularly significant is the appearance on Beaker pottery of this late phase, at Fuente Palmera near Córdoba, Palmela and Las Carolinas near Madrid, of the schematized cervids *Fig. 550* already mentioned as characteristic of later rockshelter art in the peninsula. It is to this late horizon that the great bulk of the Beaker pottery from the northern parts of the Meseta belong; the fabric of this incised and encrusted ware is not all of the fine quality of the well-known vessels from Ciempozuelos and the red slip is often replaced by a burnished grey or black body. Plate 36 The tall Bell Beakers at Ciempozuelos are, indeed, comparatively early in the series and relate to Andalusian ones, like that from a secondary burial in the Passage Grave of Cañada de *Fig. 55j* Carrascal, Carmona, which are notched but shows zone contraction. The later incised Beaker ware of the Meseta is much Plates 38, 39 coarser and shows a tendency to false relief zigzag bands, which appear also in the closely related pottery of south Catalonia and in the later Beaker ware of southern France (chiefly the Rhône valley) and central Europe; in view of radiocarbon dates – 2150 ± 140 BC (GsY 704) and 2119 ± 118 BC (GsY 116) respectively, just obtained from two sites in Basses-Alpes – the lower Rhône valley was possibly the creative centre for this heavily incised Beaker Ware. There is no doubt that this ware had a long life on the Meseta and survived there in a modified form until the end of the Bronze Age (p. 216 below). For this reason the two superimposed layers in the Cueva de la Mora, Somaén (Soria), which were at one time supposed to throw much light on the typological series, are of very little help, for the material from them all belongs to stages in the slow evolution of the late incised group of Beaker wares.

As with earlier Beaker pottery in the peninsula, the later wares mainly come from ill-recorded excavations of pit-graves

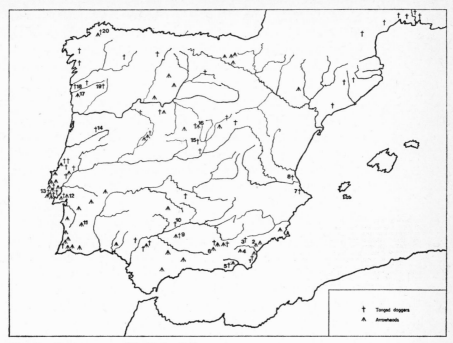

Fig. 58. Copper weapons of the Beaker Folk

1 Loma de Bel-
monte, Mojácar
(Almería)
2 Almizaraque
(Almería)
3 Velez Blanco
(Almería)
4 Loma de la
Atalaya de
Purchena
(Almería)

5 Loma de Huechar
(Almería)
6 La Sabina de
Gorafe (Granada)
7 Rocafort
(Valencia)
8 Cullera (Valencia)
9 Montilla
(Córdoba)
10 Fuente Palmera
(Córdoba)

11 Monte do Outeiro,
Aljustrel (Beja)
12 Palmela (Setubal)
13 Bela Vista,
Colares (Lisbon)
14 Pinhal dos Melos,
Fornos de Al-
godres (Guarda)
15 Arenero de
Miguel Ruiz
(Madrid)

16 Entretérminos
(Madrid)
17 S. Bento de
Balugães (Braga)
18 Quinta da Agua
Branca, S. Maria
de Lobelhe (Braga)
19 Ronfeiro (Orense)
20 Puentes de García
Rodríguez
(Coruña)

(on the Meseta and near Carmona), communal burial chambers constructed originally before the Bell Beaker phase and
later re-used (in the coastal areas) and unstratified settlement
sites. The latter usually yield remains of earlier cultures, as well
as various phases of the Beaker culture, and it is difficult to
relate any particular dwellings or other structures exclusively to
the Beaker Folk. The small circular huts with dry-stone walls
at Penha Verde, Sintra, however, seem to belong to the Beaker
phase. Two of them, 8 ft in diameter, were dwellings, while a
third enclosed a pit and appears to have been used for food
storage. It is likely that the Beaker Folk normally built circular
huts of a flimsy type, framed with wood, traces of which have
not been noticed by excavators, although roughly paved areas
that may have belonged to such huts were noticed in the upper,
Beaker-yielding level at Vila Nova in 1959. In Almería and
and Valencia, too, sherds of the late 'Meseta' Beaker type were
found in some of the settlements already mentioned, *e.g.* Almizaraque and Tabernas and they have lately appeared, with plain
Millaran wares, in association with circular hut foundations at
Cerro de la Virgen, Orce (Granada). As before, most burial
deposits in the coastal areas represent secondary use of communal burial chambers built long before. Most of the 'Meseta'
graves are ill-recorded, but those of Ciempozuelos, at least,
seem to have resembled the recently recorded one of Pago de la
Peña, Villabuena del Puente (Zamora); this was of a male,
flexed and lying on the right side facing westwards in an oval
pit 4½ ft by 2 ft and 15 in. deep. On the other hand the late
Beaker at Fuente Palmera (Córdoba) had been placed with a
tanged copper dagger in a small cist formed of four upright
slabs. Separate burial in cists may have become more general
among the later Beaker users, since several cist burials, without
Beakers but with metalwork of Beaker type, have been recorded,
as will be seen presently, and the custom is widespread in the
Mediterranean Bronze Age.

THE BELL BEAKER CULTURE

It has sometimes been asserted that the existence of Bell Beaker pottery is not proof of the existence of a distinctive Bell Beaker culture. This is no longer a reasonable point of view, if it ever was, in spite of the rarity of exclusive Beaker sites in the peninsula, because quite a large number of Beaker burial groups are now known from western Europe as a whole in which the same range of types of dress fastener, archer's equip-ment, copper dagger and gold ornament recur; even in the unstratified assemblages from communal graves in the penin-sula, the same types commonly appear together in those tombs where Beaker pottery appears, but very rarely where it does not. The Beaker Folk really did have their distinctive dress fastener – a bone or ivory botton, conical or tortoise-shell shaped, with a V-perforation – and their adult males were often archers equipped not only with bows and arrows tipped with flint but with stone wristguards and sometimes, in their later phase, they had copper arrowheads. Their copper daggers were tanged and of quite different type from those of the Millaran 'tholos' builders, and they used thin strips of gold to ornament

Fig. 60

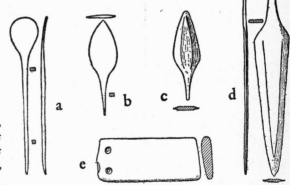

Fig. 59. Beaker metalwork: a-b, Palmela (Setubal); c, Los Millares XI (Almería); d-e, Praia das Maçãs (Lisbon) (a-b, d-e, after V. Leisner, c after Almagro and Arribas). 1:4

183

the handles of their daggers and for other decorative purposes, much more freely than the Millaran people seem to have done. The closed find, already mentioned, from near Zamora includes several of these types, together with a late, distinctively 'Meseta' range of incised Beaker ware. The button in this grave is of the simple, conical form which is associated with Beakers in Britain, but it does not follow that this type, or the other forms of V-perforated button that are more commonly met with in the peninsula, was introduced at a late stage by the supposed 'Reflux' movement. A conical button was apparently found in a Maltese tomb of early third-millennium date (Zebbuǧ) and another in an equally early communal burial at Aljezur in Algarve which yielded no Beaker pottery, while one from the Millaran 'tholos' at Almizaraque is of later date but still apparently earlier than the Beaker horizon. Tortoise-shell type buttons, too, may be related to an early Egyptian form. There are two varieties, one oval in plan with small expansions at the ends, the other with broad and angular terminals which are as wide as the body. An example of the former occurs in the third-millennium deposit in the Cueva de la Pastora, Valencia, without Beaker ware. Others appear with 'Maritime' Beakers at the 'tholoi' at São Martinho and Pedra d'Oiro north of Lisbon, while both tortoise-shell types and the conical form occur with predominantly 'Maritime' assemblages from the megalithic tombs of Trigache and Conchadas near Lisbon and the settlement of Vila Nova de São Pedro. The latter site has also yielded a single example of the square, pyramidal type of button which becomes more characteristic of the Mediterranean coast of Spain, occurring there with late, incised Beaker ware at San Antón de Orihuela, and the caves of Cova Fonda de Salamó in southern Catalonia and Aigues Vives, Solsona in northern Catalonia, and leads on to the prismatic buttons of the post-Beaker horizon in this area (p. 205 below).

Plate 57

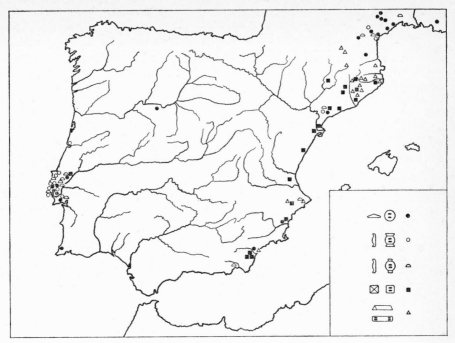

Fig. 60. V-perforated buttons and necklace elements

Like other south-west European and North African peoples before them, from the Neolithic onwards, the Beaker Folk were archers. For their arrow tips they normally used the flint weapons which had been evolved by their predecessors, the types varying from one side of the peninsula to the other, and they introduced these types to parts of central and north-western Europe that had not known them before. The archer's wristguard of stone, on the other hand, seems to have been very little used before their time in the peninsula and it is naturally one of the types which the alleged 'Reflux' move-ment is said to have introduced there from central Europe. As it happens, however, associations show that wristguards were used by the early 'Maritime' Beaker makers in Spain and are not confined to the supposed 'Reflux' horizon:

one for example was found with an early Beaker, a tanged dagger of copper, a copper arrowhead and gold strips
(one of them forming a tube) in the 'tholos' of Loma de
Belmonte, Mojácar (Almeria); another came from a 'tholos'
(XI) re-excavated by Almagro and Arribas at Los Millares,
together with part of a 'Maritime' Beaker. Iberian wristguards
are flat stone plaques, usually straight-sided and narrow, with a
single perforation at each end, as at Loma de Belmonte and
Pago de Peña. But examples with two perforations at each
end (as at Los Millares XI and a grave with two copper arrowheads at Grajal de Campos, León) and occasionally with an
even greater number of perforations occur; these are naturally
broader and sometimes have concave sides. The slender
single-holed type certainly lasted into the Argaric phase in
south-eastern Spain, but its early use is illustrated not only by
the examples just given but by its association with a 'Maritime'
Bell Beaker at Kühnheim near Colmar in Alsace. The
distinctive copper arrowheads which the Beaker Folk took
with them beyond the Pyrenees and occasionally deposited in
graves as far afield as Britain seem also to have been practically
their invention – the rare early type with elongated tang and
rounded tip does appear in the late tholos at Almizaraque with
a button but without a Beaker, and in another 'tholos' at the
Llano de la Atalaya, 6, Purchena (Almeria) with early 'Maritime' Beakers. The much more common pointed leaf-shaped
type also appears early, at Loma de Belmonte, but most frequently with incised Beaker ware of the later phase, and lasts
into the Bronze Age in association with tanged daggers and gold
ornaments which belong to the same metallurgical tradition.

Fig. 59c

Fig. 59a-b, d

Fig. 61

Plate 35

BEAKER METALLURGY

We have already noted that recent research has confirmed the
role of the Beaker Folk north of the Pyrenees as disseminators of

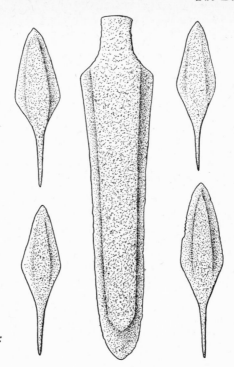

Fig. 61.   Montilla (Córdoba):
grave group. Approx. 1 : 3

metallurgy and we must now consider how this role took shape and what was its relationship to the earlier metallurgy of the Tagus and Millaran cultures. As we have seen, its leading copper type, the tanged dagger, is distinct from the characteristically Millaran midribbed dagger, which is often made in a bivalve mould. It is made by hammering after casting in an open mould, but some examples like those from Pago de la Peña and Montilla have been carefully tooled along the edges to improve the cutting edge, and this tooling can be seen on many of the associated copper arrowheads with pointed leaf-shaped blades. This type of dagger, however, cannot be a pure invention of the Beaker Folk in the peninsula, for it occurs in various

Fig. 57b
Fig. 61

187

parts of the Near East and is characteristic of western Anatolia at the beginning of the third millennium. It is certain that some tanged daggers (like those from Entretérminos and Arenero de Miguel Ruiz near Madrid, and Loma de Belmonte (Almería)) belong to an early phase of the Beaker culture – but the bulk of associated finds belong to a late phase. With these daggers seems to be associated a distinctive Iberian metallurgical tradition, using local ores and characterized by a particular set of impurities (Sangmeister's Material Group EO1), though clearly derived like the daggers from the Anatolian tradition. Analysis has shown that this indigenous Beaker industry produced not only the daggers but most of the arrowheads of the Palmela type, copper awls with quadrangular section (which occasionally occur in Beaker graves) and flat axe-heads (which never occur in Beaker graves). Owing to the absence of exclusively Beaker settlements that have been properly explored it is hardly possible to study the mining and smelting methods of this industry by themselves; it is clear, moreover, that it lasted into the Argaric Bronze Age. Comparison of the daggers reveals a certain typological progression from an early roughly straight-sided type to a late, ogival and usually large type which tends to have a slender, flanged tang and lasts into the Bronze Age (p. 207 below), but sometimes has a very broad, short tang (as at Fuente Palmera, Córdoba,) and may in this case be a halberd.

The special interest of the Beaker metallurgists in gold is made clear by a number of associations centred on the western side of the peninsula, suggesting the use of alluvial gold from the big rivers which lasted throughout the Bronze Age. Some of the Beaker types have already been mentioned – plaques, tubes and broad coiled strips probably forming part of necklaces in which perishable materials were used and bindings for dagger handles as at Pago de la Peña: the associations here are mainly late, as they are in the case of the narrow

Fig. 69c-f

Fig. 57f

spiral strips, which seem to have been finger rings, from Barro, São Pedro de Estoril, Palmela and Bela Vista (Colares), and lead on to the spiral bracelets of the Bronze Age (p. 208 below). Diadems of gold strip with perforations at the ends have a wider distribution – one was associated at Entretérminos (Madrid) with 'Maritime' Beaker ware but others come from late chieftain burials in which a dagger and 'Palmela' arrow-heads are not accompanied by Beakers – in a non-megalithic mound at Puentes de García Rodríguez (Coruña) (No. 240) and at Montilla (Córdoba). Finally, certain basket-shaped earrings, some of them associated with late Beaker ware at the Ermegeira (Torres Vedras) rock-cut tomb and the Cova da Moura cave near by, open up wider horizons, not only because of their form but because of their decoration of punctured dots, which recalls the *Blechstil* of the Copper Age sheet-metal ornaments of the Circumalpine area in south-central Europe. These earrings, like the diadems (an example of which occurs in the Late Copper Age of Hungary) have been taken to be part of the 'Reflux' movement, but the association at Entretér-minos suggests that any contact with the Danubian Copper Age was on the 'Maritime' and Corded Beaker horizon and was connected with the spread of polypod bowls to the Pyre-nean area, rather than that of incised Beakers. This question will be further examined in the next chapter (p. 210 below).

Fig. 69c

Plate 41

Fig. 69a

CHAPTER VIII

The Early Bronze Age

GENERAL

WE HAVE SEEN THAT the expansion of the Beaker Folk towards the end of the third millennium led to the collapse of the political organization represented by Millaran forts, and that this was followed, at least in the lower Tagus and Guadalquivir valleys, by the establishment of a hybrid culture using sophisticated Beaker ware of the so-called 'Reflux' type. By a long-established convention the ensuing phase in the peninsula, now to be considered, has been called the 'Bronze Age' (*Bronce II Mediterráneo* of Spanish archaeologists) although the sweeping technological change that this term would strictly imply did not in fact take place at this stage: as has now been made clear by numerous spectrographical analyses, arsenical copper continued to be the material most commonly used by metalworkers in the peninsula. What really defines this phase is the break-up of the apparent 'Beaker empire' established in the late Copper Age and the emergence, or re-emergence of regional groups some of which, chiefly represented on the Meseta, perpetuated the traditions of Beaker pottery and metallurgy for many centuries, while others, mainly in the coastal areas, revived pre-Beaker ceramic traditions or reacted to new foreign influences in their pottery and metalwork.

Among these coastal groups, that named after the large and rich site at El Argar, one of several in the province of Almeria extensively explored and published by Louis Siret, is still the best known. The settlements and burials of the Argaric culture might be taken to show the re-emergence, in some degree, of the relatively advanced, semi-urban civilization of Los Millares after the irruption of the pastoral Beaker Folk. This was, indeed, a culture of fortified villages, but many of its

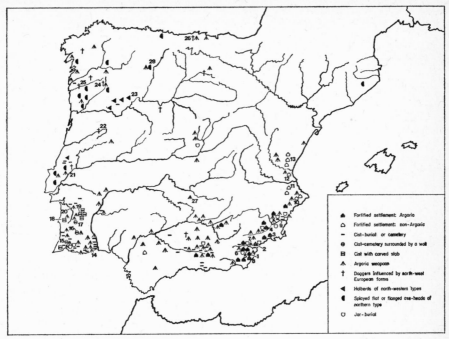

Fig. 62.   Early Bronze Age: sites and finds of metalwork

1 El Argar
(Almería)
2 El Oficio
(Almería)
3 Ifre (Murcia)
4 Bastida de Totana
(Murcia)
5 Fuente Bermeja
(Almería)
6 Lugarico Viejo
(Almería)
7 Fuente Alamo
(Almería)
8 Gatas (Almería)

9 Callosa de Segura
(Almería)
10 Mas de Menente,
Alcoy (Alicante)
11 Ereta del Pedregal
(Valencia)
12 Muntanyeta de la
Cabrera, Torrente
(Valencia)
13 Puntal de Cambra
Villar del Ar-
zobispo (Valencia)
14 Castro Marim
(Algarve)

15 Caldas de Monchi-
que (Algarve)
16 Atalaia, Aljustrel
(Beja)
17 Panoías de Ou-
rique (Beja)
18 S. Tiago do
Cacem (Setubal)
19 Mombeja (Beja)
20 Alcacer do Sal
(Setubal)
21 Vila Nova de S.
Pedro (Santarém)
22 Pinhal dos Melos,

Fornos de Algo-
dres (Guarda)
23 Carrapatas
(Bragança)
24 Ronfeiro (Orense)
25 Quinta da Agua
Branca, S. Maria de
Lobelhe (Braga)
26 Ogarrio
(Santander)
27 Puertollano
(Ciudad Real)
28 Valdevimbre
(León)

191

features – its rectangular dwellings and its practice of cist- or jar-burial within the settlement – contrast sharply with the round houses and communal extra-mural burial of Millaran culture, and most authorities have postulated a fresh infu-sion of foreign settlers in south-eastern Spain at this time. Though the characteristic metal forms and pottery of El Argar occur over a wider area, extending deeply into the Meseta, the complete culture, with its distinctive settlement and burial forms, does not seem to have established itself outside of eastern Andalusia and Murcia. In western Andalusia and much of Portugal cist-burial, singly or in small cemeteries, was common in this phase, but was extra-mural, and the pottery which replaced Beaker ware, though it reverted to plain, carinated surfaces, has a different range of forms. This addiction to cists in much of the coastal tract of the peninsula is almost the sole common factor and no doubt represents the Beaker heritage of these communities. On the east coast, in Valencia, some small fortified settlements are known, but the burial custom is different. In the north-east, though there was clearly a late survival in some areas of megalithic and Beaker traditions, there were also new cultural elements, especially in the pottery. These were evidently derived from beyond the Pyrenees and more particularly the circumalpine area of Europe. This is also true of the north-west, but here, in 'wet' Spain, the foreign elements reflect a growing dependence upon developments in the Atlantic coastal regions of Europe. However, a common feature of all these groups is that their metalwork, though linked in a general way at the outset with the contemporary achieve-ment of western and central Europe as a whole, does not accom-pany the latter in the successive stages of progress which have formed the main bases for elaborate period classifications now established for the Early and Middle Bronze Age in most parts of Europe between the North Sea and the Adriatic. For the rest of the second millennium the peninsula as a whole seems

to become increasingly isolated from the main centres of development in barbarian Europe, and to stagnate: is is natural to
suppose that increasing desiccation during the sub-Boreal
climatic phase, which may already have been a factor in the
migrations of the Beaker Folk, played a part in all this.

Within a fairly well-defined area centred on the province of
Almería but extending into the provinces of Granada, Málaga,
Jaén and Murcia, occur the characteristic settlements and house
burials of the true Argaric culture. In the area explored extensively by Siret, around Almeria, it is clear that these settlements
are regularly built on new sites, although they sometimes lie
close to sites occupied in the Copper Age. The new sites
tend to occupy higher and steeper hills and generally have
traces of strong fortifications. This and the prominence of
weapons in the grave goods give the culture a military air and
the reason is not difficult to guess: the late, 'Meseta' group of
the Beaker culture was contemporary and liable to overflow
into the Mediterranean seaboard, as a number of finds, mainly
on the older settlement sites of Almería but also at El Argar
itself, show. At the same time, the relationship of the main
groups of Argaric settlements to mineral concentrations at the
eastern end of the Sierra Morena as well as nearer the coast,
and the prominence of remains connected with metallurgy in
the settlements, suggest that the Argar culture had revived the
role of the Millaran as an organizing force in relation to industry and trade which, as finds suggest, was able at times to
expand on to the Meseta at the expense of the more loosely
organized Beaker pastoralists.

Among all these sites El Argar itself seems to have been the
largest, but Siret found it in a badly eroded condition, with
none of its defences and only vague traces of dwellings left, but

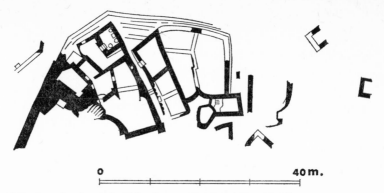

Fig. 63. An Argaric fortified settlement: El Oficio (Almería) (after L Siret)

Fig. 63

many of the underlying burials – 950 altogether – remained and these covered a plateau 300 yards by 100 and rising 100 ft above the near-by river Antas. More typical was the smaller site of El Oficio (Almería), strongly sited on a plateau covering $2\frac{1}{2}$ acres on the summit of a steep isolated hill rising 300 ft above the surrounding country, with a massive wall on the east barring the easiest approach and reinforced by outer walls at suitable points further down the slope, one of them protecting a cistern. Most of the houses are on the summit: they are rough-ly rectangular, of varying sizes, and arranged in rows flanking narrow streets. Some seem to have had a wooden upper story, others a cellar with descending steps. The burials, within the settlement and often under the floors, numbered about 200. Rather better preserved is the stronghold of Ifre, near Parazue-los (Murcia), on a rock rising 400 ft above the *rambla* of Morata, with a good water supply, a strongly walled 'acropolis' and an annexe with a larger number of dwellings, some of which again had stairs leading to an upper story and outbuildings, including an oven for baking bread and firing pottery. Frag-ments of clay, baked by a conflagration which ended the life of this settlement, like so many others, bore impressions of esparto rope that were here interpreted as structural elements of a lath and plaster clay-covered roof. Ifre had a strong outer wall which may have protected livestock, like the outer enclosures of Iron Age *castros* in the north-west. Another Murcian site, the Bastida of Totana, must have been one of the largest Argaric sites, to judge by the number of the burials – several hundreds – under and around the houses. The houses were rectangular, often from 20 to 25 ft long and 12 to 15 ft wide and built in tiers bedded into the slopes of a conical hill 600 ft high, and had been badly eroded. The settlement with its flat roofs may once have looked like one of the modern hill villages (*e.g.* Mojácar) of the same district. Here, too, burnt layers seem to record the destruction of wooden upper stories.

In some ways the material culture associated with Argaric settlements seems to reflect continuity with earlier phases. Wheat and barley were still harvested with the aid of composite sickles fitted with serrated flints, and the grain ground on saddle querns; subrectangular clay plaques with perforations at the corner were still used as loom-weights or for some other purpose, and many of the ceramic forms with their plain grey- or brown-burnished ware could be regarded as a revival of local pre-Beaker traditions with some help from foreign sources connected with 'Reflux'metalwork. But the rectangular houses and streets of the settlements contrast with almost everything known about previous cultures in the peninsula – it is true that some rectangular huts are known at Los Millares – and look forward to the Iberian Iron Age settlements of the Mediterranean coast: indeed Cortes de Navarra in the Ebro valley, as we shall see in the next chapter, provides, with its floor-burials, a connecting link between the two groups of settlements. Rectangular construction could, of course, have developed without much outside stimulus as a result of adaptation to a restricted space on hill-tops, but the break in burial ritual and the religious ideas associated with it is decisive. The Millarans worshipped their ancestors and a

Plate 42

Mother Goddess, and a series of 'idols' and amulets connected
with these cults occurs in burials and settlements alike. There
is virtually no trace of all this on Argaric sites. Separate burial
in cists, jars or pits has replaced communal burial and at El
Argar many of the double burials recorded – some fifty in
number – appear to be of man and wife, as though suttee
were practised and and a patriarchical society had replaced the
matriarchical one. It is hardly surprising that various authorities
have sought a foreign element in the origins of the Argaric
culture – from Siret and Déchelette, who looked to central
Europe, to John Evans and Bernabò Brea, who look to the
central and eastern Mediterranean. In fact house-burial and
jar-burial are both practices that are above all characteristic of
Anatolia and might have reached south-eastern Spain *via*
certain groups which flourished about the middle of the second
millennium in the western Peloponnese and the Ionian Islands,
the Aeolian Islands, Sicily and Malta. Cist-burials occur
about this time on Leukas, and jar-burials in the Milazzese
culture of Sicily, while the intrusive culture represented at the
Hal Tarxien cemetery on Malta has bronze riveted daggers not
unlike those of El Argar. Jar-burial, however, also occurs in
the Aunjetitz (Unétice) culture of central Europe, and the
same general area has also been suggested by Sangmeister and
Blance as the source of some of the 'Reflux' metal types
adopted by the Argaric culture.

These problems of origin have lately been clarified, to some
extent, by Dr Blance's analysis of Argaric grave-groups, which
have shown that two horizons can be distinguished in them,
the first characterized by cist-burials and the second by jar-
burials: the specifically Anatolian influences thus do not belong to the opening phase of the culture, but to the fifteenth or
fourteenth century BC. Moreover, the first phase has its distinctive metal types – halberds and small triangular daggers with
riveted handles – some of which seem to relate to central Euro-

Plate 43
Plate 44

Fig. 64

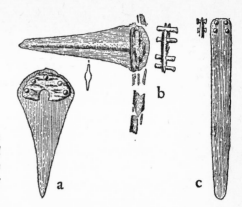

Fig. 64. Argaric weapons: a, copper dagger from El Oficio (Almería) and b, copper halberd from El Argar (Almería), with parts of their wooden handles preserved; c, copper dirk from El Argar (after L. Siret). 1 : 4

pean or north Italian types – bone pyramidal or prismatic buttons with V-perforations and tall bowls with low carinations. As we have seen the idea that these types were brought back to the peninsula by the returning Beaker Folk is an over-simplification. The metal halberd, in particular, cannot be regarded as an alien form which now appears in the peninsula for the first time; flint halberds had been familiar there well over a thousand years before, and these must have had copper prototypes. At a later stage, indeed, in the Millaran culture these prototypes appear in the archaeological record (p. 146 above) and the early Argaric halberds may indeed represent a 'Reflux' of this tradition, the intermediate stages of which are found chiefly in northern and central Italy about the beginning of the second millennium. As we shall see, the spread of button-handled, carinated cups of Polada tradition to northern Catalonia and the spread of Catalan Early Bronze types of V-perforated buttons about the same time to south-eastern Spain are clues to the diffusion of contemporary metal types in a west Mediterranean cultural zone through which the eastern Spanish type of 'Maritime' Beaker had spread two or three centuries before. There is no need to postulate much direct influence from central Europe at this time, apart from that associated with polypod bowls and Danubian gold and copper

197

ornaments with puncture-dot patterns, such as are imitated on a silver strip diadem or belt from El Oficio which relates to the gold strip from Quinta da Agua Branca in northern Portugal, later referred to (p. 207 below). In the early Argaric phase the local silver resources are already being exploited for small rings and other ornaments, and gold is rare.

Plate 50

Fig. 64c

Plate 53

Plate 42

The second, jar-burial phase at El Argar brought the development of new types: swords which are waisted immediately below the riveted butt; daggers with four rivets grouped in a rectangle; diadems for women, with nasal disc attached: these are usually made of silver (now used lavishly in the south-east) though one from Cehegín (Murcia) is of gold and bears the linear decoration of punctured dots which we have already met on the 'Reflux Horizon' and pottery chalices occur – a form which has been attributed to indirect Mycenaen influence (*via* the Milazzese culture) but was known to makers of late Beaker wares in the south-west. To this horizon belongs the celebrated find of segmented fayence beads, like those well known in the British Middle Bronze Age 'Wessex culture', in cist burial No. 9 at Fuente Alamo, with a sword, part of a silver diadem and a pottery chalice. This and a disc-bead of blue glass from a small megalithic tomb at la Sabina, Gorafe (Granada), which also has Wessex analogues, seem to indicate a revival of contacts between Egypt and the western Mediterranean in the fifteenth or fourteenth century BC, *via* Sicily (Aeolian Islands) and Malta, where segmented fayence beads have also been found. About the same time renewed Anatolian influence in the central Mediterranean is reflected by the jar-burials at Thapsus in Sicily, and Mycenaean imports are reaching the same area. To this horizon also belongs the spread of Argaric swords on to the southern Meseta, represented in particular by one with silver rivets from Puertollano (Ciudad Real) and another, said to be from the province of Toledo and preserved in the Rodríguez collection in Madrid, which has a

Plate 50

gold-cased pommel with pricked dot decoration and resem-bles the swords depicted on certain southern Portuguese cist cover-slabs. The relative frequency of swords in these northern peripheral areas and in central Andalusia suggests that the Argar culture did not expand from its original home until the fifteenth century or later, and there is as yet no evidence that the culture established itself in its entirety in these areas.

THE SOUTH-WEST

The western limits of the Argar culture are still rather vaguely defined because, though characteristic pottery and metalwork is known from central Andalusia, this comes from burials or chance finds rather than settlements; it has hardly been explored in a way that provides a basis for comparison with the sites which Siret explored, and there are hints that elements from earlier cultures had a long survival here. Though in the pro-vinces of Granada, Málaga, Jaén and Córdoba it has been mostly groups of cists and pit-burials that have been explored, some good Argaric material has come from megalithic tombs in the interior, especially at Los Eriales, Laborcillas (Granada), and both grave goods and architectural features, like rectangu-lar, rebated doorways in Sicilian cemeteries of the Thapsus group, suggest that the Alcaide (Málaga) group of rock-cut tombs lasted into this phase. Further west still, as we have seen, the old ill-explored sites around Carmona on the lower Guadalquivir have not produced much Argaric pottery – there is a chalice from Mairena del Alcor – but there are a number of isolated finds of Argaric metalwork from the area and there is much late Beaker ware, some of it grey-surfaced like that from the Meseta and south Catalonia. To this horizon belong the Beaker chalices of Carmona and the lower Tagus, which may not have been inspired by those of El Argar, since they can hardly be later than the fifteenth century.

Fig. 38g

In most of Portugal south of the Tagus, however, the Beaker culture had never been able wholly to displace the numerous communities which built the local 'tholoi' and megalithic tombs. The Early Bronze Age apparently saw the gradual replacement of the old custom of communal burial among the indigenous megalith-builders by one of single burial in cists. In the wellnigh complete absence of settlement sites, the degree to which this change was due to external influences can be judged only by the contents of these graves. In the Algarve there are some records of jar-burials which might denote Argaric influence, but the cists are better known and these are clearly extra-mural. The pottery is generally plain and the characteristic form is a low carinated bowl which is never handled and could be derived from local Copper Age forms: the typical Argaric 'tulips' and chalices are absent. A few cists, however, contained round-heeled, riveted daggers of Argaric type. The cists are generally rectangular, with four lateral slabs, and usually occur in groups, as at Castro Marim. Further north, in the Alemtejo, recent discoveries have made the picture seem more complex. To old discoveries of groups of cists, sometimes surrounded by a circular dry-stone wall, as at Panoías de Ourique and at Caldas de Monchique, have now been added several groups of cist- and pit-burials, at Atalaia near Ourique, which represent a somewhat different tradition: here irregular cists and pits, with slab-covers, are each covered by a small, low mound revetted by curving dry-stone walls and are clustered together against a primary circular mound. This might represent a reassertion, in a different form, of the idea of communal burial, after imposition from outside of the practice of separate burial in cists. A radiocarbon date of 790 ± 120 BC (KN-201) has recently been obtained for one of the cists in this cemetery. The grave goods at Atalaia are poor, but the use of handles on the pottery and the occasional decoration of punctured dots suggest connections with Catalonia and

Fig. 73a, b

Fig. 65b

Fig. 65a

Fig. 67f

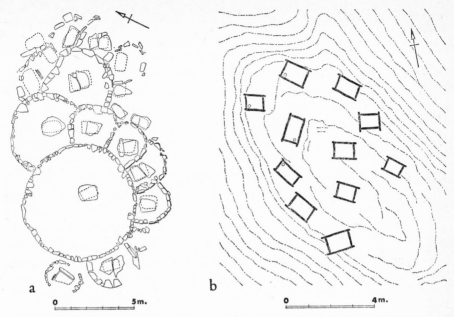

Fig. 65. Early Bronze Age cist cemeteries: a, Atalaia, Ourique (Beja); b, Castro Marim (Algarve) (a after Schubart, b after E. da Veiga)

northern Italy. North Italian connections in the Early Bronze Age may also be the explanation of the practice of occasionally carving weapons on the cist-covers as at S. Tiago do Cacém. Here the accompanying slender and widely splayed ceremonial axe-head is a north-west European type, as we shall see (p. 210 below). We must note, however, that another slab, from Assento, Santa Victoria (Beja) has a double axe or anchor, which may be purely symbolic, carved alongside a halberd. Several cists of this type have been recorded from the neighbourhood of Beja, and one, at Trigaxes, has a sword like the one just described at S. Tiago. It would seem that this practice began in the second Argaric phase in the fifteenth century or later, but it clearly lasted until the end of the Bronze Age because there are cist-covers in the same south Portuguese

Fig. 70a

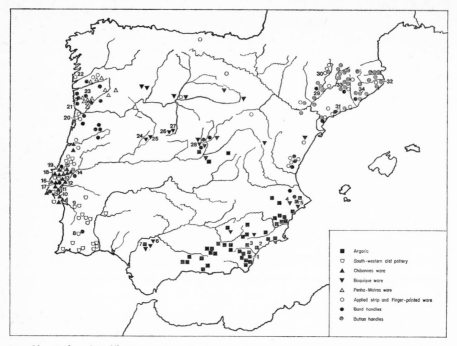

Fig. 66.   Early and Middle Bronze Age pottery groups

1 El Argar (Almería)	11 Licêa (Lisbon)	20 Gulpilhares, Vila	Cardeñosa
2 El Oficio	12 Pedra de Oiro	Nova (Porto)	(Ávila)
(Almería)	(Lisbon)	21 Antela de	28 Areneros de Val-
3 Fuente Alamo	13 Castro de Ota	Portelagem	divia (Madrid)
(Almería)	(Lisbon)	(Porto)	29 Cueva de Joan
4 Cabezo Redondo,	14 Vila Nova de S.	22 Castro de S. Tecla	d'Os, Tartareu
Villena (Alicante)	Pedro (Santarém)	(Pontevedra)	(Lérida)
5 Mas de Menente,	15 Pragança (Lisbon)	23 Penha, Guimarães	30 Cueva de Toralla
Alcoy (Alicante)	16 Castro da Fornea,	(Braga)	(Lérida)
6 Carmona (Seville)	Matacães (Lisbon)	24 Cueva del Boqui-	31 Cueva Fonda de
7 Mairena del Alcor	17 Castro do Penedo,	que, Plasencia	Salamó
(Seville)	Torres Vedras	(Cáceres)	(Tarragona)
8 Atalaia, Aljustrel	(Lisbon)	25 Cerro del Berrueco	32 Puig Roíg,
(Beja)	18 Castro de S. Ma-	(Salamanca)	Torrent (Gerona)
9 Alcacer do Sal	mede de Obidos	26 Los Castillejos en	33 Riñer (Lérida)
(Evora)	(Lisbon)	Sanchorreja	34 Mas Clamí,
10 Chibannes	19 Outeiro da Assenta,	(Ávila)	Castelltersol
(Setubal)	Obidos (Lisbon)	27 Las Cogotas de	(Barcelona)

group which have swords and shields of much later types, as we shall see (p. 234 below), and the tradition of the sharply carinated bowl has an equally long life. Pottery of Atalaia forms has also been found in burials near Alcacer do Sal at the mouth of the Sado, with daggers of Argaric form, but in one case, most significantly, with rivets of gold instead of silver.

Fig. 73

The Mediterranean coast of Spain beyond Murcia and Carta-gena presents a curious contrast to the south-west. Here, in the provinces of Alicante and Valencia where settlements in the open had been so rare in the Copper Age – the marsh settle-ment of Ereta del Pedregal, which at some time in its history was surrounded by a wall, has not yet been adequately explor-ed – small fortified hill-top settlements with rectangular dwellings, not unlike those of the Argar culture now become fairly common, but burials, which previously had supplied most of the archaeological record, become rare. At least it is clear that house-burial was not normally practised, and though the metalwork is similar to the Argaric, the pottery forms a different though closely related group, in which the 'tulip' shape as well as the low carinated bowl appears, but handles are fairly common, as in Catalonia and southern Portugal. The characteristic settlement in this group is the Mas de Menente, Alcoy, which has traces of eight houses arranged in a terrace each with a hearth, saddle querns and subrectangular clay plaques with four perforations, surrounded by a wall. The Muntanyeta de Cabrera, Torrente (Valencia) is a small pro-montory fort with a strong wall containing a guard chamber with a ditch outside it. It produced sickle flints of the tradi-tional kind and saddle querns, also bronze arrowheads with barbs. The site of Puntal de Cambra, Villar del Arzobispo (Valencia) is remarkable for the rectangular and circular bastions which defend the easier approaches to its walls. The pottery is linked on the one hand with that of El Argar by its carinated forms and plain surfaces, and with Catalonia by its handles, curvilinear furrowed and applied strip (sometimes finger-printed) decoration and perforated (cheese-making?) vessels, on the other.

Like the south-west, the north-east of the peninsula shows a remarkable persistence of Copper Age elements alongside Early Bronze Age ones introduced from beyond the Pyrenees. The late phase of the 'Meseta' Beaker ware lasted late there in the caves near the Ebro mouth, but the Pyrenean area had a fresh infusion, represented chiefly by the carinated bowls with band handles, often decorated on the top with axe- or button-shaped excrescences, which clearly denote infiltration in the Early Bronze Age from the Polada culture of northern Italy and its heirs. We have already noted the influence of this in-trusive group, with the handle excrescences omitted, in Valencia and southern Portugal. It also appears in the 'Argaric' pottery of the Madrid area and in central Portugal (there is a button-handle at Vila Nova de São Pedro) and this move-ment, following on that associated, in the Pyrenean area, with the polypod bowls, probably played an important part in spreading other north Italian ceramic forms (punctured deco-ration, multi-perforated walls) and metal types in the penin-sula. But settlements are as little known as in the south-west and our knowledge depends largely upon normally ill-stratified cave-deposits and burials. Among the former that of Toralla (Lérida) is important for its rare stratification, which included a layer with late 'Meseta' Beaker ware on which 'false-relief' is prominent, as in southern France; in the layer above lies pottery with finger-printed cordons and furrowed

Plate 48

decoration. The latter pottery is a connecting link between the late channelled and cordoned pottery of Languedoc and the Early Bronze Age pottery of Valencia already mentioned. It is well represented in various caves in southern Catalonia, notably Cueva Fonda de Salamó and Joan d'Os, Tartareu, and persists into the Iron Age, when its styles were modified under the influence of the Urnfield invaders. In the same upper layer at Toralla was a V-perforated pyramidal button like ones from Vila Nova de São Pedro, the Early Bronze Age level at the Ereta del Pedregal (Valencia) and sites in the south-east already mentioned. But the normal V-perforated button in this phase, both in Catalonia and the south-east, is an elongated, triangular sectioned one '(prismatic'). Such ornaments, along with button-handled cups, are common in a large series of cists which closes the megalithic sequence in the Pyrenean area, including the Basque region, and are often no larger than the southern cists used for separate burials. To this same horizon belong the sherds from the Puig Roig (Gerona) Passage Grave which have the same punctured decoration as that on the bowl from Atalaia. The only open-air settlement which clearly relates to this phase is that located near a copper mine at Riner (Lerida) which produced carinated bowls, handled jars with furrowed decoration, and moulds for flat axes.

Plates 45, 46

Plate 25

Plate 51

CENTRAL PORTUGAL AND THE MESETA

We have already seen that the large and mixed population of the fertile region around the Tagus mouth continued in the Early Bronze Age to use Beaker ware in its final heavily incised stage, as at S. Pedro de Estoril and Montes Claros, probably at least until the fifteenth century. But at a number of hill-top settlement sites that have yielded an abundance of ill-stratified material in this area, notably Chibannes near Palmela, another class of ware occurs in which regular channelled patterns of

Fig. 67a, e

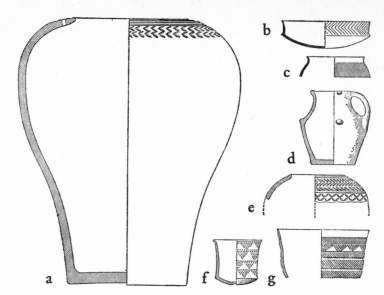

Fig. 67. Early Bronze Age pottery types (Portugal): a, Castro de Chibannes, Setubal; b, Gruta de Vimeiro (Leiria); c, Cova de Moura, Torres Vedras (Lisbon); d, Antela de Portelagem (Porto); e, S. Martinho, Sintra (Lisbon); f, Atalaia, Ourique (Beja); g, Penha, Guimarães (Braga) (a after Da Costa, e after V. Leisner, f after A. Viana). 1 : 6

herring-bones and lattices between horizontal furrows are applied to well-made ovoid jars, sometimes very large but with small mouths. The fine micaceous ware and the use of a dark wash for smaller vessels seems to indicate technical continuity with the *copas* of the pre-Beaker phase. This ware is well represented at Vila Nova, Licêa, the Outeiros of Assenta and S. Mamede near Obidos, the Castros of Penedo and Fornea near Torres Vedras and the Castros of Ota and Pedra d'Oiro near Alemquer, but it is impossible to relate it to a well-defined culture. It seems to have lasted until the time when the

Fig. 73d

Fig. 67b, c

characteristic handled carinated bowls of the Alemtejan cist group spread, with the practice of building cists, north of the Tagus, and sometimes had decoration in Chibannes style applied to them. Near the lower Douro a related channelled decoration, sometimes combined with elements from Beaker patterns, is applied to pottery of the Penha-Mairos group and the curious hat-shaped bowls. In addition, we have already noted a tendency for pottery styles of north Italian or southern French origin to spread across the Meseta in the Early Bronze Age, and the truncated cone-shaped vessels found in late megaliths in the north-west, jugs like that from the *antela* of Portelagem and the jars with multiple applied bands found on some open sites on the Minho appear to be examples of this. The most important site for this plan in northern Portugal is the cemetery of Gulpilhares near Oporto, which yielded jugs like that from Portelagem, decorated on the shoulders with bosses or applied rings and plain bowls with flat, spreading rims which seem to be ancestral to the 'hat'-shaped bowls.

Fig. 67g

Fig. 67d

The persistence of Beaker ceramic traditions in the Tagus and Douro basins has its counterpart in the continued existence of a distinctive Beaker metallurgy, represented by tanged daggers and arrowheads and gold ornaments. Even further north in the Galician province of Orense, the Ronfeiro hoard gives an association of a normal 'Beaker' tanged dagger with several riveted daggers of Argaric type. Later examples of the Beaker dagger have an ogival blade and a narrow flanged tang, as in the case of the dagger associated with a strip diadem or belt with pricked ornament in a cist at Quinta da Agua Branca in the Minho; later still, swords in the same tradition were produced, no doubt in competition with Argaric swords, like the one, still made of arsenical copper, from Pinhal dos Melos in Beira Alta. The grooves following the blade in this example relate to those on the distinctive north Portuguese group of halberds and suggest influences from north-west Europe. 'Palmela' arrowheads continued to be used throughout the millennium, but there is a tendency to an angular blade, and ultimately to barbs. Gold ornaments grow more plentiful

Plate 49

Fig. 68

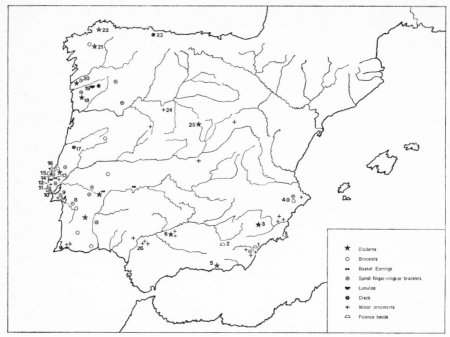

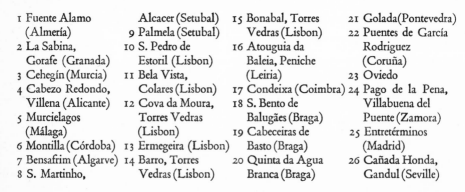

Fig. 68.   Early and Middle Bronze Age gold ornaments

1 Fuente Alamo (Almería)
2 La Sabina, Gorafe (Granada)
3 Cehegín (Murcia)
4 Cabezo Redondo, Villena (Alicante)
5 Murcielagos (Málaga)
6 Montilla (Córdoba)
7 Bensafrim (Algarve)
8 S. Martinho,
Alcacer (Setubal)
9 Palmela (Setubal)
10 S. Pedro de Estoril (Lisbon)
11 Bela Vista, Colares (Lisbon)
12 Cova da Moura, Torres Vedras (Lisbon)
13 Ermegeira (Lisbon)
14 Barro, Torres Vedras (Lisbon)
15 Bonabal, Torres Vedras (Lisbon)
16 Atouguia da Baleia, Peniche (Leiria)
17 Condeixa (Coimbra)
18 S. Bento de Balugães (Braga)
19 Cabeceiras de Basto (Braga)
20 Quinta da Agua Branca (Braga)
21 Golada (Pontevedra)
22 Puentes de García Rodriguez (Coruña)
23 Oviedo
24 Pago de la Pena, Villabuena del Puente (Zamora)
25 Entretérminos (Madrid)
26 Cañada Honda, Gandul (Seville)

and more massive, and many of the spiral and simple open bracelets from the western side of the peninsula, like those from Atouguia da Baleia, Peniche and Bonabal, Torres

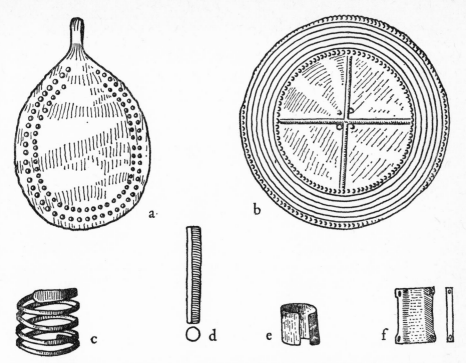

Fig. 69. Early Bronze Age gold ornaments: a, d, Ermegeira, Torres Vedras (Lisbon); b, Oviedo; c, S. Pedro de Estoril; e, Cañada del Carrascal, Gandul (Seville); f, Palmela (Setubal) (after G. and V. Leisner and MacWhite (b)). 1 : 1

Vedras (Estremadura), probably belong to the early Bronze Age; in the Bonabal hoard and at São Martinho, Alcacer do Sal several multiple-spiral bracelets were found linked together in a chain. But some of the gold ornaments of this phase are best considered in connection with the special cultural development in the north-west part of the peninsula.

THE NORTH-WEST

Even more than in northern Portugal, appraisal of the Early Bronze Age in Galicia and the Biscayan seaboard of Spain is rendered theoretical by the lack of stratified settlement sites and the paucity of associated finds of any kind. This is all the more unfortunate because there are signs that from the beginning of this period, if not earlier, the area was already exercising a special role as a stage on a coast-wise route by which ideas or products spread southwards from the creative metal industries of northern Europe: a role, indeed, in keeping with its geographical character as an extension of the north-west European climatic and vegetational zone. That seems to be the implication of the flint dagger of north European appearance from a *mâmoa* at Cela, Redondela (Pontevedra), certain mace-heads, and the stone battle-axe of French rather than Nordic appearance from a *mâmoa* in the Sierra Faladora, Puentes de García Rodríguez (Coruña). Later on, northern influences are reflected in the three broad swords with broad, rivetted butts and ornamental grooves from Ogarrio (Santander), which recall early Breton weapons but are waisted near the butt in the Argaric manner. Daggers of Argaric tradition are known from several sites in Galicia, but the evidence of a reverse trend from the north in this area helps to explain the long and widely splayed axe-

Fig. 70a, b

heads portrayed not only on Alemtejan cist-covers but on rock carvings with daggers and halberds in Morocco. This exaggerated type is known from an actual specimen at Kersoufflet (Morbihan) but there is a more practical, short form of

Plate 52b

splayed axe which contrasts with native types such as that shown in Fig. 50; whilst characteristic of northern Portugal and Galicia, it reaches Vila Nova de São Pedro and also reflects relations with north-western or central Europe. MacWhite

Plate 54

and others have been tempted to add the gold lunula and discs from Cabeceiras de Basto in the Minho and other discs like

Fig. 69b

those from Oviedo, Condeixa (Beira) and Bensafrim (Algarve) to this list of north-west European and, indeed, specifically Irish exports to the Atlantic seaboard of south-west Europe. But caution is necessary here as with the basket earrings

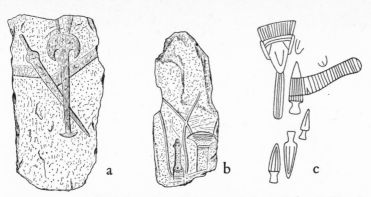

Fig. 70.   Early Bronze Age carved cist slabs and petroglyphs: a, Defesa, S. Tiago do Cacem (Setubal); b, Mombeja (Beja); c, Conjo (Pontevedra) (a-b after L. de Vasconcellos, c after Michael J. Walker)

already mentioned (p. 189 above). The Portuguese ornaments have pricked pellets in the central European '*Blechstil*' and the lunula stands closer to the silver one from Vilafranca de Verona than to any Irish example. We must attribute these forms to the immigrants who brought polypod bowls to south-western France and button-handled cups to Catalonia, but their dispersal northwards as well as southwards along the Atlantic coast is no doubt due to the same contacts as those which spread true north European types to Galicia. At a later stage, these contacts produced a distinctive 'Biscayan' type of gold ornament, the 'collar' of Golada (Pontevedra) type derived from the Argaric diadem of which several examples are known from Galicia and western France. The diffusion of the practice of carving weapons on rock-surfaces or memorial slabs from the Remedello and later, Bronze Age, cultures of northern Italy and Corsica to Galicia, southern Portugal and Morocco on the one hand, and the British Isles on the other, is part of the same phenomenon. In Galicia daggers appear in the remarkable group at Conjo, Santiago de Compostela; they are sometimes associated with cup and ring carvings which are common in the area and may conceivably be a genuine

Fig. 71

Fig. 70c
Fig. 71

211

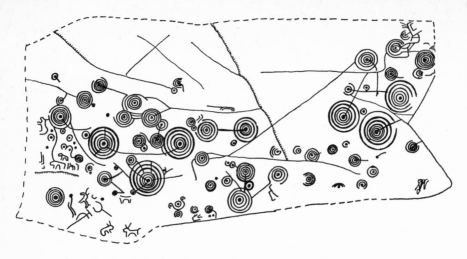

Fig. 71. Cup and ring-marked rock surface at S. Jorge de Sacos, Cotobad (Pontevedra) (after Michael J. Walker). Length 8.25 m.

'Reflux' element from the British Isles. The associated human head at Conjo, with its Philistine-like head-dress gains interest from Grosjean's recent recognition (on statue-menhirs in south-ern Corsica) of accoutrements like those of the Sherdana on Egyptian bas-reliefs.

METALLURGY

The Early Bronze Age did not bring immediate and sweeping technical changes in peninsular metallurgy. Recent analytical studies, especially those of Sangmeister and Junghans, show that influences from beyond the Pyrenees such as have been described in this chapter are indeed reflected in the composition of certain tools, mostly axe-heads with the widely splayed blades found in the centres from which these influences came, which prove to contain enough tin to justify calling them bronze: many of these tools, coming from the western side of the peninsula and especially from Vila Nova de São Pedro,

Fig. 72. Chip-carved mug: Areneros de Valdivia (Madrid) (after a photograph supplied by Barcelona Museum).
1 : 2

have been assigned to various 'material groups' thought to characterize the British Isles, Rhône basin, central Europe and northern Italy. The immigrants may have brought bronzes with them or imported them, but it should be noted that hammered-flange axes are rare and cast-flange axes almost unknown. On the other hand, though a small number of Argaric daggers and swords have proved to contain a little tin, it is certain that the Argaric and Beaker schools of metallurgy alike continued until late in the second millennium to make daggers, halberds, swords and even axe-heads of arsenical copper and to use open moulds of stone for their manufacture. This is all the more surprising when one considers the relatively extensive resources in tin ore of the north-western areas of the peninsula, no evidence for the prehistoric working of which seems so far to have been produced. Up to the present, modern work on implement analysis has not been followed up by further work on the numerous ancient copper mines of the peninsula which have produced waisted mauls like those found at El Argar itself. Some of these mines appear in fact to have yielded Early Bronze Age implements: Argaric daggers and flat axes at the Mina de Milagro (Asturias), a 'Palmela' arrowhead and a flat axe at mines in the Alemtejo, and flat axe-moulds at Riner (Lérida) and the Mola Alta de Serelles (Alicante) pl. 51.

Plate 51

CHAPTER IX

The Late Bronze Age and the Dawn of History

GENERAL

ABOUT THE BEGINNING of the first millennium BC the
Iberian peninsula began to emerge from its long cultural
isolation and stagnation. Perhaps climatic improvement, corresponding to the revived damp conditions of the sub-Atlantic
phase in northern Europe, made the arid regions of the Meseta
and the south more attractive to settlers. At any rate the archaeological material of the peninsula now recovers some of its old
wealth and variety and seems to reflect not only a reinvigoration
of native cultures, partly as a result of a renewed stimulus
from neighbouring Mediterranean lands, but the arrival of new
cultural, and even ethnic, elements from central and north-
western Europe. The native groups in the Mediterranean
coastal areas, the south-west and the Meseta now tend to merge
and, after absorbing new elements from beyond the Pyrenees, to
evolve a culture which is clearly ancestral to that of the historical Iberians. In 'wet' Spain, on the other hand, maritime
contacts transformed the retarded Early Bronze Age metal
industry into a Late Bronze Age one of north-west European
affinity without, as far as can yet be seen, introducing any
important new element in the population – in complete contrast to the north-east, where the apparent introduction of a
large foreign element in the population, with new ceramic
forms and new burial rites, did not at first have any marked
impact on the metal industry of the peninsula. This cultural
diversity during the first quarter of the millennium renders the
use of the phrase 'Atlantic Bronze Age', introduced to cover
the whole peninsula by Santa Olalla and followed by other
Spanish archaeologists, rather unsatisfactory.

During the latter part of the eighth century BC the Iberian
culture of the south, and its special form, associated with the

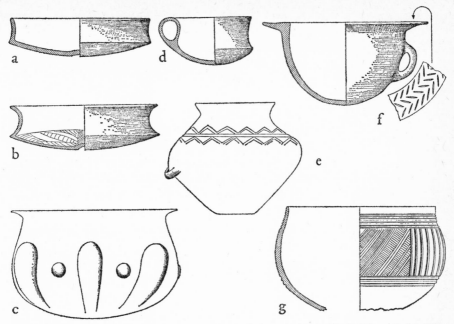

Fig. 73. Late Bronze Age pottery: a, Castro Marim (Algarve); b, Ervidel (Beja); c, Pedra d'Oiro Alemquer (Lisbon); d, Pragança (Lisbon); e, Azaila (Teruel); f, Caldelas, Guimarães (Braga); g, Penha, Guimarães (Braga) (a after E. da Veiga, b after L. de Vasconcellos, e after M. Almagro, f after M. Cardozo). 1 : 4

semi-historical Tartessus (Tarshish) at the mouth of the Guadalquivir, were beginning to come under the influence of the higher civilizations of the eastern Mediterranean and particularly that of the Phoenicians, first of all through trade and later through the foundation of actual colonies, and the use of iron spread among them along with exotic forms of metalwork and pottery. At this time Semitic writers in the Levant began to refer to the 'Land of Tarshish' as a source of gold, silver, tin and lead. The advanced culture of the south, which from now on we may call Tartessian or Iberian, had a dominating influence in the peninsula, strong enough to prevent a pure Hallstatt or Early La Tène Iron Age culture from developing even in its northern parts, in spite of the strong folk movements from beyond the Pyrenees which undoubtedly took place in this phase and led to the establishment of Celtic speech over a very large area.

THE NATIVE CULTURE: *c.* 1000–700 BC

At the end of the second millennium the two main cultural traditions described in the last chapter – the Argaric and Beaker cultures – can still be distinguished; the latter was a mainly pastoral culture, occupying open settlements and using pottery which departed more and more from Beaker forms under Argaric and other influences, but preferred all-over decoration derived in the main from that of 'Meseta' Beakers. Various styles can be distinguished among these late 'Meseta' wares, but in the almost complete absence of carefully observed and published stratifications their sequence and chronology cannot yet be worked out in detail. The main styles had a very wide distribution and at a certain, probably late, stage they spread into the coastal areas of Andalusia, Murcia and Valencia, as the original Beaker wares had many centuries before. One of these styles has been named after the cave of Boquique near Plasencia (Cáceres), where characteristic sherds were first recognized long ago. Its favourite form is a bowl or platter with a flaring rim and its typical decoration is one of 'stab and drag' furrows arranged in hanging concentric semicircles, often combined with 'barbed wire' lines and triangles and zigzag bands filled with punched dots. This group is now best defined by material from scattered oblong hut-floors explored by Maluquer de Motes at the Cerro del Berrueco (Salamanca). Here and at Las Cogotas de Cardeñosa and Los Castillejos, Sanchorreja (Ávila) it would seem to precede Early Iron Age occupation and the building of hill-forts. It is also well represented in the gravel pits of the Manzanares near Madrid, at

Plate 47

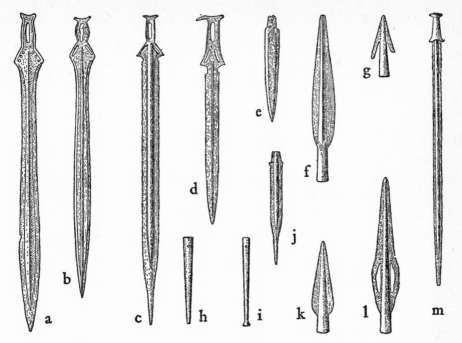

Fig. 74. Late Bronze Age weapons: a, Vila Maior, Sabugal (Guarda); b, Sobrefoz, Ponga (Asturias); c, h-m, Huelva; d, Elvas (Portalegre); e, Porto de Móz (Leiria); f, Río Sil, S. Esteban (León); Pragança (Lisbon) (a after Castro Nunes, b-d, h-m, after M. Almagro). Approx. 1:8

sites on the mountainous verge of the coastal plain of Valencia, and on the lower Guadalquivir, at Carmona, where a care-fully recorded trial section has shown it underlying a layer with Tartessian stroke-burnished ware and Phoenician pottery.

The other style, which is sometimes associated on the same pot with Boquique decoration but is generally distinct, with its own range of forms, makes great use of chip-carved decora-tion related to that found on some late 'Meseta' Beakers and on Middle Bronze Age 'Tumulus' pottery in southern Germany and eastern France. It commonly occurs on jugs and pedestal-bowls and is found at the Cerro del Berrueco, on the Manza-nares, near Soria, and at the important new site of Cabezo

Fig. 72

Redondo near Villena (Alicante), where the finds include late 'Meseta' Beaker and Boquique ware. In recent years work by J.M. Soler García in this area, combined with stratifications established by Pellicer Catalan and Schüle at Orce and Galera, have begun to reveal a post-Argaric phase, preceding the proto-Iberian culture of the area, *c.* 1000–700 BC, which some of these workers have called '*Bronce Mediterráneo III*'. The remarkable hoards of gold and silver vessels and ornaments which Soler García has brought to light near Villena seem to belong to this horizon, but it is necessary before considering them to glance at the contemporary situation in the Atlantic coastal regions of the peninsula, where, as we have seen, the manufacture of gold ornaments centred in the Early Bronze Age. Here the ceramic forms of the Meseta which we have just described do not seem to have gained a foothold; instead the indigenous tradition associated with southern Portuguese cists, represented chiefly by sharply carinated and often handled bowls, persisted down to the beginning of the Iron Age, together with the associated carved cist-covers and steles, as we shall see, spreading into Spanish Estremadura and the neighbourhood of the Douro mouth. In the latter area the 'Penha' ceramic style also persisted and large plain jars in the

Fig. 73g   Minho area and at Santa Tecla (Pontevedra), with decorative bosses or rings on the shoulder, seem to belong here, together

Fig. 73f   with the 'hat-shaped' bowls which have sometimes been found with cremated burials but never, apparently, with other datable objects.

There are, however, in the southern Atlantic regions of the peninsula, a number of metal types which seem to be related to a 'post-Argaric' native Bronze Age phase by associations in the hut-floors explored by Maluquer at Cerro del Berrueco: the

Fig. 74e   special 'Porto de Mós' form of bronze dagger, which is almost confined to Portugal but appears in the Huelva hoard; bronze

Fig. 75a   spits of the Painho type, which have a similar distribution;

bronze bracelets hung with leech-shaped pendants which also
appear independently in north-western Spain as well as
Portugal and bronze bracelets with engraved geometric decoration very much like that on the remarkable gold gorget from
Sintra near Lisbon, in the British Museum, which relates to
other gold gorgets and neck-rings from Berzocana (Cáceres),
Penela (Estremadura), Evora and Moura in the Alemtejo, and
a gold bracelet from Guimarães. It is clear that the gold supplies
on the western side of the peninsula were still being exploited in
the latter part of the Bronze Age and that the accomplished
goldsmiths of the native culture went on developing their art
then and even in the Early Iron Age, after Punic influence had
begun, and in spite of the upheavals of the Celtic invasions.
Though their art, like their supplies of metal, was rooted in the
west, they no doubt travelled throughout the peninsula and
served customers on the south-eastern seaboard, as the two
remarkable hoards recently published by Soler García show.
For the smaller of these from Cabezo Redondo itself not only
contained gold-strip diadems, plain open bracelets and spirals
of the types already familiar in the Early Bronze Age, but raw
material suggestive of an itinerant metalworker; it also contained
conical beads of sheet gold, related to ones in the São Martinho,
Alcacer do Sal hoard and moulded rings which are small
editions of the elaborate bracelets which form an important
feature of the great hoard found in a jar of Argaric tradition in
1963 north-east of Villena. These bracelets are elaborately
profiled bangles, which in some cases have rows of teeth like
those of a cog wheel – a form hitherto known only from scattered finds in Portugal and Galicia. Even more remarkable are
the eleven gold carinated bowls and the two gold and three
silver bottles. The former are decorated with embossed dots – a
technique apparently derived from the Early Bronze Age
'*Blechstil*' of the peninsula but greatly elaborated by the Atlantic jewellers, as we see in the embossed gold bracteate from

Fig. 75b

Fig. 75d
Plate 56

Plate 55

Fig. 76

Plate 59

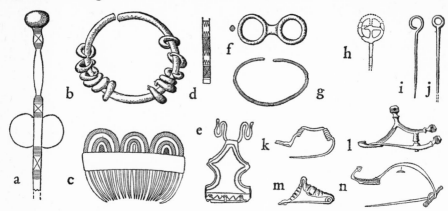

Fig. 75.   Late Bronze Age ornaments: a, bronze 'spit', Painho (Leiria); b, bronze 'leach' bracelet, Casti-llejos en Sanchorreja (Ávila); c, gold comb, Caldas de Reyes (Pontevedra); d, detail of bronze bracelet, Cerro del Berrueco (Salamanca); e, bronze belt-hook from Agullana (Gerona); f, bronze link from Huelva hoard; g, bronze bracelet with alternating torsion from Tosseta (Tarragona); h-j, bronze pins from Agullana; k-n, bronze brooches from Molá (Tarragona), Agullana, Huelva hoard and Cruz del Negro, Carmona (Seville) (a after E.da Veiga, b and d after Maluquer, c after MacWhite, e, h-j, l, after Palol, f after Almagro, g after Vilaseca and k and n after Schüle). 1: 4

Ninho do Açor (Castelo Branco) – and have forms and patterns which seem on the one hand to inherit much from the late 'Meseta' Beaker ware and on the other to greatly influence the native pottery of the final Bronze Age and Early Iron Age. The identical nature of the concentric semicircle patterns on the metal bowls and those on Boquique pottery vessels can hardly be accidental, and the low carinated form appears again on painted pottery dishes, with internal decoration of red zigzag and trellis patterns on a yellow ground, from the late Bronze Age layer at Galera (Granada). The embossed dot patterns on the well-known silver 'helmet' from Caudete (Teruel) are now explained. The bottles with their vertical ribs formed by folding the sheet-metal, in the manner of My-cenaean sheet-metalwork, also influenced later pottery forms,

Plate 47
Fig. 76c

Fig. 76

like the vertically ribbed cremation urn from near the site of Castulo (Jaén). Other pottery vessels, from the *castro* of Pedra d'Oiro, Alemquer (Estremadura) combine local Early Bronze Age traditions with Punic influences – reflected particularly in the bowl with its metallic decoration of leaves and medallions in relief. The extraordinary openwork trun-cated cone-shaped ornaments from the Villena hoard may be related to gorgets of Golada type, as may also be the fragmen-tary collar found with gold cups bearing engraved patterns in Beaker tradition and a gold comb, no doubt a woman's hair ornament, in the Galician Late Bronze Age hoard of Caldas de Reyes (Pontevedra).

Fig. 73c

Fig. 76b

Fig. 75c

THE ATLANTIC BRONZE AGE (FIRST PHASE): c. 1000–700 BC

Already before the end of the second millennium the flourish-ing bronze industry characterized by palstaves, socketed spearheads and dirks or rapiers which developed during the local Middle Bronze Age on either side of the English Channel

Fig. 76. The Villena Hoard (Alicante): a, flask; b, ornament; c, bowl (after J. N. Soler García). 1:3

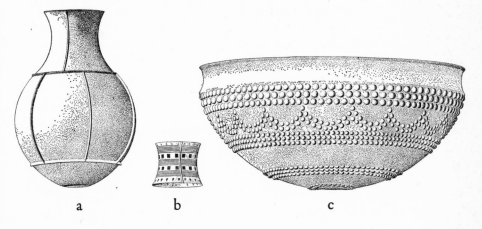

a   b   c

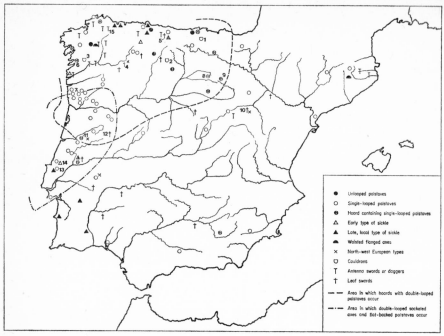

Fig. 77. Late Bronze Age: Atlantic types

1 Cabárceno
  (Santander)
2 Lois (León)
3 Peneda
  (Pontevedra)
4 Rio Sil, S. Esteban
  (Léon)

5 Sobrefoz, Ponga
  (Asturias)
6 Hio (Pontevedra)
7 Penha, Guimarães
  (Braga)
8 Padilla de Abajo
  (Burgos)

9 Huerta de Arriba
  (Burgos)
10 Alhama de
   Aragón
11 Arganil (Coimbra)
12 Vila Maior
   Sabugal (Guarda)

13 Pragança (Lisbon)
14 S. Martinho, Río
   Maior (Santarém)
15 Castro de Coubuei-
   ra, Mondoñedo
   (Lugo)

had begun to spread its products and perhaps its craftsmen towards south-western France, and to some degree to the northern seaboard of Spain; a few plain, slender, unlooped palstaves from the Cantabrian area and the personal hoard of Valdevimbre (León), in which a socketed spearhead, conical spear ferrule and miniature anvil of north-west European types are associated with a saw, a flanged axe and a riveted dagger of Argaric affinity, may belong to this early horizon, during which foreign metalworkers from across the Bay of Biscay may have been establishing themselves in the copper mining areas of the north-west. It was, however, probably not until the beginning of the first millennium that a distinctive north-west Iberian bronze-using industry became established, manufac-

Fig. 78. Late Bronze Age tools: a, S. Martinho, Río Maior (Santarém); b, Castro-pol (Asturias); c-d, Arganil (Coimbra); e, Minho; f, Ripoll (Gerona); g-i, Hio (Pontevedra); j, Roriz (Minho) (a after Do Paço, b and e after L. Siret, c-d after Castro Nunes, f-h after M. Almagro). 1:4

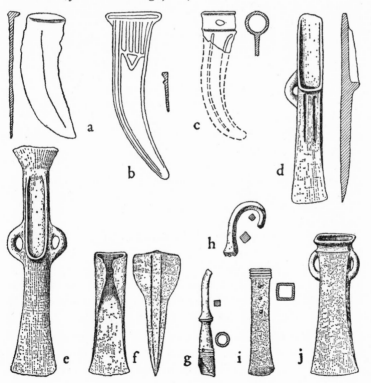

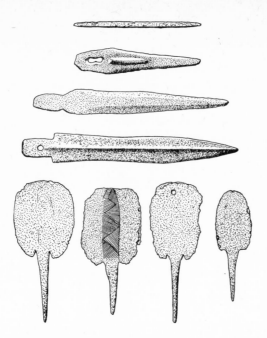

Fig. 79. Huerta de Arriba (Burgos): part of the hoard (after a photograph supplied by Valencia Museum). 1:3

Fig. 78a, b

Plate 52c, d

Fig. 79

turing types of palstave and sickle which clearly originate in north-west Europe but develop an increasingly local character. The earlier palstaves with single loops usually have a single central rib below the stop, and frequently combine this with vestigial flanes. Such forms are closely related to the palstaves of western France as well as Britain, but there are special traits which seem to suggest an extension to the Iberian north-west of a specifically British element in the north-west European tradition, among them, probably, the double loops which came to be so distinctively 'Iberian'.

The beginning of the Iberian development, after inspiration from north-west Europe, is probably seen in the hoard of Padilla de Abajo (Burgos) in which a slender flat axe, with widely splayed blade and double loops and a plain socketed spearhead are associated with a 'Palmela' arrowhead and open bracelets of native Early Bronze Age form. The 'maple leaf' razors

associated with single and double-looped palstaves of Iberian *Fig. 79*
type in the Huerta de Arriba (Burgos) hoard and the curv-
bladed, ridge-button type of sickle which begins the west *Fig. 78a, b*
Iberian series, afterwards so peculiar in its development, are
part of the same north-west European influence. So too, is the
unique, ring-socketed sickle found in a hoard at Arganil *Fig. 78c*
(Beira Alta) with an Iberian double-looped palstave of the
midribbed and flanged type and an example of the strange
central Portuguese 'flat-backed' palstave, as well as the *Fig. 78d*
occasional basal-looped spearheads like the one associated in
the Río Sil, San Esteban (León) hoard with a normal spear- *Fig. 74f*
head, a leech pendant of native type and a leaf-shaped flange-
hilted sword of north-west European ('Wilburton') affinity.
Swords of this kind are relatively common in the northern and *Fig. 74a, b*
western parts of the peninsula and one, from Alhama de
Aragón, near Saragossa, still retains its ogival chape – a form
distinctive of Britain and the Atlantic coast regions of France.
There is no doubt, however, that the palstaves of Iberian type
reflect the arrival of new metallurgical processes as well as
types in the north-west of the peninsula, because a number of
analyses have shown that these implements were normally of
true bronze, even though a few contain an admixture of arsenic, possibly due to the melting-down of obsolete native
tools and weapons. Presumably, therefore, north-western tin
ores were now being exploited, in the form of cassiterite used
in the reductive fusion of copper to produce bronze, instead of
metallic tin. This, at any rate, was the type of bronze production
practised in the 'Nuraghi' of Sardinia about this time; and that
the cassiterite here may in fact have come from the Iberian
north-west is suggested by the presence of double-looped
palstaves at Forraxi Nioi and in the well-known Sardinian
hoard of Monte Sa Idda, which also contained sickles of west
Iberian type, and the fact that about this time Sicilian bronze
shaft-hole axes were being exported to Galicia and the Bis-

Fig. 80.   Late Bronze Age to Early Iron Age migration period

1 Can Bech de Baix, Agullana (Gerona)	6 El Marcó, Tivisa (Tarragona)	11 Roquizal del Rulló, Fabara (Zaragoza)	16 Miraveche (Burgos)
2 Sabadell (Barcelona)	7 Cueva de Janet, Tivisa (Tarragona)	12 Azaila (Zaragoza)	17 Las Cogotas de Cardeñosa (Ávila)
3 Can Missert, Tarrassa (Barcelona)	8 S. Cristobal de Mazaleón (Teruel)	13 Almohaja (Teruel)	18 Los Castillejos de Sanchorreja (Ávila)
4 El Molá (Tarragona)	9 Tossal Redó (Teruel)	14 Cortes de Navarra	19 Santarém
5 Tosseta (Tarragona)	10 Cabezo de Monleón (Teruel)	15 El Redal (Logroño)	20 Alpiarça (Santarém)

cayan area of France. As we have already indicated, however, there is as yet no sign that the introduction of Atlantic metallurgy was accompanied by any marked change in other aspects of culture in the peninsula. Although Atlantic bronzes

226

are usually isolated finds, whether made singly or in hoards, some have been found on the old-established settlements of the native culture like Penha, Guimarães and Pragança (Estrema- dura), which though unplanned and unstratified have yielded bronzes of all phases of the Atlantic industry as well as late native types like the barbed and socketed spearhead.

Plate 52

Fig. 74g

THE URNFIELD INVADERS OF THE NORTH-EAST: c. 750–500 BC

In complete contrast to the north-west, Catalonia has yielded remarkably few bronzes that can be assigned to the Atlantic industry. Indeed, towards the end of the second millennium and in the early part of the first, north-eastern Spain seems to have been an even greater backwater than the adjacent regions of southern France. On the other hand no other region in the peninsula can show such clear evidence, from burials and set- tlements, of the irruption of new settlers from beyond the Pyre- nees at the end of the Bronze Age.

Fig. 80

The Urnfield culture of Catalonia does, indeed, represent a complete break with the traditional burial customs of the peninsula, with cremation substituted for inhumation and the ashes placed in separate pits, usually in a large urn which often has a lid and sometimes a number of small 'accessory' vessels. Occasionally there are bronzes with the burial – bracelets, brooches, pins, tweezers, razors, belt plaques. The graves are grouped close together, sometimes in large numbers – about 200, for example, were counted in two cemeteries near Agul- lana on the Pyrenean foothills north of Gerona and nearly as many at El Molá (Tarragona) – and though the urn may be covered with stone slabs or surrounded by a ring of stones they were apparently rarely marked by a cairn; at Sabadell it seems that a row of graves were separated from each other by upright slabs. The number of sites which have yielded material of this culture is considerable, chiefly because very many of the

Fig. 75e

numerous caves of Catalonia were used for burial or settlement in this phase, although the deposits, being comparatively superficial, are usually badly disturbed. Settlements occupied by users of the highly characteristic Urnfield pottery, at least in the later stages of its development, are also common, not only in Catalonia but further up the Ebro valley in Aragon and Navarre.

The burial rite and the ceramic tradition of this intrusive group in the north-east alike speak clearly of an extension beyond the Pyrenees of the Urnfield culture which had been carried westwards from its original home in central Europe by a series of folk-movements lasting centuries and spread over the latter part of the Bronze Age of western Europe and the Bronze Age D and Hallstatt A and B of Reinecke's period system for central Europe. The greater part of the Catalan pottery has a special character which links it more particularly with that of the Languedoc urnfields, recently so thoroughly studied by the Taffanels, which begin during the latter part of Hallstatt B, in the eighth century BC, but persist far into Hallstatt C, in the Early Iron Age. The earliest pottery of the Catalan urnfields, which is also the finest ware, tends to have broadly fluted decoration and is well represented at the cemetery of Can Missert, Terrassá (Barcelona) and in the caves of Janet and El Marcó (Tarragona); it seems to represent the initial settlement on the better agricultural land near the coast. In the later stages, well represented in Languedoc, and in Catalonia chiefly on the Pyrenean foothills, the decoration tends to consist of paired narrow grooves often arranged in meander patterns, and the urns develop low pedestals. Here new influences are at work coming not from central Europe but from the Villanovan culture of northern Italy, and Catalonia has now become part of a special province extending along the north-western shores of the Mediterranean; the great cemetery of Can Bech de Baix, Agullana, gives most definition

Plate 60

Plate 61

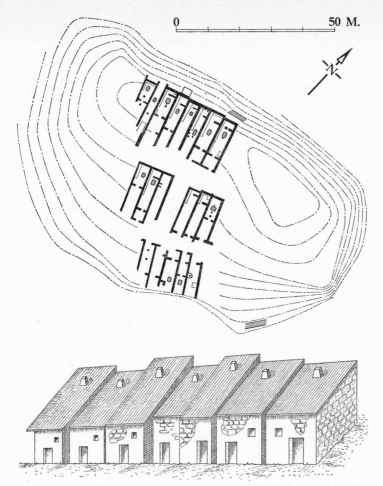

Fig. 81. An Urnfield settlement: Cortes de Navarra (after Maluquer) plan and re-construction

to this phase in Catalonia. The metalwork from Agullana shows more clearly than the pottery how mixed the Catalan Urnfield group became after its initial phase. The pins echo those of Languedoc and are derived ultimately from central Europe, but the razors with their rectangular tendency are

Fig. 75b,j

Fig. 79

Fig. 75k–m

more specifically Iberian, with analogues in the Huerta de Arriba hoard and in Andalusia; while the brooches, as we shall see later, are definitely of types evolved in the native culture of the peninsular south, which now spread northwards to Catalonia and Languedoc. The view, sometimes put for-ward, that the Catalan Urnfield group can be equated with the first band of Celts to arrive in Spain, encounters even greater difficulties when the evidence of the settlements is considered. For here not only are the native and Atlantic Bronze Age elements in the metalwork even more prominent, but the architecture and layout often seems to represent a deve-lopment of Argaric rather than of central European Bronze Age traditions and at many of the sites there appears to be continuity of occupation into Iberian Iron Age times; so much so, that one might be tempted to regard the Urnfield culture as Iberian rather than Celtic. These settlements will therefore be consid-ered more fully in a later section.

Not all the Urnfield pottery of north-eastern Spain, however, can be treated as an extension of that of Languedoc. Certain urnfields and settlements in the neighbourhood of the Ebro, in use during the seventh century BC and later, have yielded pottery which seems to indicate a fresh cultural infusion from much further north than Languedoc – one, indeed, which seems to have hampered the spread of later Languedocian pottery forms southward from the Pyrenean foothills and to have instituted a cultural cleavage in the north-east. This new pottery includes: a) urns which tend to an ovoid form, with

Fig. 73e

truncated cone-shaped neck, often bearing chevron patterns, and flaring rim, as seen at Azaila and the two cemeteries of El Molá and Tosseta in the Lower Priorato (Tarragona) – a form relating to the characteristic '*Halsurn*' of Hallstatt C burials in west-central Europe. With this, painted ware is associated, not only in the Ebro valley but at Almohaja near Teruel and far across the Meseta at Sanchorreja (Avila) and is followed by

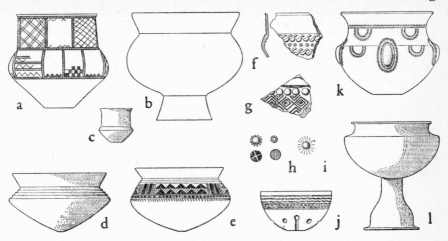

Fig. 82. Early Iron Age pottery: a, painted jar from Cortes de Navarra; b, plain pedestal urn from Cortes; c, 'Marnian' cup from Alpiarça (Santarém); d-e, El Redal (Logroño): f, Simancas (Valladolid); g, j-k, Osera (Ávila); h-i, l, Las Cogotas de Cardeñosa (Ávila) (a-b after Maluquer, d-e after Almagro, f after F. Wattenberg, g-l after J. Cabré)

other related painted pottery in the sixth century at the settle-ments of Cortes de Navarra, S. Cristobal de Mazaleón and Tossal Redó in the Ebro valley; b) chip-carved pottery with patterns like those on the painted pottery, much more elaborate than the post-Beaker chip-carving of the native 'Meseta' group, particularly well represented at Roquizal del Rulló and lasting like the painted ware into the sixth century on the northern Meseta as well as the Ebro valley with a growing fondness for stamped concentric circles; c) *kernoi* – large vases with small vessels attached to the rim, like those of the Rhineland Hallstatt C, from settlements in Cabezo de Monleón, Caspe (Saragossa) and Cortes de Navarra; and d) clay firedogs, of central Euro-pean tradition at Roquizal. But most significant of all is the appearance of cast bronze neck-rings with alternating torsion at Tosseta (Tarragona) and El Molá – a type which occurs in a

Figs. 82, 81

Plate 63

Fig. 75g
Plate 63

seventh-century context at the Languedocian urnfield of Le Moulin (Aude) but is otherwise virtually confined to the Hall-statt C culture of the hill country between the Rhine and the Moselle and certain Danish hoards of Montelius' Period VI. It seems, in short that in the seventh century BC a series of folk movements began which brought people from the neighbour-hood of the Middle Rhine initially, and later from various parts of France, through the western passes of the Pyrenees to the Ebro valley and the Meseta – and here we must seek the origins of those Celtic-speaking populations in the northern Meseta whose culture we shall examine in the next chapter.

TARTESSUS AND THE 'CARP'S-TONGUE' COMPLEX: *c.* 700–500 BC

During the period of the 'Urnfield' invasions of the north-east, the south-western areas of the peninsula also saw important changes of culture. Precisely how these came about is still ob-scure, for here there is no wealth of published material from burials and settlements and any attempt to reconstruct the process must be based mainly upon isolated finds of metalwork, a few poorly recorded settlement and burial finds, and study of a remarkable series of carved cist-covers and steles which perpet-uate the local Early Bronze Age ritual but commemorate warriors whose equipment owed much to barbarian Europe north of the Pyrenees as well as to contacts with Mediterranean lands. Many years ago I drew attention to the mainly south-western distribution in the peninsula of the characteristically west-European cut and thrust sword with 'carp's-tongue' tip, which now seems to have developed in the first place chiefly in the Atlantic regions of France, especially Brittany, from the late eighth century BC onward. This type of sword is represen-ted by many examples in the great bronze hoard found in 1923 in the estuary of the Odiel at Huelva – a hoard unique in Spain for its size, variety and character as a collection of scrap

Fig. 74c

metal. Associated with it were a few solid-handled swords probably derived from a central European type; daggers with riveted butts like the native 'Porto de Mós' type but often with 'carp's-tongue' tips; spearheads and butts; fragments of a helmet like the well-known Urnfield culture ones from Bernières d'Ailly, Normandy; belt-hooks; and brooches which will be discussed later. Some of these types recur in the more recently discovered hoard from Cabezo de Araya, Cáceres, and variants of the 'carp's-tongue' sword type are fairly plentifully represented in southern Spain and Portugal, with some outliers in the northern Meseta. Their distribution clearly does not correspond to that of the Atlantic palstave industry even its later, specialized stage, and I was at one time inclined to attribute their introduction to the makers of the French late Hallstatt pottery which accompanied various ill-recorded burials on the lower Tagus and Guadalquivir, whom I supposed to have arrived by sea-routes from western France, where the 'carp's-tongue' sword remained long in use. Now, however, it seems likelier that these people were late colonists from the valleys of the Upper Ebro and Tagus, and that the swords were adapted by the Tartessians themselves – for so we may reasonably name the people of the south-west – as a result of their trade with the Oestrymnici of Brittany, which a Greek *periplus* of the sixth century BC, used by Avienus, records. It was, no doubt, this trade which brought specifically Irish types of cauldron to Cabárceno (Santander) and Lois (León), two Irish 'flesh hooks' to Hio (Pontevedra) to be deposited in a hoard with fragments of a 'carp's-tongue' sword, and the Irish type of lunate spearhead to Huelva. The Tartessians may also have been middlemen in the trade of north-western cassiterite to Sardinia, for the late, south-west Iberian and southern French type of short 'carp's-tongue' sword with elongated guards above and below the hilt-plate occurs in the Monte Sa Idda hoard.

Fig. 74m

Fig. 74j

Fig. 74h, i, k, l

Fig. 78g, h

Fig. 74l

Fig. 74d

The composite nature of the Tartessian culture is well illustrated by the late carved cist-covers and steles of the south-
west, which clearly perpetuate an ancient local tradition of
warrior symbolism. One cist-cover, from Mombeja (Beja),

Fig. 70b

shows a late, flange-hilted type of sword alongside one of the
long splayed flat axes traditional in the area. The later slabs,
moreover, sometimes show the warrior himself, with his sword
or dagger, spear, shield and ornaments. The slab from Solana

Plate 62

de Cabañas (Cáceres) shows a sword which appears to be of
the late 'carp's-tongue' type with guards, a mirror, an elbowed
brooch of a type we shall meet in the next section, and a four-
wheeled vehicle; a bow and a two-wheeled vehicle are shown
at Torrejón del Rubio (Cáceres). The warrior of Megacela

Fig. 84

(Badajoz) has a horned helmet like the actual ones from Viksø,
Denmark, and what appears to be an antenna-handled dagger
of the Early Iron Age type. A helmet of a more familiar central
European type seems to be represented on a slab from Santa
Ana de Trujillo (Cáceres). Shields are seen on slabs from as
far apart as Figueira (Algarve), Penamacor (Beira), Carmona
(Seville) and Haza del Trillo (Jaén). Most V-shaped indentations known from actual specimens or votive models found
in Ireland and the east Mediterranean are now thought to be
derived from the central European '*Herzsprung*' type with
U-shaped indentations. There is little information about grave
goods connected with these slabs, but it seems that the finely
made and sharply carinated bowls of the earlier southern
Portuguese cists persisted and were sometimes decorated, in

Fig. 85

the final Bronze Age, with stroke-burnished patterns, as at
the Lapa de Fumo, Sesimbra cave, in brown or beige or dark
grey on light grey. This ware is known from a number of
recent, not yet fully published excavations on *castro* sites in the
Alemtejo, at Carmona, Lora del Rio and Carambolo near
Seville and Asta Regia near Jérez. On some of these sites this
ware appears to have been mistakenly compared with 'stroke-

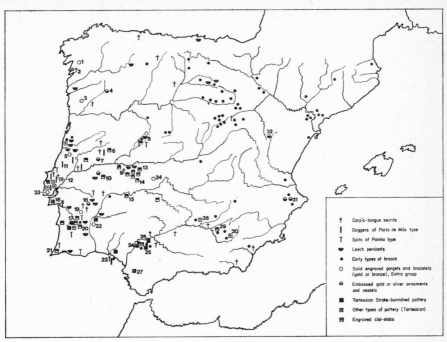

Fig. 83. Late Bronze Age: Tartessian types

1 Caldas de Reyes (Pontevedra)	9 Cabezo de Araya (Cáceres)	Cezimbra (Setubal)	26 Lora del Río (Seville)
2 Hio (Pontevedra)	10 Portalegre	17 Mombeja (Beja)	27 Asta Regia, Jerez (Cádiz)
3 Guimarães (Braga)	11 Porto de Mós	18 Estremoz (Evora)	28 Castulo (Jaén)
4 Chaves (Vila Real)	12 Pedra de Oiro (Lisbon)	19 Evora	29 Haza del Trillo (Jaén)
5 Penela (Coimbra)	13 Torrejón del Rubio (Cáceres)	20 Ervidel (Beja)	30 Galera (Granada)
6 Meimão, Penamacor (Castelo Branco)	14 Solana de las Cabañas (Cáceres)	21 Figueira (Algarve)	31 Villena (Alicante)
7 Ninho do Açor (Castelo Branco)	15 Megacela (Badajoz)	22 Moura (Beja)	32 Caudete (Teruel)
8 Cerro del Berrueco (Salamanca)	16 Lapa de Fumo,	23 Huelva	33 Sintra (Lisbon)
		24 Carambolo, (Seville)	34 Berzocana (Cáceres)
		25 Carmona (Seville)	

burnished' wares of much earlier Aegean Copper Age groups; but at Carmona, at least, carefully recorded stratifications show that it is later than native Boquique ware and fine grey wheel-turned ware probably connected with Phoenician trade and colonization, and contemporary with other Phoenician and early Iberian wares. To sum up, the Tartessians were a trading people who acted as intermediaries between the advanced Mediterranean cultures and the barbarians of Atlantic Europe and absorbed ideas from both directions. Not until modern excavations have been extensively carried out in western Andalusia, and published, will we have a proper understanding of their role; but it already seems likely that they and their Iberian neighbours to the east absorbed the northern barbarians, who settled among them and transformed the culture of those who remained in the north-eastern parts of the peninsula.

Fig. 84.   Megacela (Badajoz): warrior stele (after Soutou). Height 1.42 m.

THE TRANSITION TO THE EARLY IRON AGE: *c.* 700–500 BC

It has already been said that many of the Urnfield burials in Catalonia and Languedoc contain metal types, especially brooches, which cannot be derived from the parent culture of central Europe. The most common type of brooch, with double unilateral coils, also occurs in Andalusia and is evidently derived from the Early Iron Age cultures of Italy and Sicily, as must also be the pivoting type of brooch found in the seventh century at Agullana, El Molá and Sanchorreja (Avila). On the other hand the elbowed type of brooch represented by several examples in the Huelva hoard and isolated finds on the Meseta is now seen to be a Cypriot type brought to Andalusia by the Phoenicians in the seventh century BC. These contacts with the central and eastern Mediterranean, mainly due to the Phoenicians, who were now establishing trade posts on the

Fig. 75k

Fig. 75l

Fig. 75m

southern coasts of the peninsula (see D. B. Harden, *The Phoeni-cians*, in this series), must have been the principal factor in spreading the use of iron along with bronze brooches and other finer metal types, including bronze vessels and gold jewellery, from the south upwards towards the Pyrenees (iron has been found with proto-Corinthian *kotyloi* in a grave at Laurita de Almuñecar near Málaga). But the Tartessians themselves contributed types to this northward movement – not only bow brooches with crossbow coils and upturned, knob-bed foot which reached Catalonia by the middle of the sixth century BC and belt hooks like that from Agullana, but the mysterious double rings which occur in the Huelva hoard and various north-eastern and Languedocian urn burials of the seventh century. But we know from moulds found in the lower Ebro settlement of Roquizal del Rullo that these rings, and even 'carp's-tongue' swords, which must be derived from the south-west, were being made in the north-east in the seventh century. When we consider these Ebro valley settle-ments more closely, as we are able to do particularly well at Cortes de Navarra, thanks to the careful work of Maluquer de Motes, we can see that the allegedly 'Celtic' culture they represent was in fact composed of elements derived as much from the earlier Bronze Age culture of the Mediterranean coast as from beyond the Pyrenees. Cortes is a *tell* built up by the decay or destruction of successive walled villages of mud-

Fig. 75n

Fig. 75e

Fig. 75f

Fig. 81

Fig. 85. Tartessian stroke-burnished bowl: Lapa de Fumo, Sesimbra (Setubal) (after Da Cunha Serrão). Approx. 1 : 3

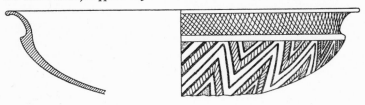

brick houses built in straight terraces, often with a vestibule in front of a main living room with central hearth and benches along the walls. In the later phases of this settlement painted wall-plaster and burials of children under the floor seem to indicate a revival of native Iberian traditions. The lower Ebro villages of Roquizal del Rulló, Cabezo de Monleón and Tossal Redó have a similar layout and show a steady evolution into the 'Iberian' culture described by Dr Arribas in this series. They represent agricultural communities exploiting the possibilities of the middle Ebro basin, in particular, for the growth of cereals.

Bronze implements long remained in use in this transitional phase, but in the north-east flat axes were apparently still being made, to judge by moulds found at Cabezo de Mon-

Fig. 78f

león, alongside of the end-winged axes and socketed axes (often unlooped) introduced by the Urnfield immigrants and associated in the hoard found at Ripoll (Gerona). In the north-west the replacement of bronze by iron for making implements was probably slower. The socketed axe, in an early form

Fig. 78i

known from Brittany, already appears in the Hio (Pontevedra) hoard but many examples, especially in central Portugal are a

Fig. 78j

local adaptation with double loops. The late type of double-looped palstave, without decorative ribs or vestigial flanges, must have been made mainly in the transitional period, but its occurrence in numerous large hoards in Galicia and northern Portugal, unaccompanied by other types and frequently without the casting jets removed and with a high admixture of lead, suggest that its use was by then largely votive, as seems to be the case with similar hoards of socketed axes in Brittany, at a time when working tools were made increasingly of iron.

CHAPTER X

The Celtic Iron Age

THE HISTORICAL BACKGROUND

WE SAW IN THE LAST CHAPTER that the earliest surviving literary references to the Iberian peninsula arose from Phoenician trading expeditions in the ninth and eighth centuries BC. But the decline of Phoenician enterprise as a result of Assyrian assaults in the seventh century gave the Greek maritime powers of the time, particularly Phocaea, an opportunity to establish trading posts along the west Mediterranean coasts, the chief of which was Massilia. The naval victory of Alalia (535 BC) enabled the Carthaginians to eliminate the more southerly of these posts in Spain. It seems that the Phocaean or Massiliot *periplus* upon which the late Roman writer Avienus is generally thought to have based much of his account of the Mediterranean coasts of Spain in his *Ora Maritima*, was composed before this battle, and comparison of this account with statements by Greek writers of the late fifth and fourth centuries BC provides a control for the archaeological evidence suggesting Celtic invasions of the peninsula in this period. For Avienus' sources make no clear reference to Celts in the peninsula, only to particular tribes like the Saefes and the Cempsi which some authorities have taken to be Celtic, without general acceptance, and which are not mentioned in later, more detailed classical accounts of peninsular geography. In fact, they seem to describe conditions in which Iberians or Tartessians are in control of the eastern and southern maritime regions of the peninsula, with Phoenician or Greek settlers in a few places, while the Atlantic seaboard appears to be occupied by tribes that are more likely to be pre-Celtic (though possibly speaking an 'Indo-European' language) than Celtic. On the other hand the later writers, including Herodotus, clearly refer to Celts as a people who by the late fifth century, at any rate, were established in the northern and western regions of the peninsula. At a later date still, writers of the Roman period give much information about tribal and place names in the peninsula which is supplemented by inscriptions and coins, and this enables us to form a general picture of the distribution of Celtic and Iberian speech in the last few centuries of the pre-Christian era. From it we can

Fig. 86

deduce, for example, that there is no great overlap between the distribution of the characteristically Celtic place-name ending *-briga*, on the Meseta and in the Atlantic coastal regions, on the one hand, and the typically Iberian endings in *-ilti, -ili, -iltu, -ilu* and *-urris* in the Mediterranean areas, on the other. But there is a much greater overlap between the Celtic place-name ending just mentioned and what seem to be specifically Tartessian endings, *-ippo, -uba, -igi, -ucci* and *-urgi*, extending across the southern regions of the peninsula. On this historical and philological evidence one might expect to find that the sixth and fifth centuries BC saw the most extensive Celtic folk-movements south of the Pyrenees.

During the last forty years archaeologists and ethnologists have propounded many and varying reconstructions, based partly on archaeological evidence, of the folk-movements which established the historically Celtic or 'Celtiberian' character of non-Mediterranean Spain as the Romans found it. Professor P. Bosch-Gimpera has played a prominent part in these discussions, with a series of papers which have built up a picture of two Celtic 'waves': the first, 'Late Bronze Age' and repesented by the 'Urnfield' invasion of Catalonia, which we have already considered; the second, 'Hallstatt Iron Age' and represented by various archaeological groups in the Ebro valley and on the Meseta, some of which are equated with the Cempsi and Saefes mentioned by Avienus, while others are equated with tribes like the Vaccaei, Vettones and Gallaeci which first appear in much later sources. The archaeological

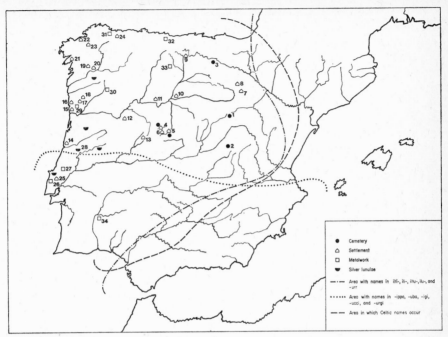

Fig. 86.   Celtic Early Iron Age

1 Aguilar de Anguita (Guadalajara)
2 Madrigueras, Carrascosa del Campo (Cuenca)
3 Miraveche (Burgos)
4 Osera and Mesas de Asta, Chamartín de la Sierra (Ávila)
5 Las Cogotas de Cardeños (Ávila)
6 Los Castillejos de Sanchorreja (Ávila)

7 Castilfrío de la Sierra (Soria)
8 Arevalo de la Sierra (Soria)
9 Monte Bernorio (Palencia)
10 Soto de Medinilla (Valladolid)
11 Mota del Marqués (Valladolid)
12 Saldeana (Salamanca)
13 Cerro del Berrueco (Salamanca)

14 Santa Olaya (Coimbra)
15 Terroso (Porto)
16 Laundos (Porto)
17 Sabroso (Braga)
18 Briteiros (Braga)
19 Cameixa (Orense)
20 S. Ciprián de Lás (Orense)
21 Rianxo (Coruña)
22 Elviña (Coruña)
23 Meirás (Coruña)
24 Coaña (Asturias)
25 Pragança (Lisbon)
26 Outeiro da

Cabeça, Torres Vedras (Lisbon)
27 Mira de Aire (Lisbon)
28 Chã de Lamas, Miranda do Corvo (Coimbra)
29 Bougado (Porto)
30 Chaves (Vila Real)
31 Ribadeo (Lugo)
32 Cangas de Onis (Asturias)
33 Saldaña (Palencia)
34 Moura (Beja)

241

and ethnological elements gathered together by Bosch in his second wave are so disparate and the Celtic character of some of them so doubtful, that later students have tended to react increasingly against it, culminating in Professor Sangmeister, who has recently asserted that real Celtic influences and immigrations in the peninsula did not begin until the middle of the fifth century BC – a view no more closely related to the evidence than Bosch-Gimpera's. We have already noted, in the previous chapter, that though the main Catalan Urnfield culture is not likely to have been Celtic, there are Hallstatt C elements in the urnfields and settlements of the Ebro valley which seem to owe something to immigration from the neighbourhood of the middle Rhine. In fact, as we shall now see, these movements began a series which continued in the later Hallstatt periods, and it must be admitted that the seventh and sixth centuries BC were the period of maximum contact between the Celtic World of west-central Europe and the native cultures of the peninsula even though the Celts may not have established themselves on the northern and western seaboards until later.

THE CELTIC INVASIONS

The characteristics of the 'Hierro Celtico' of Spanish archaeologists have long been familiar, thanks chiefly to the extensive excavations of cremation cemeteries on the Meseta, in the early part of this century, by the Marqués de Cerralbo, D.B. Taracena Aguirre and J. Cabré Aguiló. These cemeteries have yielded a great quantity of metalwork and pottery which has a distinctively Iberian, post-Hallstatt character and many of the forms are proper to the distinctive Iberian culture of the Mediterranean seaboard which Professor Arribas has dealt with in this series (*The Iberians*, 1965). It seems to confirm the historical evidence that many of the tribes of the Meseta and

Atlantic seaboard in the fifth century and later were only partly Celtic in origin and in fact largely represent a reassertion of pre-Celtic elements, no doubt greatly helped by the continued existence of a much more advanced Iberian culture on the Mediterranean seaboard. But closer examination reveals different cultural provinces in this vast area, which must have had diverse origins, in so far as they were not due to geographical and economical differences between the regions. The traditional cereal-raising areas of New Castile were occupied by agricultural tribes like the Arevaci and Vaccaei, who came increasingly under Iberian ('Celtiberian') influence. León and central Portugal were occupied by the stock-raising Vettones and Lusitani, while the north-west with its mixed agriculture had many tribes, some Celtic, among whom the Gallaeci were prominent. It is necessary, however, to go back beyond this fully evolved and localized Iberian Hallstatt culture to find the origins of its Celtic elements beyond the Pyrenees. The fact that these are most plainly seen in the earlier, hand-made pottery from the burials and settlements rather than the metalwork, which mostly belongs to later phases in the cemeteries, when the hybrid culture was fully evolved, is a reflection of the strength and superiority of the native Iberian culture, as well as the newcomers' isolation from their homeland.

In the light of recent research on the later Hallstatt cultures of west-central Europe and France by Kossack, Kimmig and others, it is now possible to see a little more clearly the sources of particular ceramic styles and the likely date of their introduction into the peninsula. Two main groups can be distinguished corresponding to two major cultural provinces of the Celtic world between the Upper Danube and the Pyrenees. The most important is the French Hallstatt group characterized by large ovoid or biconical jars with cylindrical necks, smaller vessels, with globular or carinated bodies and cylindrical or flaring rims, and a tendency to use tall truncated cone-shaped

Fig. 82a

Fig. 82b

pedestals for the larger jars and broad horizontal fluting above the carination of bowls. This repertoire is widespread among the later Hallstatt groups of the sixth century BC in various parts of France, is still important in the early La Tène 'Marnian' culture of Champagne in the fifth century, and lasts until much later in south-western France, as in Spain. This western Celtic group contrasts markedly with the elaborate pottery of the sixth century in southern Germany and the Swiss plateau, and has been called the 'Urnfield Renaissance' by Kimmig. In certain early groups in France and Spain fine, small vessels with chip-carved decoration, using more elaborate patterns than those associated with the earlier 'Boquique'

Fig. 82d, e

group on the Meseta occur – El Redal (Logroño) is a type-site – and the ware is found further down the Ebro valley and at sites at either end of the northern Meseta but not apparently

Fig. 82a

in the Tagus basin or further south. Polychrome painted ware also occurs, notably at Cortes de Navarra and as far west as Sanchorreja (Avila): there is a general relationship to the geometric painted patterns which occasionally occur in contemporary groups in France, chiefly in Burgundy; at Cortes

Fig. 75k

the ware is associated with several double, unilateral coil brooches and is probably early seventh-century. But the great mass of the pottery, as in France, is plain, though often of fine, well burnished, hand-made ware, and this applies particularly to the wider and probably later range of distribution, which includes the Tagus valley, as far as Portugal, where a cremation cemetery at Tanchoal dos Patudos, Alpiarça (Ribatejo)

Fig. 82c

is the principal site, and curiously 'Marnian' looking carinated cups occur. Scattered finds of cremation burials with pottery resembling Alpiarça ware, and very little else have been made in the lower Guadalquivir valley, at several sites near Almería and in the province of Castellón. These intrusions into the Iberian area may represent mercenary warriors employed by the Tartessians, such as may have been commemorated by the

later steles, one of which, as we noted, shows an antenna
dagger which could hardly be earlier than the sixth century.
The group is not, as yet, well represented in the north-west,
and its place in Galicia, León, Asturias and central Portugal
seems to have been taken by our second group.

Fig. 84

The second group is represented by pottery with stamped or
combed decoration; this tends to cover much of the surface of
the pot and is sometimes associated with bosses of metal or
amber set in round or oval hollows, which were often left
empty, or became empty, ringed by dotted rays or *tremolo* lines
executed with a rocked tracing tool like those commonly
engraved on late Hallstatt bronze belt-plaques in south-west
Germany. As with the first group, there are regional variants,
one on the western Meseta in León, chiefly known from the
hill-forts and associated cemeteries of Las Cogotas de Cardeñosa and Osera, Chamartín de la Sierra (Ávila). Many of the
patterns on the stamped ware from these sites closely resemble
those on the Hallstatt D pottery of southern Bavaria and some
of the associated forms seem to point in the same direction.
Another variant – pottery decorated in horizontal friezes
separated by girth-grooves, filled with stamped ring-and-dot,
cables and rows of schematized 'ducks' – is above all characteristic of the *castros* of Galicia, northern Portugal and Asturias
although examples occur as far east as the neighbourhood of
Valladolid in what became the territory of the Vaccaei. This
pottery seems to be related to the La Tène A ware of the
fifth century BC in western Austria, Bohemia, Moravia and
eastern Bavaria. It would seem, then, that in addition to a
series of folk-movements from eastern and southern France,
beginning about the end of the seventh century with a movement into the Upper Ebro basin and continuing in the sixth
century with expansion in the southern areas of the peninsula,
there was another series of movements in the late sixth and
extending into the fifth century BC from the neighbourhood of

Fig. 82i, j
Fig. 82k

Fig. 82g, h

Fig. 82f
Plate 64

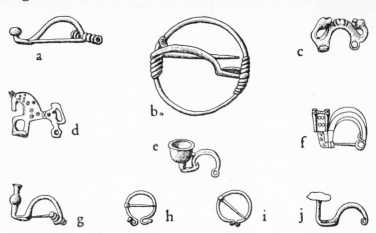

Fig. 87. Early Iron Age brooch types of the north-west: a, Ampurias (Gerona); b, Lara (Burgos); c, Tineo (Asturias); d, Numantia (Soria); e, Miraveche (Burgos); f, Osera (Avila); g, Sabroso (Braga); h-i, Briteiros (Braga); j, Cidade Velha, Santa Luzia (Pontevedra) (a, c-e after Schüle, b after Cuadrado, f after J. Cabré, g-i after M. Cardozo, j after Leeds). a, b 1 :2; c-j 1 : 4

the upper Danube into the north-western areas of the peninsula, possibly passing mainly overland through the western Pyrenees but to some extent by sea from the Gironde to Galicia.

As we have said, the invaders do not seem to have brought with them metalworkers in sufficient numbers or of a high enough standard to establish an independent industry of Celtic Hallstatt tradition comparable with that founded by their potters: they were soon content with the output of the native metalworkers. There are, indeed, a few types which may have been introduced by the Celtic invaders in the seventh or sixth century BC, or have reached the peninsula after the inva-sion as a result of some continuing contact with the homeland: antenna-handled swords and daggers akin to ones found in some Celtic areas north of the Pyrenees in Hallstatt C or D; belt-clasps of types related to the early example from Agullana,

Fig. 88

Fig. 75e

246

and a few brooches of Hallstatt D2-3 or early La Tène types. *Fig. 87a-c* But there is now some uncertainty, as a result of the work of Sangmeister and Schüle, as to whether all of these types really were of Celtic origin. The antenna-handled sword may, in fact, have been transmitted to the Celts north of the Pyrenees and the late Urnfield people of Languedoc and Catalonia alike by the Ligurians of north-west Italy, along with special ceramic forms like pedestals decorated with openwork or horizontal godrooning and brooches in the form of a horse, *Fig. 87d* which are equally popular in northern Italy and the north-eastern Meseta (Miraveche, Mota del Marqués, Las Cogotas, etc.) at this time. It is striking that the peninsular series of antenna-handled daggers seems to begin with ones made entirely of bronze, fairly common in Galicia and Asturias, *Fig. 88a* some of which have deeply incurving ricassos like those on late examples of the 'carp's-tongue' group from northern Italy and the Monte Sa Idda hoard, Sardinia. One of these was apparently found with a leaf-shaped bronze sword at Sobre- *Fig. 74b* foz, Ponga (Asturias). One might suspect a survival of the 'Atlantic' bronze industry of the north-west in this context, influenced by contacts with northern Italy, and it is still possible that some of the late 'carp's-tongue' swords from the upper Tagus and lower Guadiana and Guadalquivir basins were wielded by Celtic settlers of the sixth century BC. It is certainly true that the iron-using 'post-Hallstatic' industry, whose metalwork is so plentiful in the cremation cemeteries of the northern Meseta, is never associated with the earliest, hand-made pottery found in these cemeteries, which we have already referred to as showing the closest connection with west-central European late Hallstatt groups. On the other hand there is no doubt as to the Celtic origin of the kettledrum – or *Fig. 87e, f* tower-footed – brooches so common in the Douro basin and the north-west, or of the influence of the Celtic Hallstatt D3 crossbow brooch on the evolution of the specifically Iberian

annular brooches, some of which seem to have taken over the
characteristically western Hallstatt kettledrum foot and developed it in a local manner. In the fifth century, too, specifically
early La Tène forms of brooch reached the peninsula – not
only the La Tène A cast double bird-headed form but the La
Tène Ia wire-made form which appears occasionally in
Catalonia and on the northern Meseta. At the cemetery of Las
Cogotas (Avila) associations show that the latter belongs to
the horizon of the north-western combed and stamped ware.

Fig, 87b

Fig. 87c

THE NATIVE REACTION

We have already referred to the power of the Iberian and
Tartessian cultures of the eastern and southern coastal areas to
absorb the barbarian invaders who were continually being
attracted towards them by their wealth. Under Punic and
Greek influence these cultures became increasingly urban in
character and developed industrial centres producing sophisticated wheel-turned and even painted pottery and an elaborate
metalwork; this formed an important element in the 'post-
Hallstattico' which developed on the Meseta from the fifth
century BC onwards. In its early stages already described above
(p. 237) that metal industry may well, as Schüle has argued,
have influenced the development of western Hallstatt D2–3
metal forms, especially of brooches of the 'crossbow' type with
turned-up, knobbed foot; and its sophisticated jewellery,
directly or through the pre-Celtic jewellers of the Atlantic
regions of the peninsula, may have influenced the style of gold
ornaments found in Celtic Hallstatt 'chieftain' graves north
and west of the Alps. But the hybrid cultures which we find
developing on the Meseta and along the Atlantic coasts from
the fifth century onwards owed a great deal not only to the
'Iberian' culture of the Mediterranean seaboard but to the more
backward pre-Celtic peoples of the Meseta – the makers of the

Fig. 87a

Fig. 75n

'Boquique' and early chip-carved pottery. These may well have been the 'Cempsi' of the early historical sources among whom the Celts infiltrated from their original centres along the Ebro and on the north-eastern Meseta – and those of the northwest, – the makers of the final Beaker ware and other Bronze Age wares of northern Portugal and Galicia, who transmitted the axe and snake cults which survived in the north-west to the time of the Roman conquest and may have been the Saefes of the *Periplus*.

The distinctive metal types of the 'post-Hallstattico' will be discussed presently when we consider the 'Meseta' cultures, but the most striking contribution of the pre-Celtic and pre-Iberian communities to Iron Age culture in the peninsula is probably the remarkable gold and silver jewellery which was produced in Portugal and Galicia during the last few centuries before the Roman conquest. This jewellery seems to carry on the traditions represented by the Villena hoard and various Late Bronze Age finds from Portugal already mentioned (p. 219). The craftsmen who produced it seem at first to have been centred on the *Castro* culture of central Portugal, represented by such sites as Pragança (Estramadura) and Santa Olaya near Figueira da Foz, which is far less well known to us from published excavations than that of the north-west, but seems to have remained relatively unaffected by Celtic immigration. This industry apparently revived the Early Bronze Age lunula form, represented notably by a silver example with embossed boars and human masks of Middle La Tène inspiration, associated with silver torcs formed of multiple twisted strands like some British Early Iron Age torcs, at Chã de Lamas, Miranda do Corvo (Beira Alta), and now preserved at the National Museum in Madrid. The technique of embossed dots and cones was similarly transmitted by the later Atlantic jewellers through the gold diadem and cones from Mira de Aire, Porto de Mós, the bracelet from Bougado and the discs from Outeiro da Cabeça, Torres Vedras, not only to various Celtic Hallstatt ornaments but to gold earrings of the

Plate 58   north-western *Castro* culture, like that from Laundos, Povoa de Varzim, which probably last into the Roman period. The hooked terminals of the late lunulae appear also on certain

Plate 56   gorgets formed of solid bars or curving strips, which recall

Fig. 88.   Early Iron Age weapons: a, bronze dagger from the Castro de Coubueira (Lugo); b, iron short sword from Aguilar de Anguita (Guadalajara); c, iron short sword from Osera (Ávila); d, iron dagger (Miraveche type) from Osera (Ávila) (a-b after Schüle, c-d after J. Cabré). 1 : 4

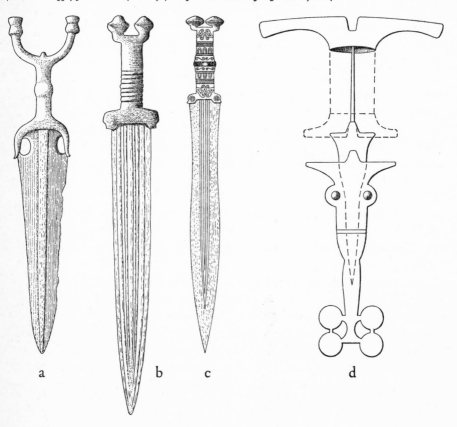

a   b   c   d

those of Sintra and Penela (p. 000 above), but one of which, associated with other ornaments of Sintra affinity in the hoard from Herdade do Alamo, Moura (Alemtejo), bears ring and dot decoration probably derived from the Celtic Hallstatt culture. These same jewellers may have been the source of various gold bracelets, torcs, earrings and hollow spherical pendants found in Celtic Hallstatt 'chieftain' graves in eastern France, southern Germany and Switzerland and perhaps even of the elaborate 'diadem' worn by the princess at Vix-sur-Châtillon; so at any rate, Schüle has argued on the strength of many resemblances in technique and decorative detail.

Plate 55

Further north-east, in Old Castile and further north, in Galicia, regional schools of jewellery developed as the Iron Age advanced. The outstanding products of the former are the gold horse-head terminals from Saldaña (Palencia). The latter is the most remarkable, however, for the variety of its types, which include the strange 'diadems' formed of rectangular sheets of gold leaf with embossed decoration – one from Cangas de Onís (Asturias) combining embossed dots of ancient tradition with rows of S-motifs of immigrant Hallstatt origin, and others from Ribadeo (Lugo) with processions of infantry-men and cavalrymen like those on certain Hallstatt D belt-plaques from southern Germany but some of them wearing crested helmets of an Iberian type, alternating with bearers of *situlae* recalling those on the Certosa *situla* of the fifth century BC. The similarly constructed brassards from Elviña (Coruña) combine the usual embossed dots with whirligigs of Middle La Tène inspiration. Commonest of all in the north-west are the gold and silver torcs, sometimes seen on the warrior statues of the same area, and represented by the simple example from Chaves (Traz-os-Montes). Many examples have more elaborate decoration of the hoop and the terminals, some of it of La Tène inspiration, like 'duck' pattern and multiple S-friezes similar to those found on the stamped pottery of the

Plate 57

same region, while some terminals, like certain earrings and pendants from necklaces, have whirligigs like those on the Elviña brassards.

THE MESETA CEMETERIES

As has been said, most of our systematic knowledge of the Celtic invasions of the Meseta, spreading from, or through, the original areas of settlement in the Ebro valley and on the north-eastern Meseta, down the great river valleys to the Atlantic and the Andalusian coast, is derived from study of material from cremation cemeteries which at some sites, at least, includes a considerable number of recorded grave-groups that permit the construction of a rough typological sequence of pottery, arms and personal ornaments. Unfortunately the earlier graves in these cemeteries contain little but the hand-made pottery which indicates the presence of a cultural element akin to that of the sixth-century 'Urnfield Renaissance' in France. These, at any rate, show the uniformity over a large area that one might expect in a migration period. Thereafter there is a divergence: as grave goods become more plentiful, in the fifth and fourth centuries BC, regional groups appear, partly defined by their degree of assimilation to the Ibero-Punic culture of the coasts. The characteristic 'post-Hallstatic' metalwork originally devel-oped from Celtic foundations, but with much Iberian in-fluence, in the upper valley of the Tagus, where the cemetery ples of the narrow antenna-handled iron dagger with parallel-

Fig. 88b   sided blade, is the chief site; such early types do not appear in Portugal or Andalusia, where it is clear that Iberian culture soon got the upper hand; but they spread northwards through Navarre and the Basque area into south-western France where they must be associated with the semi-Iberian Aquitanians of Caesar. Even among the Carpetani, in part of the Upper Tagus basin, Iberian and indeed Greek imported wheel-turned pottery was displacing the native hand-made wares as early as the fourth century BC, as the finds from Las Madrigueras, Carrascosa del Campo (Cuenca) suggest; at the same time Celtiberian material culture, as the excavations at Numantia showed, had lost most of its Celtic aspect a century later.

Further north, in what had become the territory of the Vaccaei by the third century BC, and in the middle basin of the Douro, a different culture was implanted about the beginning of the fifth century by the makers of stamped and combed ware coming probably from the Loire mouth, and this later evolved its own type of dagger known as that of Miraveche from a cemetery in the province of Burgos, and had its own range of brooch types in which the late Hallstatt and La Tène element is much stronger than further south. In what became the territory of the Vettones the cemeteries of Las Cogotas de Cardeñosa and Osera (Ávila) show the later stage of the Tagus group, with its leaf-bladed dagger, often decorated on the pommel and scabbard with silver-and-copper-inlaid patterns which only occasionally echo those of Middle La Tène, mingling with products of the Douro culture in the fourth and third centuries BC. In this group contact with the Middle La Tène culture beyond the Pyrenees is also reflected by the occasional plain, wheel-turned, cordoned and pedestalled bowls and by brooches of La Tène Ic and II forms: once again, sea connections with the Loire estuary are likely, and finds in the Cantabrian area are a link. The later graves in all these 'Meseta' groups reflect a warlike culture in which cavalry, to judge by the abundant horse-harness and the historical references, was important. The small, round Iberian shield (known also from statues in the north-western *Castro* culture) takes the place of the oblong Middle La Tène form, but long swords like those associated with the latter type of shield occasionally appear. The graves are sometimes arranged in rows marked by

Fig. 88d

Fig. 87c, e

Fig. 88c

Fig. 82l

Plate 66

steles (as at Aguilar de Anguita) or by small cairns (as at Osera). In the north-western *Castro* culture no rich cemeteries are known and cremation burials seem to have been deposited without grave goods in stone-lined shafts within the settlements.

SETTLEMENTS

Warfare between the various Celtic, Iberian and hybrid communities – intensified as first the Carthaginians, and then the Romans, sought to extend their influence in the peninsula and young tribesmen found a career for themselves as mercenaries in foreign wars, from the fifth century BC onwards – gave an increasing impetus, during the Early Iron Age, to the fortification of settlements. At first these fortifications drew their inspiration from the compact walled villages that the Iberians and their predecessors had long been building near the Mediterranean coasts, with a single line of defence, simple gateways and rows of oblong dwellings, built of adobe or of dry-stone, sometimes butted in a nearly continuous ring against the inner face of the defences. A number of small enclosures of this type have been explored in the eastern uplands of Old Castile, where influence from the lower Ebro basin had been strong for some time past (pp. 230-2, 252), and one site, Arévalo de la Sierra (Soria), actually had oblong huts built against the rampart in the Iberian manner. Castelfrío de la Sierra (Soria) is more typical of this early, pre-'Celtiberian' type in use from the sixth to the fourth century BC, in that the dwellings left no trace and were apparently built of perishable materials. The distinctive feature of these sites and of other early forts further west in the western Meseta and Galicia are the *chevaux de frise* (cavalry obstacles) formed of rough stone pillars placed in a broad belt immediately outside the ramparts – a feature apparently elsewhere matched only at certain early hill-forts in west and north Wales. Like the Iberian villages, these forts

Fig. 89

Fig. 90

rarely have ditches. In the area of the north-western *Castro* culture, in Galicia and Asturias, some small hill-top forts may be equally early, beginning with the introduction of the stamped ware already mentioned, *c.* 500 BC. The first phase of the fort of Cameixa, Carballino (Orense), which Cuevillas explored, would belong to this stage, as would the promontory fort at Cespón, Rianxo (Coruña).

After the fourth century BC the growth of large towns in the Iberian areas affected by Greek or Punic influence is reflected in the Celtic areas, by the appearance of large fortified

Fig. 89. *Hill-fort with chevaux-de-frise: Castilfrio de la Sierra (Soria) (after B. Taracena)*

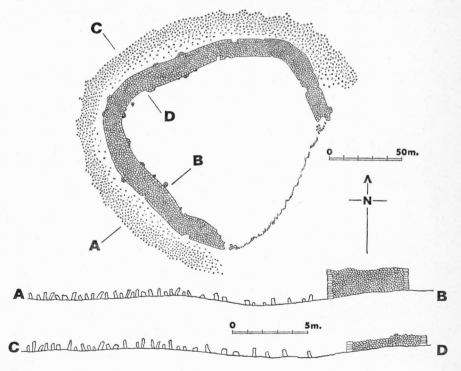

enclosures or *oppida*, which however differ from each other regionally according to the local economy and the degree of true urbanization. Strong Iberian influences from the Ebro valley finally led to the replacement of the Celtic Arevaci of eastern Old Castile by the 'Celtiberians', whose culture is represented by the town of Numantia, so extensively explored by Adolf Schulten. Here the system of streets and compact rectangular housing, with the painted pottery of Iberian affinity, illustrate the triumph of Mediterranean civilization over the rustic traditions of north-western Europe. Further north-west, in the territories of the corn-growing Vaccaei and the Cantabrian tribes, large hill-top *oppida* occur, as at Monte Bernorio (Palencia), but here the single or double walls only seem to enclose scattered round or oblong huts and the local 'Miraveche' culture lives on in the associated cemeteries. Further west and south in the territory of the Vettones, Lusitani and Carpetani the pastoral economy shaped a different development. Existing simple enclosures had annexes added to them laterally and at Mesas de Miranda (Chamartín de la Sierra) the walls of the third, outermost annexe were built over the cemetery (Osera). The *Castro* of Castillejos de Sanchorreja (Ávila) belongs to this segmented type in which one at least of the annexes served as a cattle compound, while at Las Cogotas (Ávila), a similar site, the road passing through the annexes was lined with examples of the crudely carved stone *verracos* (bulls or boars) which occur throughout the territories of these pastoral tribes in the western Meseta and, like the north-eastern warrior statues, reflect the influence of the contemporary Iberian sculptures of Andalusia. In the *Castro* culture of the north-west a more complex development is found: small hill-top forts like Cameixa (Orense), Meirás (Coruña) and S. Ciprián de Lás (Orense) come to be surrounded by concentric outer enclosures defended by widely-spaced walls or banks and ditches. These and other peculiar features

Fig. 90

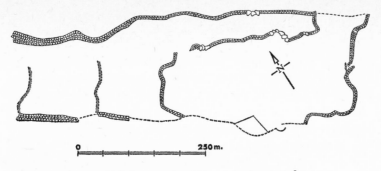

Fig. 90.   A segmented hill-fort: Los Castillejos en Sanchorreja (Ávila)

Fig. 91

Plate 65

seem to be echoed in the distinctive earthworks of the western and south-western B cultures of Britain. Other sites, however, developed by segmentation, as at Elviña (Coruña) and fresh sites built in the immediate pre-Roman phase, have single or double lines of walling which enclose a larger area, as at Terroso and Sabroso in the Minho province of Portugal, covered by scattered mainly circular huts; while a very large site, the Citania de Briteiros, Guimarães, with occupation continuing into the Roman period, has a concentric lay-out with numerous sub-rectangular as well as circular huts. All these sites show common technical features due to classical and Iberian influence – more massive ramparts, with multiple internal revetments, complicated overlapping entrances, bastions and guard chambers – these too echoed in British hill-forts – but local cultural differences emerge in the type and layout of the dwellings. At the beginning of the Early Iron Age circular huts built of adobe (as at Soto de Medinilla, Valladolid, in association with cultural elements derived from the final Urnfield and late Hallstatt groups of the middle Ebro) or perishable materials, were widespread in the upper Meseta – *e.g.* at the Castro de Saldeana (Salamanca) – as well as in the north-west, but the ancient tradition of oblong huts in the Vettonian area found in the Late Bronze Age at Berruecos

(Avila) persists in the Iron Age at Sanchorreja and Las Cogotas, where some of the huts were butted against the back of the
rampart. In the north-west the earlier round huts were generally
constructed of perishable materials, but stone construction,
sometimes with polygonal blocks established itself near the
coast in the immediate pre-Roman period (*c.* second century
BC), along with rotary querns which now at last replaced the
saddle-quern, and later spread further inland.

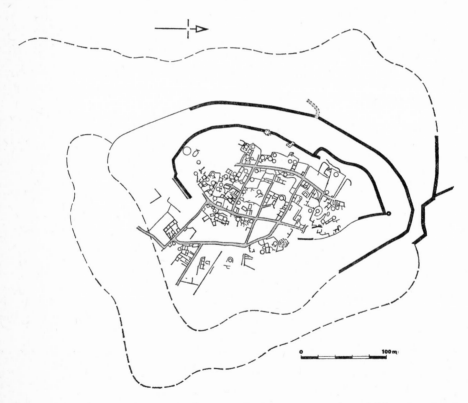

Fig. 91. A north-western concentric site: the Citania of Briteiros, Guimarães (Braga) (after M. Cardozo)

THE FINAL PHASE

The north-west, formerly the main centre of the final Atlantic bronze industry, became the last stronghold of prehistoric (if not Iberian) cultural forms in the peninsula. When the power of Rome finally asserted itself, in this area too, towards the end of the first century BC, some of those forms persisted on sites like Briteiros and Coaña in the Asturias, where scattered circular and subrectangular houses, only occasionally incor-porated in a system of streets, for long continued to be inhabited and the art of carving the doorways of the more important dwellings with raditional designs persisted. Circular houses are, indeed, still inhabited by the peasants in some remote mountain villages in the interior of Galicia. In this remote region of the north-west, it was the pre-Iberian and pre-Celtic that had the longest survival.

Chronological Table

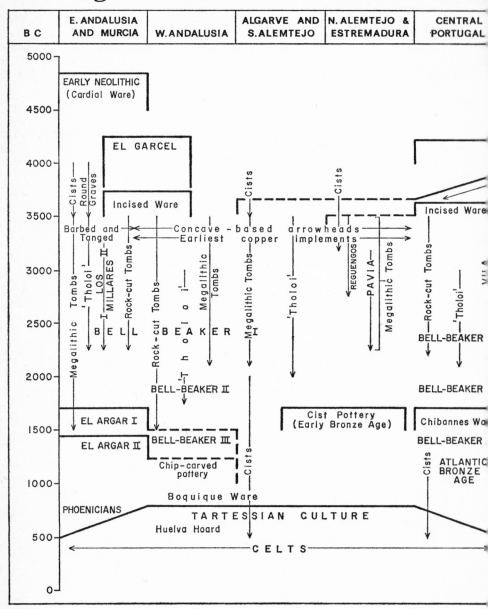

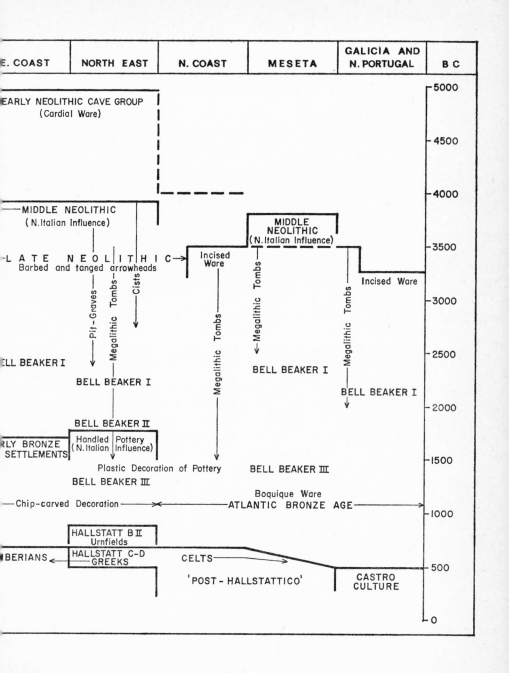

E. COAST	NORTH EAST	N. COAST	MESETA	GALICIA AND N. PORTUGAL	B C

Bibliography

General works

ALMAGRO, M., *Orígen y Formación del Pueblo Hispano*, Barcelona, 1958.
BOSCH-GIMPERA, P., *Etnología de la península Ibérica*, Barcelona, 1932.
—, *La Formación de los Pueblos de España*, Mexico City, D.F., 1945.
PERICOT, L., *La España primitiva y Romana* (Vol. I of *Historia de España*, Instituto Gallach, Barcelona, 1942).
—, *La España Primitiva*, Barcelona, 1950.
PIDAL, R. Menéndez (*ed.*), *Historia de España*, Vol. I, Parts 1–3. Madrid, 1947, 1952, 1954.
SANTA OLALLA, J. M., *Esquema Paletnológico de la Península Ibérica*, Madrid, 1946.

CHAPTER I

AGUIRRE, E., *Las Gándaras de Budiño, Porriño (Pontevedra)* (Excavaciones Arqueológicas en España, 31), Madrid, 1963.
ALMAGRO, M., El Paleolítico Español (Part III, chapters I–IV of Pidal, *Historia...* 1947).
—, El Paleolítico Superior en España: sus problemas y peculiaridades. (Chapter V in *Manual de Historia Universal*, Vol. I), Madrid, 1960.
—, *Las pinturas rupestres cuaternarias de la cueva de Maltravieso en Cáceres*, Madrid, 1960.
BREUIL, H., *et al.*, *La Pileta de Benaoján*, Monaco, 1913.
BREUIL, H. and OBERMAIER, H., *The Cave of Altamira*, Madrid, 1935.
BREUIL, H. and ZBYSZEWSKI, G., Contribution à l'étude des industries paléolithiques du Portugal et de leurs rapports avec la géologie du Quaternaire. *Comunicações dos Serviços Geológicos de Portugal*, XXIII (1942), 3–369 and XXVI (1945), 3–662.
GLORY, A., *et al.* La Grotte ornée d'Escoural (Portugal), *Bulletin de la Société Préhistorique Française*, 1965, 110–117.
JORDÁ, F., La Cova Negra de Bellús (Játiva) y sus industrias líticas, *Archivo de Prehistoria Levantina*, II, (1945), 11–29.
—, *El Solutrense en España y sus Problemas*, Oviedo, 1955.

LEROI-GOURHAN, A., *Préhistoire de l'art occidental,* Paris, 1965. (English ed. *The Art of Prehistoric Man,* London, 1968).

McBURNEY, C. B. M., *The Stone Age of Northern Africa,* Harmonds-worth, 1960.

OBERMAIER, H., *Fossil Man in Spain,* London, 1925.

PERICOT, L., *La Cueva de Parpalló,* Madrid, 1942.

ROCHE, J., Le Paléolithique supérieur portugais. Bilan de nos connais-sances et problèmes, *Bulletin de la Société Préhistorique Française,* 1965, 11–27.

SIEVEKING, A. and G., *The Caves of France and North Spain,* London, 1962.

SMITH, P. E. L., The Solutrean Culture, *Scientific American,* Aug., 1964, 86–94.

CHAPTER II

ALMAGRO, M., In Pidal, *Historia...,* Part III, chapters V–VI.

—, *Manual de Historia Universal,* I, 1960, chapter VII.

—, *El Covacho con pinturas rupestres de Cogul (Lérida),* Lérida, 1952.

BREUIL, H., *Les peintures rupestres schématiques de la Péninsule Ibérique,* 4 vols. 1933–5.

BREUIL H. and BURKITT, M., *Rock Paintings of Southern Andalusia,* Oxford, 1929.

CABRÉ, J., *El Arte rupestre en España,* Madrid, 1916.

CAMÓN, J., *Las Artes y los Pueblos de la España Primitiva,* Madrid, 1954, 303–477.

HERNANDEZ PACHECO, E., *Prehistoria del Solar Hispano,* Madrid, 1959, chapters VI–VII.

OBERMAIER, H., *Fossil Man in Spain,* 1925.

PERICOT, L., La Cueva de la Cocina (Dos Aguas), *Archivo de Prehis-toria Levantina,* II, (1945), 39–71.

PERICOT, L. and RIPOLL E.*(eds.),* *Prehistoric Art of the Western Mediter-ranean and the Sahara,* Chicago, 1965.

ROCHE, J., *Le Gisement Mésolithique de Moita do Sebastião,* Lisbon, 1960.

—, Observations sur la stratigraphie et la chronologie des amas de coquil-liers mésolithiques de Muge (Portugal), *Bulletin de la Société Préhistorique Française,* 1965, 130–38.

CHAPTER III

ÅBERG, N., *La Civilisation Enéolithique dans la Péninsule Ibérique*, Upp-sala, 1921.

BREA, L. BERNABÒ, *Arene Candide*, I-II, Bordighera, 1946 and 1956.

COLOMINAS, J., *La Prehistoria de Montserrat*, Montserrat, 1925.

CUNHA, E. DA and PRESCOTT, E., O Castro eneolitico de Olelas, *Comunicações dos Serviços Geológicos de Portugal*, XXXIX (1958), 87-125.

FONTON, M. ESCALON DE, Préhistoire de la Basse Provence, *Préhistoire*, XII, 1956.

GOMEZ-MORENO, M., La Cerámica primitiva Ibérica, *Homenagem a Martins Sarmento*, Guimarães, 1933, 125-36.

JIMENEZ, J., Excavaciones en Cueva Ambrosio, *Noticiario Arqueológico Hispanico*, V (1956-61), 13-48.

MUÑOZ, A. M. *Cultura Neolítica Catalana*, Barcelona, 1965.

PELLICER, M., *El Neolítico y el Bronce de la Cueva de la Carigüela de Piñar (Granada)* Madrid, 1964.

—, *Estratigrafía Prehistórica de la Cueva de Nerja*, Madrid, 1963.

SANTA OLALLA, J. M., La fecha de la cerámica a la almagre en el Neo-lítico Hispano-Mauritano, *Cuadernos de Historia Primitiva*, III (1948), 95-106.

SAN VALERO, J., *La Cueva de la Sarsa*, Valencia, 1950.

—, El Neolítico Europeo y sus Raíces, *Cuadernos de Historia Primitiva*, IX-X (1954-5) 16-24.

SANTOS, J. R. DOS, Jr. *As pinturas pré-históricas do Cachão da Rapa*, Opor-to, 1933.

SOBRINO, R., *Corpus Petroglyphorum Gallaeciae*, Santiago, 1935.

TARRADELL, M., Problemas Neolíticos, *Primer Symposium de Prehistoria Peninsular*, Pamplona, 1959.

TEIXEIRA, C. and MENDES CORRÊA, A., *A Jazida Pré-histórica de Eira Pedrinha* (Serviços Geológicos de Portugal), Lisbon, 1949.

CHAPTER IV

ALBUQUERQUE E CASTRO, L. DE and VEIGA FERREIRA, O. DA, O Dólmen pintado de Antelas, *Comunicações dos Serviços Geológicos de Por-tugal*, XXXVIII i (1957), 325-46.

BALLESTER, I., Excavaciones en 'Cova de la Pastora' (Alcoy), *La Labor del Servicio de Investigación Prehistórica, 1940–1948,* Valencia, 1949, 41–65.

BARANDIARAN J. M. DE and MEDRANO, D. F., Excavaciones en Alava, *Zephyrus,* IX (1958), 5–33.

CORREIA, V., *El Neolítico de Pavia* (Memória 27, Comisión de Investigaciones Paleolíticas y Prehistóricas), Madrid, 1921.

DANIEL, G. E., *The Megalith Builders of Western Europe,* Harmondsworth, 1962.

—, *Corpus de Sepulcros Megalíticos,* fasc. 1–4 (1961–65). Instituto de Prehistoria y Arqueología de la Deputación Provincial de Barcelona.

LEISNER, G. and V., *Die Megalithgräber der Iberischen Halbinsel,* I: *Der Süden,* Berlin, 1943.

—, *Die Megalithgräber der Iberischen Halbinsel,* I: *Der Westen* (Madrider Forschungen, I, 1–2), Berlin, 1956–9.

LEISNER, V., *Die Megalithgräber der Iberischen Halbinsel,* I: *Der Westen* (Madrider Forschungen I, 3) Berlin, 1965.

LEISNER, G. and V., *Antas do Concelho de Reguengos de Monsaraz,* Lisbon, 1951.

LEISNER, G. and V. and CERDÁN MARQUEZ, C., *Los Sepulcros Megalíticos de Huelva* (Informes y Memorias, No. 26, Comisaría General de Excavaciones Arqueológicas), Madrid, 1952.

—, *Antas dos Arredores de Evora,* Evora, 1949.

—, *Antas nas herdades da Casa de Bragança no Concelho de Estremoz,* Lisbon, 1955.

MALUQUER DE MOTES, J., Arquitectura Megalítica Pyrenaíca, *Arquitectura Megalítica y Ciclopea Catalano-Balear* (ed. Pericot), Barcelona, 1965, 25–40.

MORÁN, P. C., *Excavaciones en Dolmenes de Salamanca y de Zamora* (Memórias 113 and 135 de la Junta Superior de Excavaciones), 1930 and 1935.

OBERMAIER, H., *El Dolmen de Matarrubilla* (Memória 26, Comisión de Investigaciones Paleolíticas y Prehistóricas), Madrid, 1919.

PERICOT, L., *Los Sepulcros Megalíticos Catalanes y la Cultura Pirenaïca,* 2 edn., Barcelona, 1950.

SANTOS ROCHA, A. DOS, *Antigüedades prehistóricas do Concelho de Figueira da Foz,* Coimbra, 1898–1900 (reprinted, Coimbra, 1949).

CHAPTER V

ÅBERG, N., *La Civilisation Enéolithique dans la Péninsule Ibérique,* Uppsala, 1921.

BLANCE, B., Early Bronze Age Colonists in Iberia, *Antiquity,* 1961, 192–202.

JALHAY, E. and PAÇO, A. DO, A Gruta II da Necropole de Alapraia, *Anais da Academia Portuguesa da Historia,* Lisbon, Vol. IV (1941), 107–40.

LEISNER, V., *Die Megalithgräber der Iberischen Halbinsel:* I: *Der Westen* (Madrider Forschungen, 1/3) Berlin, 1965.

LEISNER, V. et al., *Les Grottes Artificielles de Casal do Pardo (Palmela) et la Culture du Vase Campaniforme* (Memória 8 (n.s.) dos Serviços Geológicos de Portugal), Lisbon, 1961.

—, *Grutas Artificiais de São Pedro de Estoril,* Lisbon, 1964.

NIETO, G., La Cueva Artificial de la Loma de los Peregrinos en Alguazas (Murcia), *Ampurias,* XXI (1959), 189–244.

PAÇO, A. DO, El Castro de Vila Nova de San Pedro, *Actas y Memorias dela Sociedad Española de Antropología, Etnografía y Prehistoria,* XX (1945), 5–93.

—, *cf. Ampurias* XXI (1959), 252–60; *Arqueología e Historia* 8s. iii (1954), 3–80 and vii (1956), 95–114; *Anais da Academia Portuguesa da História,* 2s. VIII (1958), 43–91.

PAÇO, A. Do and SANGMEISTER, E., Vila Nova de S. Pedro, eine befestigte Siedlung der Kupferzeit in Portugal, *Germania,* XXXIV (1956), 211–30.

—, Necropole de Alapraia, *Anais da Academia Portuguesa da Historia,* 2s. VI (1955), 25–140.

PELLICER, M., Cerro del Greal, Iznalloz (Granada), *Ampurias,* XIX–XX (1957–8) 123–33.

SCHER, S. B. *Los Enterramientos en Cuevas Artificiales del Bronce,* I *Hispánico* (Biblioteca Praehistoria Hispana, VI) Madrid, 1964.

CHAPTER VI

ÅBERG, N., *La Civilisation Enéolithique dans la Péninsule Ibérique,* Uppsala, 1921.

ALMAGRO, M. and ARRIBAS, A., *El Poblado y la Necrópolis Megalíticos de los Millares* (Biblioteca Praehistorica Hispana, Vol. III) Madrid, 1963.

ARRIBAS, A., El Urbanismo peninsular durante el bronce primitivo, *Zephyrus*, X (1959), 81–128.

—, Megalitismo peninsular, *Primer Symposium de Prehistoria de la Peninsula Ibérica*, Pamplona, 1960, 69–102.

ARRIBAS, A. with TOPP, C., A Survey of the Tabernas Material lodged in the Museum of Almeria, *Bulletin of the Institute of Archaeology*, London, V (1965), 69–89.

CRAWFORD, O. G. S., *The Eye Goddess*, London, 1956.

CUADRADO, J., Almizaraque: la mas antigua explotación de la plata en España, *Congreso Arqueológico del Sudeste Español* III (1946), 168–85.

LEISNER, G. and V., works cited for Chapter V.

PAÇO, A. DO, works cited for Chapter V.

SANGMEISTER, E. *et al.*, *Excavacões no castro eneolítico do Zambujal, Torres Vedras, 1964.* Torres Vedras, 1967.

SCHUBART, H., As duas fases de ocupação do túmulo de cúpula do Monte do Outeiro, nos arredores de Aljustrel, *Revista de Guimarães*, 1965, 195–204.

SIRET, L., *Questions de Chronologie et d'Ethnographie Ibériques*, I, Paris, 1913 (Chapters II–IV).

VEIGA, E. DA, *Antiguidades monumentães do Algarve*, I–IV, Lisbon, 1886–91

CHAPTER VII

ARNAL, J., Les boutons perforés en V, *Bulletin de la Société Préhistorique. Française*, 1954, 255–68.

BRAY, W., Sardinian Beakers, *Proceedings of the Prehistoric Society*, 1964, 75–98.

DEL CASTILLO, A., *La Cultura del Vaso Campaniforme*, Barcelona, 1928.

—, La Gran Cultura Hispanica del pleno Eneolítico: el Vaso Campaniforme' (Pidal, *Historia...*, I. 1, part IV, Chapter III).

—, Las tres capas de la cueva de la Mora de Somaén (Soria), *Anuario de Prehistoria Levantina*, 1953, 135–50.

—, El Vaso Campaniforme, *IVth International Congress of Prehistoric and Protohistoric Sciences*, Madrid, 1954.

JODIN, A., Nouveaux documents sur la civilisation du vase campani‚ forme au Maroc. *Congrès préhistorique de France* XVI (1959) 677–86.

LEISNER, G. and V., works cited for Chapters V–VI.

MALUQUER, J., Nuevos hallazgos de la cultura del vaso campaniforme en la Meseta. *Zephyrus,* XI (1960), 119–30.

PAÇO, A. DO, works cited for Chapters V–VI.

—, A Estacão pré‚histórica de Montes Claros (Monsanto), *Lisboa e seu Termo,* I (1948), 51–8.

ROCHE, J. and VEIGA FERREIRA, O. DA, Revision des boutons per‚ forés en V de l'Enéolithique Portuguaise, *l'Anthropologie,* Paris 1961, 67–72.

SANGMEISTER, E., Exposé sur la civilisation du vase campaniforme, *Actes du Premier Colloque Atlantique,* Brest, 1961, 25–56.

SANTA OLALLA, J. M., Obras maestras hispánicas de la cerámica de estilo campaniforme, *Cuadernos de Historia Primitiva,* Madrid II (1947), 65–94.

SCHÜLE, W. and PELLICER, M., *El Cerro de la Virgen, Orce (Granada),* I (Excavaciones Arqueológicas en España, 46) Madrid, 1966.

TARADELL, M., Gar Cahal, *Germania,* 1955, 13–23.

—, Caf Taht El Gar, *Ampurias,* XIX‚XX (1957–8) 137–56.

CHAPTER VIII

ÅBERG, N., *La Civilisation Enéolithique dans la Péninsule Ibérique,* Uppsala, 1921.

ALCACER, J., El Puntal de Cambra, *Archivo de Prehistoria Levantina,* V (1954), 65–84.

BLANCE, B., The Argaric Bronze Age in Iberia, *Revista de Guimarães,* 1964, 129–42.

CARRIAZO, J. DE M., La Edad del Bronce, (Pidal, *Historia...* I. I. VI).

CASTILLO, A. DEL, El Pleno Eneolítico, (Pidal, *Historia...* I. I. IV, Chapter II).

FLETCHER D. and ALCACER, J., El Castillarejo de los Moros, *Archivo de Prehistoria Levantina,* VII (1958), 93–110.

GARCIA, M., El Poblado Argárico del cerro del Culantrillo en Gorafe (Granada), *Archivo de Prehistoria Levantina,* X (1963) 69–96.

HELENO, M., Joias pré‚romanas, *Ethnos,* I (1935), 229–257.

JUNGHANS, S., *et al.*, *Metallanalysen kupferzeitlicher und früh-bronzezeitlicher Bodenfunde aus Europa*, Berlin, 1960.

MACWHITE, E., *Estudios sobre las relaciones Atlánticas de la Península Ibérica en la edad del Bronce*, Madrid, 1951.

PERICOT, L., and PONSELL, F., El Poblado de 'Mas de Menente, Alcoy, *Archivo de Prehistoria Levantina*, I (1935), 101–110.

SANTA OLALLA, J. M., *Excavaciones en la Ciudad del Bronce Mediterráneo II, dela Bastida de Totana (Murcia)* (Informes y Memorias de la Comisión de Excavaciones Arqueologicas 16, 1947).

SANTOS, J. R. DOS, JR., A ceramica campaniforme de Mairos (Traz-os-Montes) *Homenagem*, 364–72.

SCHUBART, H., Grabungen auf dem bronzezeitlichen Gräberfeld von Atalaia in Süd Portugal, *Madrider Mitteilungen* V (1964), 11–54.

SERRA RAFOLS, J. DE C., Els Començos de la Mineria la Metallurgia del Coure a la Peninsula Ibérica, *Butlletí de l'Associació Catalana d'Antropologia, Etnologia y Prehistoria*, II (1924), 147–75.

SIRET, L., *Las primeras edades del metal en el Sudeste de España*, Barcelona, 1890.

—, *Questions de Chronologie et d'Ethnographie Ibériques*, Paris, 1913, Chapters VI and VII.

TARADELL, M., Sobre la delimitación geográfica de la cultura del Argar, *Congreso Arqueológico del Sudeste Español*, II (1946) 139–45.

TRINDADE L. and VEIGA FERREIRA, O. DA, Tesouro pré-histórico de Bonabal (Torres Vedras), *Revista de Guimarães*, 1964, 271–280.

CHAPTER IX

ALMAGRO, M., El Hallazgo de la Ría de Huelva y el Final de la Edad del Bronce en el Occidente de Europa, *Ampurias*, II (1940), 85–143.

—, Los Campos de Urnas de España (Part 1, Chapter III of Pidal, *Historia...* 1952).

—, España, *Inventaria Archaeologica*, fasc. 1–6, Madrid, 1958–62.

—, *Las Estelas Decoradas del Suroeste Peninsular* (Biblioteca Praehistorica Hispana) Madrid, 1966.

BOSCH-GIMPERA, P., *Two Celtic Waves in Spain*, Proceedings of the British Academy 1939.

CARDOZO, M., Novas urnas de largo Bôrdo horizontal, *Trabalhos da Sociedade Portuguesa de Antropologia,* Porto, 1936, 5–27.

—, 'Joalharia Lusitana', *Conimbriga,* I (1959), 13–27.

CARRIAZO J. M. and RADDATZ, D., *Madrider Mitteilungen* II (1961), 100–112.

HAWKES, C. F. C., Las Relaciones en el bronce final, entre la Peninsula Ibérica y las Islas Británicas con respecto a Francia y la Europa Central y Mediterránea, *Ampurias,* XIV (1952), 81–118.

HENCKEN, H., Carp's tongue swords in Spain, France and Italy, *Zephyrus,* VII (1956), 125–178.

MACWHITE, E., *op. cit.* VIII.

MALUQUER, J. M., *El Castro de los Castellejos en Sanchorreja,* Salamanca, 1958.

PALOL, P., *La Necropolis Hallstáttica de Agullana,* Madrid, 1958.

PELLICER, M. and SCHÜLE, W., *El Cerro del Real, Galera (Granada)* Excavaciones Arqueológicas en España, 52.

SAVORY, H. N., The Atlantic Bronze Age in south-west Europe, *Proceedings of the Prehistoric Society,* 1949, 128–155.

SCHÜLE, W., *Las Mas Antiguas Fibulas con Pié Alto y Ballesta,* Madrid, 1961.

—, Probleme der Eisenzeit auf der Iberischen Halbinsel, *Jahrbuch des Römisch-Germanischen Zentralmuseums Mainz,* VII, (1960), 59–125.

SOLER, J. M., *El Tesoro de Villena,* Madrid, 1965.

CHAPTER X

CABRÉ, J., Excaviones de las Cogotas, Cardeñosa (Avila), *Memórias de la Junta Superior de Excavaciones,* 110 (1929), and 120 (1932).

CARDOZO, M., *Citânia e Sabroso,* 5th ed. Guimarães, 1960.

—, Das Origens e Tecnica do Trabalho do Ouro, *Revista de Guimarães,* LXVII (1957), 5–46.

CUADRADO, E., *Precedentes y Prototipos de la Fibula Anular Hispanica,* Madrid, 1963.

CUEVILLAS, F. L., *Las Joyas Castreñas,* Madrid, 1951.

—, *La Civilización Celtica en Galicia,* Santiago, 1953.

—, Notas arqueolóxicas do castro de Cameixa, *Revista de Guimarães,* LVIII (1948), 288–305.

MALUQUER, J. M., Los Pueblos y las Tribus Celtas de España, (Chapter I of Pidal, *Historia...*, 1954, 5–194).

SANGMEISTER, E., Die Kelten in Spanien, *Madrider Mitteilungen*, I, 75–85.

SCHÜLE, W., *Las Mas Antigas Fibulas con Pié Alto y Ballesta*, Madrid, 1961.

—, Probleme der Eisenzeit, *Jahrbuch des Römisch-Germanischen Zentral-museums Mainz*, VII (1960), 59–125.

—, Frühe Antennenwaffen in Südwesteuropa, *Germania*, 38 (1960), 1–19.

Sources of Illustrations

The author wishes to thank Dr A. Arribas and the Barcelona Archae-ological Museum for the use of the following photographs: 6–8, 10, 20, 22, 25, 38, 41–8 and 60–61; the National Archaeological Museum, Madrid for 1, 26, 33a, e-g, 35–6, 39–40, 50, 53 and 62–3; Dr V. Leisner and Messrs Walter De Gruyter of Berlin for 14–19, 23–4, 29–30, 34 and 37; Dr M. Cardozo and the Museu Sarmento, Guimarães, for 33b–c, 49, 52, 54–5, 57–9 and 64–6; Dr D. Fletcher Valls and The Museum of the Service of Prehistoric Investigations, Valencia, for 4–5, 9, 11–12, 33d and 51; Dr J. M. Santa Olalla for 2–3 and 21; the Ashmolean Mu-seum, Oxford for 27–8 and the British Museum, London, for 56. Nos. 13 and 31–2 are the author's own photographs.

The line illustrations have all been redrawn from publications or from the author's own unpublished drawings, mostly by Mr Colin Williams of the Department of Archaeology, National Museum of Wales, but the following were redrawn by the author: figs. 9–17 and 84. Mr Michael Walker has kindly permitted the use of his own unpublished drawings, figs. 70c, 71. The sources of redrawn illustrations, which have already been published, may be gathered from the captions and the bibliog-raphy: the author's debt here to Dr. V. Leisner and Messrs Walter De Gruyter, publishers of *Die Megalithgräber der Iberischen Halbinsel*, 1943–65 is particularly obvious.

1

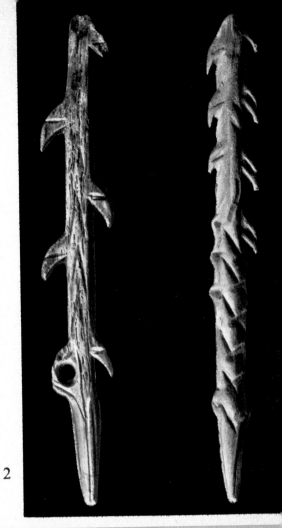

2

3

4

5

6

7

8

a

b

c

9   d   e

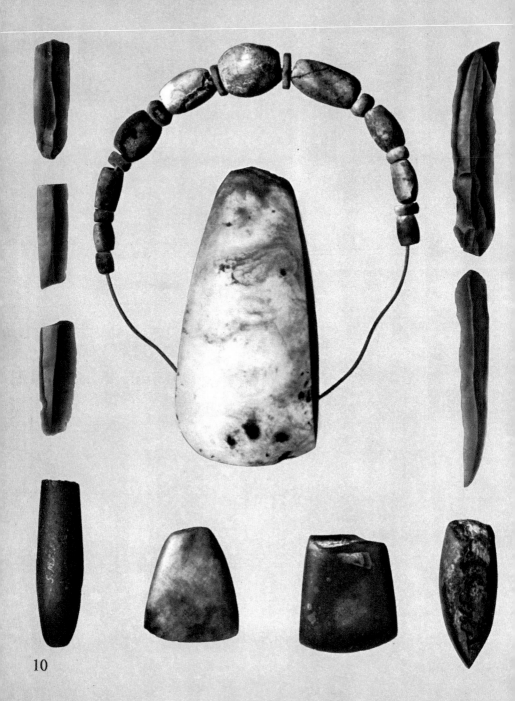

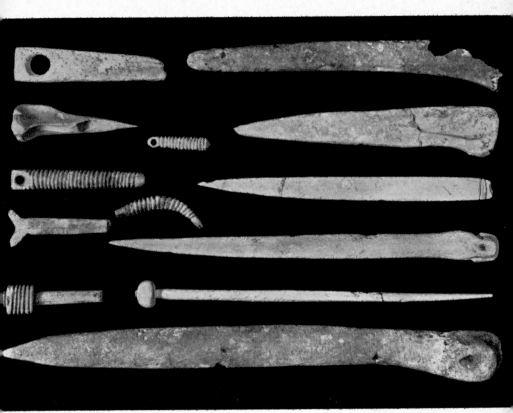

11

12

13

14

17

18

a

b

c

d

e

f

19

20

21

22

23

24

25

26

27

28

29

30

31

32

a

b

c

33

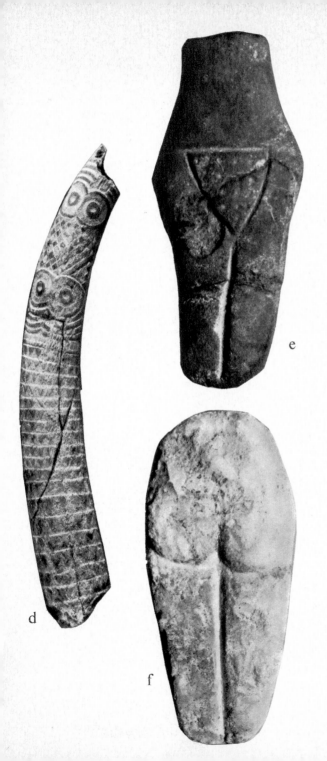

d

e

f

g

34

35

36

37

38

39

40

41

42

43

44

45

46

47

48

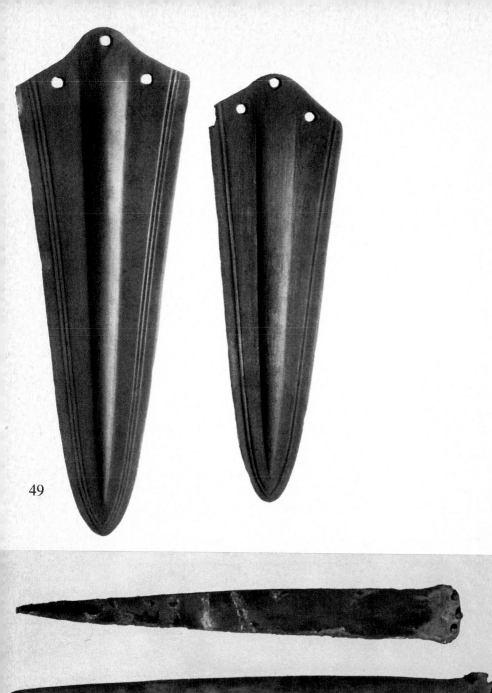

49

50

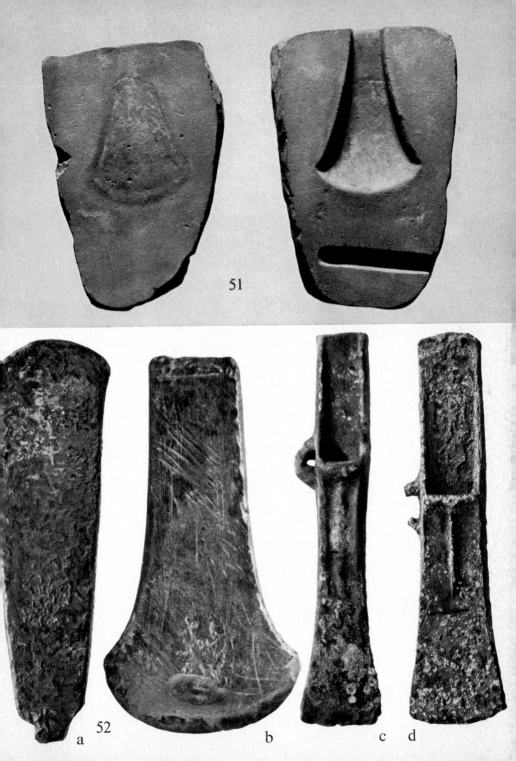

51

52   a   b   c   d

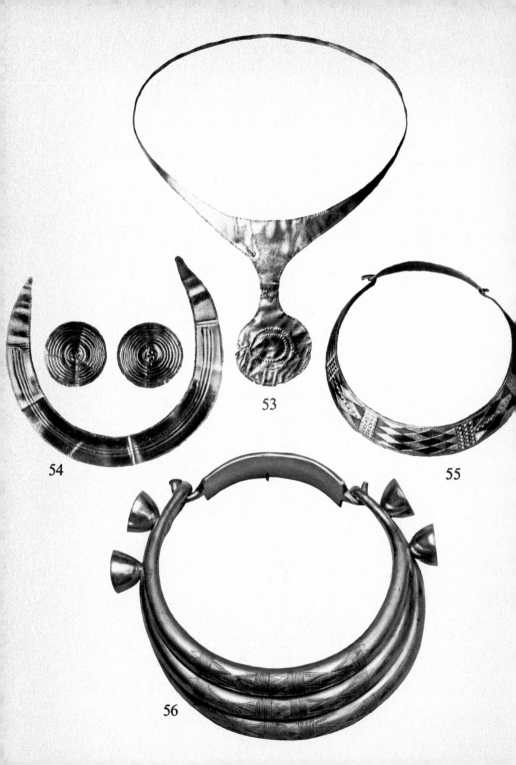

53

54

55

56

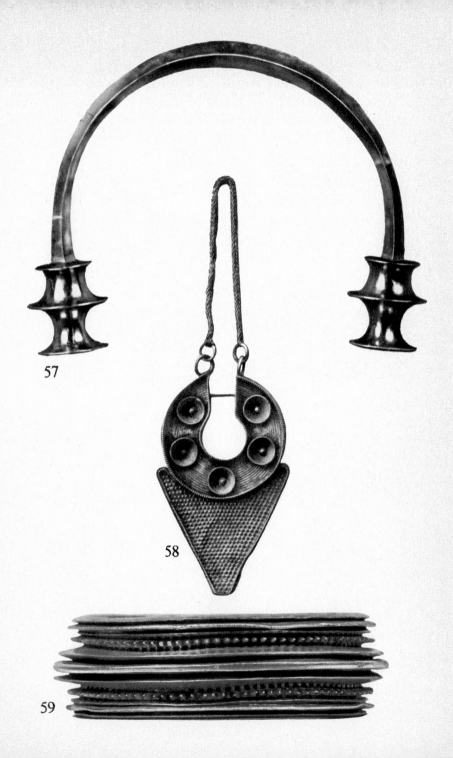

57

58

59

60

61

62

63

64

65

66

Notes on the Plates

1 S. Isidro (Madrid). Flaked flint hand-axe of advanced Acheulian type. Anthropological Museum, Madrid. Length: 15 cm.

2 Cave of El Pendo, Camargo (Santander). Late Magdalenian bone harpoons, one of them with a lateral loop for attachment – a feature anticipating the later Azilian harpoons. Santander Museum.

3 Cave of El Pendo, Camargo (Santander). 'Bâton de Commandement' (spear-shaft straightener?) of antler with engraved heads of deer. Santander Museum. Length: 16.5 cm.

4, 5 Cave of Parpalló, Gandia (Valencia). Two stone plaques, possibly artists' trial-pieces, of which 4983 were found in the cave. 4, like the majority of the plaques, is engraved, in this case with a horse's head. 5, with a horse's head painted in red (length: 38 cm.), comes from a late Solutrean level. Museum of the Service of Prehistoric Investigation, Valencia. L. Pericot, *La Cueva de Parpalló*, 1942.

6 Ancora (Viana do Castelo). Pebble tools of Asturian type, as found on raised beaches at many points on the coasts of northern Spain and Portugal. Archaeological Museum, Barcelona.

7 Cueva Bonica, Vallirana (Barcelona). Cardial pottery, with decoration impressed with a shell edge. Archaeological Museum, Barcelona. *Carta Arqueológica de España: Barcelona* (1955), 220.

8 Abric Romaní, Capellades (Barcelona). Necklace of *cypraea* shells, each about 3 × 2.5 cm., from an Upper Palaeolithic deposit. Archaeological Museum, Barcelona. *Anuari d'Estudis Catalans*, IV, 267.

9 Cueva de la Sarsa, Bocairente (Valencia) (a-c) and Coveta de l'Or, Beniarrés (Alicante) (d-e). Examples of cardial ware. Some of the impressed decoration, notably on c (20 cm. wide), is not made with a shell

Spain and Portugal

edge but with a comb-like tool, as in the later Bell Beaker ware. The hanging concentric semicircular patterns should be compared with those on Copper Age channelled ware (Fig. 42). Museum of the Service of Prehistoric Investigation, Valencia. *Noticiario Arqueológico Hispánico VI*.

10 S. Maria de Miralles, Igualada (Barcelona). Equipment of a pit grave, including a large polished axe-head of fibrolite, two small plump axe-heads of the same material, two stone chisels, flint knives and a necklace of large 'callais' beads – a green material of uncertain origin which first appears in the Neolithic graves of Catalonia. Archaeological Museum, Barcelona. The largest axe-head is 10 cm. long. *Anuari d'Estudis Catalans*, V, 811.

11 Cueva de la Pastora, Alcoy (Alicante). Selection of bone pins and pendants found with collective burials totalling over 40 in the cave. Many of the burials consisted of heaps of disarticulated bones, apparently re-buried, with the skulls (in some cases trepanned) placed on top, with the pins alongside, as though they had been worn in the hair. The crutch-headed pin relates to a Danubian form. The segmented pendant above it is 6 cm. long. Museum of the Service of Prehistoric Investigation, Valencia. *La Labor del S.I.P. y su Museo en los años 1940–48*, Pl. V.

12 Cueva de la Pastora. Black stone (steatite) pendant of anthropomorphic form, resembling one of ivory, said to be predynastic, in Cairo Museum. Length: 6.5 cm. Museum of the Service of Prehistoric Investigation, Valencia. *La Labor del S.I.P. y su Museo en los años 1940–48* IVB.

13 Dolmen do Porto de Cima de D. Miguel, Fontalva, Elvas (Evora). An example of the early form of megalithic cist and one of a group which was excavated in 1937 and yielded primitive grave goods – asymmetrical trapeze arrowheads and plump axe-heads. Photo H. N. Savory.

14 Anta do Silval, Evora. Exceptionally well-preserved megalithic Passage Grave, with entrance passage opening ESE and large slab sealing the gap between the innermost cover slab of the passage and the capstone of the high chamber, which would have been filled, in 'tholos' tombs,

306

by drystone vaulting. The greater part of the circular covering mound has been removed by wind erosion. The over/all length of chamber and passage is 8.3 m. G. and V. Leisner, *Die Megalithgräber der Iberischen Halbinsel: Der Westen (Madrider Forschungen I)*, Pl. 43.1.

15 Anta Grande da Comenda da Igreja, Montemor/o/Novo (Evora). Un/ usual not only in its size – the overall length of the chamber and passage is 15.30 m. and the chamber has a mean diameter of 4.65 m. and a height of 5 m. – but in its retention of most of its circular covering mound, diam. 35m. G. and V. Leisner, *ibid.*, Pl. 46.1.

16 Antela de Castillejo, Sardoeira, Vila Nova de Paiva (Viseu). Small rectangular chamber with door carved out of end slab: the sealing slabs have been removed. The carved door is a rare feature in the north/west of the peninsula, reflecting influences in the third millennium BC from the Millaran 'Tholos' Culture. The length of the cist is 2.4 m. G. and V. Leisner, *ibid.*, Pl. 63.2.

17 Anta Grande do Olival da Pega, Monsaraz (Evora). Selection of grave goods, including flint asymmetrical trapeze and concave/based arrow/ heads, segmented bone pin/heads and animal pendants, an undecorated anthropomorphic schist plaque (9.2 cm. long) and a miniature en/ graved schist crozier amulet. Portuguese Ethnological Museum, Belém. G. and V. Leisner, *Antas do Concelho de Reguengos de Monsaraz*, Lisbon, 1951.

18 Anta Grande do Olival da Pega. Sherds of decorated pottery, unusual for an Alemtejan megalithic tomb. The fragment of hemispherical bowl, bottom left, with impressed (nail) decoration in friezes and panels (10 cm. wide) recalls very early Neolithic pottery from the east Mediterranean. Two sherds (top left and bottom right) with punctured, white encrusted triangles resemble pottery from settlements of the Millaran culture (especially Almizaraque) and the ocular ('Mother Goddess') pattern on the remaining sherd also shows Millaran influence. Portuguese Ethno/ logical Museum, Belém. G. and V. Leisner, *ibid.*

19 Types of decorated schist plaque from the Alemtejo. The plaques accompanied individual corpses in the megalithic Passage Graves of

Spain and Portugal

advanced type. The earliest (a/b, from Olival da Pega (16 cm. long) and Anta do Paço, Reguengos) are engraved with purely geometric patterns. Later come sub-rectangular plaques (c–d) with ocular patterns added, possibly as a result of contact with the Millaran 'tholos' builders. Other late plaques (e–f) are plain or engraved with purely geometric patterns but have a schematic anthropomorphic outline reflecting the influence of the Almerian type of plaque-amulet (c–d from Anta 2 da Comenda (15 cm. long) Reguengos, e–f (18 and 15 cm. long) from Anta da Marquesa, Marvão (Portalegre). Portuguese Ethnological Museum, Belém.

20 Los Millares (Almería). Reconstruction model of 'tholos' tomb No. 17 (Leisner) (= No. 1, Almagro and Arribas), showing the chamber (right), 3.4 m. in diameter with its delicate orthostats, corbelled roof and low central pillar. The passage has three segments, separated by septal slabs with 'portholes'; the segment nearest to the chamber has small sub-rectangular side chambers. The circular cairn had two concentric perista-liths. Archaeological Museum, Barcelona. Almagro and Arribas, *El Poblado y la Necrópolis Megalíticos da los Millares*, Pl. 137a.

21 Cueva de Romeral, Antequera (Málaga). The entrance passage, looking in towards the door leading into the main chamber (see fig. 46).

22 Model of the Cova d'en Daina transitional Passage-Gallery Grave, Romañá de la Selva, Gabarras (Gerona). The actual chamber and passage are 8.25 m. long over-all and are set in a circular mound with peristalith. Archaeological Museum, Barcelona.

23 Praia das Maçãs, Sintra (Lisbon). View from the primary chamber on the western edge of the mound, with the passage leading to the ante-chamber of the primary chamber in the foreground and the secondary ('tholos') chamber in the background. V. Leisner, *Die Megalithgräber der Iberischen Halbinsel: Der Westen* (*Madrider Forschungen* I/3), Pl. 138.

24 Carenque, Lisbon, Rock-cut tomb No 3 from the east. The chamber is seen in the background: the 'man-hole' and the upper part of the vault

308

has been destroyed by weathering; the diameter near the base is 3.8 m. A broad entrance pit in the foregound leads, at an angle, into a long antechamber with curving recesses at the far end. G. and V. Leisner, *Die Megalithgräber der Iberischen Halbinsel: Der Westen (Madrider Forschungen 1)*, Pl. 40.3.

25 Puig Roig, Torrent (Gerona). Grave goods from a transitional Passage-Gallery grave with an over-all length of 11 m. set in a circular cairn nearly 18 m. in diameter. The plain pottery includes handled forms, probably of Early Bronze Age date (early second millennium BC); the long flint blades are characteristic of the Copper Age in all parts of the peninsula, the plain sub-rectangular schist plaques are characteristic of megalithic tombs in Catalonia and Languedoc and the prismatic V-perforated bone buttons are found on the Mediterranean coast of Spain in the Early Bronze Age. Archaeological Museum, Barcelona Ampurias, V (1943) 133; VII-VIII (1945–6) 323 and IX-X (1947–8) 317.

26 Los Millares (Almería). 'Tholos' No. 9. Bowl with incised 'wing' motif similar to that on Millaran 'Eye-Goddess' amulets. National Archaeological Museum, Madrid. Diameter: 11 cm.

27, 28 Los Millares (Almería). 'Tholos' No. 15 (Leisner). Footed bowl with engraved oculiform motif similar to that on Millaran amulets (Pl. 27) and decoration, including schematized deer like those seen on late petroglyphs (Fig. 16) (Pl. 28). Ashmolean Museum, Oxford. Diameter: 11 cm.

29 Anta 2 and 'tholos' of A Comenda, Reguengos de Monsaraz (Evora). View from SSW, with 'tholos' in the foreground and the megalithic chamber, with its much more massive slabs, in the background The entrance passage of the 'tholos' is seen on the right; that of the megalithic chamber is similarly aligned behind it but is concealed, being constructed, like its chamber, at a lower level. The maximum diameter of the 'tholos' chamber is 3.5 m. V. and G. Leisner, *Die Megalithgräber der Iberischen Halbinsel: Der Westen (Madrider Forschungen I/2)*, Pl. 78.

30   The 'tholos' of A Farisoa, Reguengos de Monsaraz (Evora). View from the WSW, showing the thin orthostats of the chamber, the maximum diameter of which was 4.5 m. G. and V. Leisner, *Antas do Concelho de Reguengos de Monsaraz*, Pl. 49.

31   Vila Nova de São Pedro (Santarém). The north side of the inner fortifi⁄cation, showing two bastions, with surviving facing of rough masonry, bonded with mixed clay and pounded chalk ('argamassa'). Photo H. N. Savory

32   Vila Nova de São Pedro (Santarém). View from the inner defences, looking W across a rock⁄cut storage or habitation pit of the first period, sealed by occupation layers on which the defences of the second period were built. The side of a bastion is seen in the left foreground. The upper⁄most layer sealing the pit contains the remains of a hut⁄circle, built against the bastion. Photo H. N. Savory

33   The Millaran Mother Goddess. a, Cylindrical stone 'idol' from an un⁄known megalithic tomb in Estremadura, 16.5 cm. high. National Archaeological Museum, Madrid. b, Phalange 'idol' from 'tholos' of S. Martinho, Sintra (Lisbon), 8 cm. high. Portuguese Ethnological Museum, Belém. c, Pottery vessel from Monte do Outeiro 'tholos' tomb, Aljustrel (Beja), 11.5 cm. high. Geological Services Museum, Lisbon. d, Antler "idol", 24 cm. long, from Ereta del Pedregal, Navarrés (Valencia). Museum of the Service of Prehistoric Investigation, Valencia. e,f, Idols of alabaster, 10 cm. and 9.5 cm. high, from houses in the settle⁄ment at Almizaraque. National Archaeological Museum, Madrid. g, Flat bone 'idol' from Almizaraque, 15 cm. high. National Archaeological Museum, Madrid.

34   S. Pedro de Estoril (Lisbon). Beaker 'fruitstand' from rock⁄cut tomb No. 1. Height: 15 cm. V. Leisner *Die Megalithgräber der Iberischen Halbinsel: Der Westen* (*Madrider Forschungen*, I/3), Pl. 178.

35   Llano de la Atalaya 6 (Almería). Bell Beaker of Mediterranean type from 'tholos'. The decoration is encrusted with white. Height 15 cm. National Archaeological Museum, Madrid.

36 Ciempozuelos (Madrid). Tall Beaker from a pit grave, with dark burnished surface and incised decoration showing zone contraction. Height: 12.6 cm. National Archaeological Museum, Madrid.

37 Alapraia (Lisbon). Tall Beaker with red burnished surface and notched decoration throughout, from rock-cut tomb No. 2. Height: 11.6 cm. Municipal Museum, Cascais. V. Leisner, *Die Megalithgräber der Iberischen Halbinsel: Der Westen* (*Madrider Forschungen*, I/3), Pl. 170.

38 Cueva de Toralla (Lérida). Late 'Meseta' ware bowl with furrowed and chip-carved decoration. Height: 8.5 cm. Archaeological Museum, Barcelona.

39 Algodor (Toledo). Late encrusted 'Meseta' ware bowl with furrowed and chip-carved decoration. Height: 12 cm. Toledo Museum.

40 Ciempozuelos (Madrid). Carinated bowl ('cazuela') of white-encrusted, dark burnished Meseta ware. Width: 30.5 cm. National Archaeological Museum, Madrid.

41 Montilla (Córdoba). Gold diadem and two gold bracelets found with an inhumation and fragments of pottery, now lost and of unrecorded type, a copper tanged dagger of Beaker type and copper tanged arrow-heads (see fig. 61) in a cist. The diadem is formed of a strip 44 cm. long and weighs 25.30 grams. Archaeological Museum, Barcelona.

42 El Oficio (Almería). Selection of fine pottery from the Argaric cemetery. Archaeological Museum, Barcelona.

43, 44 Callosa de Segura (Alicante). Reconstructed Argaric cist and jar burial. Archaeological Museum, Barcelona.

45 Cueva Bonica, Vallirana (Barcelona). Plain bowls of Early Bronze Age type, representative of the period in the whole area on the eastern coast of Spain, northwards from Alicante. Archaeological Museum, Barcelona. *Carta Arqueologica de España: Barcelona* (1955), 220.

46 Cueva Fonda, Salamó (Tarragona). Heavily furrowed jar of Early or Middle Bronze Age date. Height: 20 cm. Archaeological Museum, Barcelona.

47 Areneros de Valdivia (Madrid). 'Boquique' bowl with chevron decoration in the characteristic 'stab and drag' technique. Height: 13 cm. National Archaeological Museum, Madrid.

48 Mas Clamí (Barcelona). Carinated bowl with button handle (*ansa a botón*). Early Bronze Age. Height: 8 cm. Archaeological Museum, Barcelona.

49 Carrapatas, Macedo de Cavaleiros (Bragança). Hoard of copper halberds; the larger is 34.5 cm., the smaller 29.5 cm. long. Guimarães Museum. *Actas e Memórias do I Congresso Nacional de Arqueologia* (Lisbon, 1959), 431–9.

50 Linares (Jaén) and Puertollano (Ciudad Real). Examples of copper swords of Argaric type, the former 51 cm. and the latter 58 cm. long. Both have the characteristic contraction of the blade close to the expanded butt; the larger sword has silver rivets. National Archaeological Museum, Madrid.

51 Stone moulds for the manufacture of widely splayed copper or bronze flat axes of Early Bronze Age type, from the settlement at Mola Alta de Serelles (Alicante). The largest mould is 19 cm. long. Museum of the Service of Prehistoric Investigation, Valencia.

52 Copper and bronze axe-heads from northern Portugal:
a, flat axe from Terras de Bouro (Braga) 165 mm. long,
b, splayed flat axe from Gondomar (Guimarães), 155 mm. long,
c, single-looped palstave from Penha (Guimarães), 185 mm. long,
d, single-looped palstave from Penha (Guimarães), 143 mm. long,
Museu Sarmento, Guimarães.

53 Cehegín (Murcia). Diadem of gold sheeting, with decoration of small embossed dots. Similar diadems of silver, with embossed decoration,

were found on the skulls of female skeletons in graves at El Argar. National Archaeological Museum, Madrid.

54 Cabeceiras de Basto (Braga). Gold 'lunula' and discs found together. The lunula has embossed ribs and rows of dots like those on the diadem from Cehegín, and is 12.35 cm. in diameter; it weighs 47 grams. The discs are 4.8 cm. in diameter and each weighs 5 grams. Portuguese Ethnological Museum, Belém.

55 Alamo, Moura (Beja). Gold gorget of Early Iron Age type, associated in a hoard with gold collars and bracelets (p. 251). Maximum diameter 14 cm. Weight: 209 grams. Portuguese Ethnological Museum.

56 Sintra (Lisbon). Gold gorget of a type which originated in the Late Bronze Age in Iberia, but in this case may rather be of Early Iron Age date. The spiked cups and the hooked detachable portion suggest a relatively late date. The maximum diameter of the opening is 11 cm., the weight 1262 grams. British Museum.

57 Chaves (Vila Real). Gold torc of Early Iron Age type. Maximum diameter: 12 cm. Weight: 212.2 grams. Private collection.

58 Castro de Laundos, Povoa de Varzim (Porto). Gold earring. The disc is 40 cm. in diameter and the total weight is 17.6 grams. Soares dos Reis Museum, Porto.

59 Portalegre. Gold bracelet with encircling ribs and spikes. The diameter is 7.8 cm., the weight 598.5 grams. Private collection.

60 Can Missert, Tarrasa (Barcelona). Urn from the earliest phase of the Catalan Urnfields. Height (with cover): 35.5 cm. Archaeological Museum, Barcelona.

61 Can Bech, Agullana (Gerona). Urn from the later phase of the Catalan Urnfield Culture (late seventh – early sixth century BC), with incised meander pattern and pedestal (Tomb 101). Height: 17 cm. Archaeological Museum, Barcelona.

62 Solana de Cabañas, Logrosán (Cáceres). Sepulchral slab of a warrior with shield of Herzsprung type, sword probably of carp's-tongue type, mirror(?), angled bow brooch and four-wheeled cart. The main axis of the slab measures approximately 1.3 m. Sixth century BC. National Archaeological Museum, Madrid.

63 Roquizal del Rulló, Fabara (Zaragoza). Firedogs and pottery with excised decoration, from the phase of Hallstatt 'C' influence at the settle-ment (sixth century BC). National Archaeological Museum, Madrid.

64 Citania de Briteiros, Guimarães (Braga). Selection of sherds of Early Iron Age 'Castro' pottery, wheel-turned, with girth-grooves and stamped 'Duck' and 'S' patterns. Guimarães Museum.

65 Citania de Briteiros, Guimarães (Braga). Street with enclosures and hut-circles.

66 S. Jorge de Vizela and S. Ovidio, Fafe (Braga). Warrior statues, about 1.6 m. high. Guimarães Museum.

Index

44167

ST. MAR...

ST. MARY'S CITY, MARYLAND